Dedicated to every teacher, student, and parent
who is committed to educational excellence

In Memory of

D. Keith Osborn, Alan J. Jaworski, and Carol Ann Colquitt. Keith and Alan will always be remembered as inspiring colleagues at The University of Georgia. Both were extraordinary teachers and Meigs Award recipients.

Carol Ann was a good friend and an extraordinary teacher in the Clarke County School System of Georgia. She taught students with behavior disorders with the love, caring, and professional competency that every child deserves.

Each of these three wonderful people made a profound impact not just on their students' lives but on the lives of every person who had the privilege of knowing them.

EXTRAORDINARY
TEACHERS

EXTRAORDINARY TEACHERS

The Essence of Excellent Teaching

Frederick J. Stephenson, Jr., Ph.D., Editor

**Andrews McMeel
Publishing**

Kansas City

01 02 03 04 05 QUF 10 9 8 7 6 5 4 3 2 1

Library of Congress Cataloging-in-Publication Data
Extraordinary teachers : the essence of excellent teaching / Frederick J. Stephenson, [editor].
   p. cm.
   ISBN 0-7407-1860-6
   1. Teachers.   2. Effective teaching.   3. Teacher effectiveness.   I. Stephenson,
Frederick J.
   LB1775 .E98 2001
   371.1—dc21

2001022999

CONTENTS

ACKNOWLEDGMENTS

A BOOK IS not written without the help of many people, and in my case, numerous individuals made important contributions. First and foremost, I recognize and thank members of my family. Sharon, my wife, best friend, and most trusted confidant, you have been there throughout. Without your love, encouragement, and computer know-how, this book would still be a work in progress. You worked hard and with great success for fourteen years as a teaching assistant in the Clarke County schools, but your greatest teaching success was at home. You taught our children well. Whatever I have achieved in the last thirty-five years, I couldn't have done it without you. You are a very special, loved lady.

To our children, daughter-in-law, and son-in-law, Katie, Jeff, Dave, Kendra, and John, thank you so much for your great ideas, editorial suggestions, and constant encouragement. As a teacher, I never made a ton of money, but I have always considered myself the richest of people because of your love for me and one another. I have been blessed with a wonderful, kind, caring family, for which I am deeply grateful. You are your mom's and my proudest accomplishments.

To Dad, my ninety-five-year-old inspiration and role model, you taught me so much about what really counts in life. Thanks for your love and for always being there for me.

To Mom, you are always with me. I never enter the classroom without you. You are my teaching benchmark.

To my sister Eleanor, who just retired after thirty-five years of elementary school teaching, thanks for your love and for being my big sister, for your book suggestions, and for the countless unselfish deeds you did for your students. Your input was very valuable in trying to address the needs of K–12 teachers.

I have had the privilege of getting to know many exceptional business leaders during my career, but three men are very special mentors and friends, Paul Taylor, Harry Norris, and Dan Baker. Thank you for your wisdom, for the good times we have had together, and for your help. Your support, respect, and belief in me have made my job and life much easier. One thing, though, has significantly helped my teaching of business students. By knowing you and watching the way you so competently do your jobs, honorably lead your lives, and love and care for your families, I have been able to guide my students toward a higher ground of business leadership. You have been great role models for me and my students, and if all business leaders would run their companies and treat their employees and customers with the respect you do, how great this world would be. Integrity, as you have shown by your examples, doesn't just count. It is a cornerstone of success.

To my friends at Winterville Elementary School, thanks for the times we have spent together. Your contributions to teaching and your concerns about the welfare of your students are reflected in this book.

To George Zinkhan, Head, Department of Marketing and Distribution, Terry College of Business, The University of Georgia, you will never fully know how much your efforts to understand and appreciate who I am and what I have been trying to do have meant to me. You valued my teaching, took the initiative to nominate me for the Meigs Award, reviewed sections of this book, and cheered the book's development. Your respect was highly motivational.

To my colleague Kevin Ellis and his wife, Isobelle, thank you for listening. The wonderful evening at your home kept me focused and driven to do this book right. Kevin, you have been a good friend and my sounding board for the book since day one. You always saw a great need for, and the potential of, the book. Thank you for your dedication and hard work on behalf of your students.

To my new colleague Tom McPeak, thanks for reading the book materials and believing in the project. I have enjoyed being your mentor and am proud of your progress as a teacher.

Several people in the Marketing and Distribution Department have helped me with the book. Connie Autry and Mae Dell Huff were always there with professionalism and great care to assist with word processing and administrative needs. Andy Roberts, Maureen Wangensteen, Joel Tanenbaum, Yinan Wang, Katrina Chao, and Matt Fowler, my outstanding graduate teaching assistants, gave me thoughtful advice and excellent assistance. I believe in you and know you will do well in life.

Ellen Sutherland, one of my most respected former students, thoughtfully read and critiqued the manuscript. I am grateful for your excellent suggestions, efforts, and friendship.

To my student Stacy Vogel, thank you very much for your thoughtful review and perspectives on how the book would appeal to students who are considering teaching careers. I thoroughly enjoyed teaching you and encourage you to consider becoming a teacher. You would make a fine one.

To Nathan Deasey and Steve Howard, my students, backpacking partners, and friends, thanks for the memories and for helping me talk through this book while hiking together. Nathan, I am sure you will not forget your forty-five-mile hike in the rain in Joyce Kilmer-Slickrock Wilderness nor being lost in the fog on top of a mountain. Steve, I am positive you won't forget our being stalked and charged by a black bear on the Appalachian Trail. I certainly won't. Nor will I forget Nathan's wise philosophy of life or Steve's trailside cooking. I have many fond memories of my students but none so unforgettable, unique, or enjoyable as the times when I got to see these two students in codependent roles on the trail. I will always remember how resourceful young people can be from these experiences.

To Karen Holbrook, UGA's Senior Vice President for Academic Affairs and Provost, I appreciate your encouragement. You have my greatest respect for all of your contributions to the university and for being the honorable person you are. You set a great example for all of us.

To John Campbell, my good friend and library reference professional extraordinaire, thanks for all the assistance with my secondary research.

To Gail Taylor, whom it was my privilege to mentor as a young faculty member, thank you so much for your ideas and belief in the book. Your efforts and success in teaching are an inspiration to me. You taught me a lot about teaching.

To Jeff Tanner, my former student, who has accomplished so much in his short academic career at Baylor University, I am very proud of you. Thanks for believing in the book and me and valuing my teaching.

To Karen Orchard, I appreciate your thoughtful review of the manuscript. Your ideas were very helpful.

To David Robinson, thank you for the timely, thorough, and excellent editing of the original manuscript and thanks for your friendship over the years.

To Ron Simpson, former head of UGA's Office of Instructional Development, thank you for your central role in improving the quality of teaching at The University of Georgia. No one has done more to raise the status of teaching at this major research university than you have, and your contributions have had a positive effect on countless thousands of students. You were a leader in creating the Meigs Award, which has meant so much not just to me but to all the recipients. But the key thing you did for me was make me aware that I was not alone in my struggle to make teaching more important. You introduced me to dedicated teachers all over the campus, and just knowing that I didn't have to fight the battle by myself gave me hope and energy to proceed. This book is one outcome.

To the late Virginia Trotter, who as Vice President for Academic Affairs together with Ron Simpson created the Meigs Award, and to William Prokasy, who succeeded Dr. Trotter and greatly stimulated teaching on campus by expanding the Meigs Awards program and its financial rewards and status, thank you. What you did made the single biggest, most powerful statement of teaching's importance that occurred during my years at UGA.

I also want to thank Bill Jackson and Tricia Kalivoda, who, through their development of the UGA Senior Teaching Fellows program, have created an exceptional pool of teaching scholars. As a Fellow, I have met and worked with many outstanding leaders committed to teaching excellence. And I am most grateful to the members of my 1997–98 Senior Teaching Fellows class for their support for *Extraordinary Teachers*. This book is a direct result of their strong enthusiasm for the project.

I also acknowledge The University of Georgia Teaching Academy. As a charter member of this group, I discussed the development of this book and received their strong encouragement and endorsement.

To my attorneys, Bill Marianes, Mike Hobbs, and Tony Barnes of Troutman Sanders, thanks for your excellent advice and great representation in negotiating our book contract and in creating the LLC. You are exceptional listeners and fine lawyers.

To Greg Garcia of Garcia, Coy, Rose & Wiltshire, thanks for all of your excellent advice, friendship, and help through the years. I have great faith in your professional knowledge. You were always there when we needed you.

To Christine Schillig and the staff of Andrews McMeel, thanks for believing in this project and for all of your assistance. Chris, I will never forget the day you called me to tell me that Andrews McMeel wanted to publish the book. Thanks for sharing the vision and for your commitment to excellence.

In concluding these acknowledgments, let me offer special recognition to the following groups and individuals. First, I owe much gratitude to all the teachers across the UGA campus who have demonstrated such love and caring for their students, three of whom were my children. I tip my hat to each of you and encourage you to stay the course. Your work is very important.

I can't say enough about my coauthors. I wish you could have gotten to know them as I have. These are fine, outstanding people with significant accomplishments, as verified in their biographies, not just in teaching but also in research, public service, leadership roles, and families. To each of you, I express my deepest admiration and appreciation. What you have done on behalf of teaching is a legacy you can be proud of.

To all of my students, past and current, you mean a great deal to me. You are the reason I have spent my career in academia. May your lives be rich in joy and success, and may you always remember to help those around you. Be a good teacher and role model because the world needs you.

And finally, to my mentor and friend, Tom Stanley, author of *The Millionaire Next Door* and *The Millionaire Mind*, you have my utmost respect and appreciation. You are the epitome of a great teacher, and I can't thank you enough for all of your efforts to help me and on behalf of this book. And Brad, I am grateful I had the opportunity to be your teacher. I have confidence in you and wish you the best.

INTRODUCTION

Frederick J. Stephenson

Extraordinary Teachers, The Essence of Excellent Teaching is about achievement and promise. Written for every person who cares deeply about teaching and learning, its thesis is that if we are determined to solve America's educational shortcomings, we have the power and ability to do so. The book shows teachers from pre-K through graduate school how to become more effective instructors. It will help parents learn ways to help their children get a better education. It can guide school administrators and public officials as they set educational priorities and policies. And hopefully, it will both attract an increasing number of promising men and women into the teaching profession and slow the exodus of teachers, particularly top teachers, leaving the field. This is a book about what it means to be a teacher and about the love and respect that bond students and teachers together.

I have been watching teachers and schools for a long time. I sat in classrooms for twenty-two years as a student. For the past twenty-nine years I have been a high school and college teacher. And for thirty-two years I have been a parent conscientiously monitoring our three children as they passed through the schools on their educational journeys. From these experiences I have drawn one significant conclusion. America's educational system is seriously flawed, underachieving, and heavily in need of change. If I had never read a newspaper, watched television, listened to the radio, or heard a speech on educational reform, I still would know that we—parents, students, teachers, school administrators, and governmental officials—have settled for too long for mediocrity when educational excellence has always been within our reach. There is strong evidence that many of you share my disappointment. According to a *Business Week* poll, educational reform is America's number-one national priority.[1] This sense of urgency is well deserved. What we are talking about is something of enormous importance to people—our children's and grandchildren's futures and happiness. My colleagues and I wrote this book to share what we have learned in our more than one thousand years of teaching experience and to lead this country along the path to educational excellence.

Extraordinary Teachers is a rather unique book, a collection of thirty-six reflective papers about teaching excellence. Authored by outstanding teachers, the writings reveal the heart and soul of master teachers, clarify the requirements for becoming excellent classroom instructors, and establish why the objective of improved teaching is well worth the effort.

For the past three years, I have been privileged to have served as the book's editor and as a contributing author. This has been a richly rewarding endeavor during which I have developed a deep appreciation and respect for my coauthors. I have learned much from studying their papers, including many ways to improve my own teaching. I have also been reassured of the importance of teaching. It is very meaningful work. Teachers have the power to change lives, and I am convinced that nothing I do as a professor is more important than helping my students learn and develop. They, and their parents, are counting on me.

There are many lessons that I have learned from *Extraordinary Teachers*, but none is more valuable than understanding that teaching is primarily a *learned* profession. The authors were not born teachers, and many lament their inadequate and poor teacher training. Still, they have all been remarkably successful instructors, leading me to conclude that improved teaching effectiveness is within the power of every teacher determined to succeed.

By carefully reviewing the papers, I identified more than three hundred different traits that distinguish excellent teachers. I have condensed these into *six key characteristics of extraordinary teachers:*

1. Extraordinary teachers have great passion for their work.

2. Extraordinary teachers know what to teach, how to teach, and how to improve.

3. Extraordinary teachers excel at creating exciting classroom environments.

4. Extraordinary teachers connect exceptionally well with students.

5. Extraordinary teachers challenge students to reach their full potential.

6. Extraordinary teachers get extraordinary results.

In this introductory chapter, I will discuss each of these characteristics in more depth. But first, let's review the urgency of teaching reform and the background information that will both define the authors' credentials and clarify the book's purposes.

The Educational Crisis and the Demand for Reform

Although there are many fine books in print on teaching, the publication of *Extraordinary Teachers* is timely and needed. As previously noted, educational reform is a high national priority. Daily, the public is deluged with reminders of teaching and educational shortcomings. The criticism seems to appear everywhere—in the media, in government reports, and in independently published research studies and books.

What are the people's concerns? Public schools are heavily criticized for falling test scores, reduced standards, grade inflation, and too many students who are unable to do basic math, read, or communicate effectively.[2] In one highly regarded report about research universities, undergraduate education was taken to task when the authors said, "All too often they [undergraduates] graduate without knowing how to think logically, write clearly, or speak coherently. The university has given them too little that will be of real value beyond a credential that will help them find their first jobs."[3] Even teachers are critical of educational efforts. In a national survey of college and university professors, 73 percent of the faculty felt that students were not well prepared academically.[4] One outcome is the demand for more standardized testing and teacher accountability. Lawmakers want to know, for instance, why colleges have failed to make teaching a higher priority.[5]

All the news is not bad, however. Many teachers and educational programs are already highly effective. They should be recognized and praised for their contributions and considered as models for reform. There is also a rising chorus calling for increased recognition and rewards for outstanding teachers. This is very encouraging and crucial to improved teacher recruitment and retention. Teaching excellence and learning, though, are everybody's responsibility. Parents must take a more active role and interest in promoting education and preparing their children for school. Students must contribute more time and energy to making the most of their educational opportunities. But most critics agree that nothing is more crucial to educational reform than improved teaching. And at its core are competent, dedicated, caring teachers.

Ernest L. Boyer, the renowned educator and former president of the Carnegie Foundation for the Advancement of Teaching, once said, "In Japan, where my granddaughter went to school, the term 'sensei'—teacher—is a title of great honor. When all is said and done we simply must make teaching in this country an honorable profession—since it is in the classrooms of America where the battle for excellence, ultimately, will be won or lost."[6] I couldn't agree more.

The Book and the Authors

In 1998, I conceived the idea of editing a book with the objective of helping as many teachers as possible improve the quality of their teaching. I wanted to tap the wisdom of highly honored master teachers—

individuals recognized by their peers and students as being exceptional instructors. My plan was to invite recipients of The University of Georgia's Josiah Meigs Award for Excellence in Teaching, the university's highest faculty teaching honor, to participate in this endeavor. Strongly encouraged by my University of Georgia colleagues, I sent an invitation to every living Meigs Award recipient, fifty-six honorees who had earned the recognition since the awards were first presented in 1982. These professors represent the top 2 percent of all the teachers who served on the faculty from 1982–99.

Prospective authors were asked to submit individually written papers that would inspire, motivate, challenge, and uplift teachers. Teaching methods were not to be the book's focus. Rather, I wanted the writings to explain how teaching defines these extraordinary teachers, drives them toward teaching excellence, motivates them to work the extra hours, and provides so much meaning in their lives. I was primarily interested in teaching philosophy, teaching responsibilities, teaching advice, teaching myths and realities, and the characteristics of top teachers.

The response far exceeded my expectations. Thirty-six individuals contributed papers (64 percent). The authors have an average of thirty-one years of teaching experience, and they come from twenty-nine different academic disciplines and work in eight of the university's colleges and schools (see the appendix for more information on the Meigs Award and for a list of the authors, fields, and colleges). I believe their enthusiasm for *Extraordinary Teachers* verifies the major priorities of top teachers—the desire to share their knowledge of teaching, a sincere interest in helping others improve, and a knack for building confidence in people that motivates them to succeed. Each paper says something important and insightful about teaching.

Although *Extraordinary Teachers* was authored by college teachers at a major research university, the wisdom shared in the papers has broad appeal. It clearly confirms that excellent teaching is neither grade-level nor field specific but rather that teaching skills are primarily generic. Therefore, if a person knows these skills well, then he or she can apply them with customization and success to most any type of classroom environment, whether that means college, pre-K, K–12, executive education, or other settings where teachers and students converge to engage in learning. There are no real mysteries to teaching, but there are numerous skills and principles of good teaching that normally take years to master by trial and error. *Extraordinary Teachers* will make teaching success easier and faster, and any teacher can benefit from this collection of papers.

Characteristic 1: Extraordinary Teachers Have Great Passion for Their Work

As previously mentioned, the papers helped me identify more than three hundred characteristics of outstanding teachers; however, please don't jump to the wrong conclusion. None of the authors displays all of these characteristics nor is it necessary to possess each of these traits to become a master teacher. The extensiveness of the list, however, verifies that extraordinary teachers earn their titles. They are praised for doing many things that others fail to duplicate.

Extraordinary teachers have passion for four things—learning, their fields, their students, and teaching. In other words, they believe deeply in their work, the people they serve, and their mission. If teachers lack passion for any of these four elements, achieving extraordinary teaching success is unlikely.

Extraordinary teachers possess a deep understanding of the importance of teaching and feel responsible, even obligated, to help

I sincerely believe that every student is educable, but some are simply not as intellectually gifted as others are. I have also come to appreciate the very average student who works extremely hard, struggles through every examination, never makes the dean's list, but is diligent and conscientious. We have to make a place for average students, and many times, they are the most rewarding students to work with.

Dean G. Rojek, "Responsibilities of a College Teacher"

all students. Mainly, this comes from a rich comprehension of the impact teachers can have on people. In particular, they remember the profound changes that one or more teachers made in their own lives. Extraordinary teachers want to share the thrill of discovery with their students. These teachers are highly motivated, inspired men and women.

They are also serious students, curious individuals constantly searching for answers and never satisfied with what they know. By remaining lifelong learners, they have an uncanny ability to transfer this sense of inquiry to their students. It is hard to imagine highly successful teachers who are not hungry for knowledge of their fields and subjects. Research, study, and personal growth are traits that mark top teachers.

Clearly, extraordinary teachers have an uncommon and intense desire to master the craft of teaching. Whereas many instructors seek to become good teachers or even excellent ones, extraordinary teachers want to be the benchmarks of their profession. They have the Tiger Woods, Michael Jordan, Wayne Gretzky mentality. The point is not that they reach the pinnacle of success in teaching as these athletes have done in their respective sports, but that these teachers think *big* and make the effort. In return, they learn to teach as few others do.

What drives such commitment and effort? Extraordinary teachers find teaching deeply satisfying. They wear the title of "Teacher" with pride. They know they are very good at what they do. I don't mean arrogantly, but confidently. They are professionals. They are also motivated by the achievements of their students. Seeing their students learn, bloom, and succeed gives them

> ... what more life-affirming job is there than the opportunity to help shape the lives of creative, energetic, irrepressible young people?
>
> *Richard K. Hill, "Why I Teach"*

great joy, because they feel they played a part, however small, in this growth process. In summary, extraordinary teachers find their work exciting and meaningful, and this is the chief driving force that motivates their success.

In my opinion, mastery of the subject matter and staying current, having a teaching plan and being organized, and developing one's communication skills are the responsibility of every teacher. This is true whether a person teaches one class each year or several. These are components of effective teaching that teachers owe their students.

Keith J. Karnok, "Thoughts on College Teaching"

Characteristic 2: Extraordinary Teachers Know What to Teach, How to Teach, and How to Improve

As a young teacher, I was convinced that my primary job was passing on subject-matter knowledge to students. Certainly this is an important responsibility, and every teacher needs to prepare students for subsequent classes, fields, and/or careers. But to extraordinary teachers, subject matter is overrated and far from the most critical element of student learning. These teachers have a much richer understanding of what needs to be taught and what students need to learn.

In Exhibit 1 (page xxvi), I have listed what the authors try to teach their students. What conclusions can be drawn from this comprehensive list? Perhaps what is most important is that extraordinary teachers see their primary task as trying to prepare students for life. How they achieve this is by teaching students many skills to go along with facts and by influencing the way students see the world and their roles in it. An ultimate goal of master teachers is that students develop their full potential to become honorable and productive members of society.

Furthermore, extraordinary teachers know how to teach. They have extensive knowledge of both their fields and teaching, and they have a craftsman's ability to choose the best tools for each particular task. For instance, they use their research knowledge as a powerful source of energy for both teaching and student learning. The bottom line, though, is that these highly successful teachers learned the tools and *learned* to teach.

Dean G. Rojek's quote typifies the teaching dilemma of most Meigs teachers when they began their careers. A review of the book's biographies shows that the authors graduated from top universities all over America and the world, yet the vast majority say they entered their first classrooms not knowing how to

> If we can teach young people skills such as creative, reflective, and analytical thinking and values such as empathy and the worth of diversity; if we can give them confidence and passion to continue learning and not to fear the new, then we will have accomplished a feat far more important than the imparting of facts.
>
> *Katharina M. Wilson, "In Praise of Holistic Teaching"*

teach. They still can't believe that their graduate schools sent them out into the teaching profession with so little guidance and training.

So how did these extraordinary teachers evolve from such poorly prepared novices? Essentially, they credit years of hard work and on-the-job training. Teaching has primarily been a self-help, self-taught endeavor. The upside of this is that there is no really good reason why any teacher can't significantly improve his or her teaching. The downside is that no one should have to enter the teaching profession so inadequately prepared for the job nor should students have to wait so long for quality teaching results.

> As I look back at my twenty-five years of teaching, I am painfully aware that much of what I have been doing in the classroom was nothing more than on-the-job training. I had no courses in how to teach; I had no mentors to guide me through my first classes; I attended no workshops on how to be an effective college teacher. Unfortunately, I see no evidence to suggest that our most recent cohorts of newly minted Ph.D.s who are marching into their classrooms have any more experience or guidance than I had.
>
> *Dean G. Rojek, "Responsibilities of a College Teacher"*

Exhibit I

What Extraordinary Teachers Teach

they teach
knowledge of the field and subject matter
why a field is important and worth studying
the value of the mind
the joy of learning
a process of understanding
creative, reflective, and analytical thinking
logic and reasoning
standards of responsible citizenship
values
mutual respect
the value of hard work
attitudes
how to do research
how to judge the reliability of information
how to organize information so that it can be accessed efficiently
studying skills
problem-solving skills
writing skills
speaking skills
listening skills

and they teach students
to value cultural differences
to believe in themselves
to become lifelong learners
to succeed in their own ways
to function more effectively in life

I reflected on the fact that she was one of those rare teachers who created an atmosphere in class that was sheer magic. I asked her, "How do we learn to become a Mildred Morgan? How do we ever learn to be like you?" She responded, "Jim, you don't need to become Mildred Morgan—you need to become the best Jim Walters that you can be."

James Walters, "Teachers Who Meant the Most to Me as a Student"

One of the truly significant findings is that these extraordinary teachers have their own unique teaching styles. No two teachers seem to be anything close to identical. There is no blueprint of *"the"* successful teacher, and it is ludicrous to try to develop such a model that others must emulate, as many nonteachers seem determined to believe. We would neither get equal results nor maximize individual teachers' potential. To the contrary, standardizing teaching would destroy one of the most cherished incentives valued by top teachers—the personal touch of inventiveness and creativity that spark individual teaching energy and pride. As Jim Walters writes in the above quote, top teachers excel *because* they can be themselves. Certainly the authors recommend that teachers try to incorporate many of the best traits of highly effective teachers, but success will come more rapidly by customizing one's teaching to reflect his or her individual personality and talents.

What then are the secrets of teaching improvement? Top teachers seek solutions and will look anywhere and everywhere for help. Colleagues, students, books, and trial and error all helped Meigs teachers improve. They have the courage to accept risks and defy conventional wisdom. Success comes from experimenting with innovative teaching techniques. Outstanding teachers also quickly get over mistakes, failures, and disappointments and keep moving forward toward the broader objective of teaching excellence. What they have learned is the value of trying, culling, and modifying until they get it right. The key is practice, practice, practice.

Characteristic 3: Extraordinary Teachers Excel at Creating Exciting Classroom Environments

The mark of exceptional teachers is an exciting classroom that captures student interest. It's a place that both students and teachers look forward to going to each day. In such a lively setting, students are stimulated to learn.

How do top teachers accomplish this? It begins with classroom atmosphere. Extraordinary teachers seem to have boundless energy and enthusiasm, not just for their fields or teaching but for life in general. It is obvious they love what they do, and students catch the fever. While the papers provide more precise teaching tips, I am drawn to the importance of currency and relevancy. Excellent teachers keep their material fresh and meaningful. They win the learning battle by establishing the "why" before the "what." Consequently, their students understand the need for learning and thus are more motivated to make the effort.

> ...the classroom must engage and stimulate. It must be fun. Not fun in the gimmicky way that panders in order to win popularity contests, but fun in the sense of being unforgettably challenging, as in the film *Dead Poets Society.*
>
> *Lief H. Carter,* "Teaching Tricks"

Extraordinary teachers believe good things will happen every time they enter the classroom. Do they always succeed? Of course not, but the expectation of positive results dramatically increases the odds of achievement. Top teachers believe that setting a positive tone for learning is a fundamental teacher responsibility and that class attitude is set by their example.

> Monotone, half-dead teachers do not engender inspired students. Energy begets energy, enthusiasm is contagious, and inspired teachers inspire others to excel.
>
> *Brenda H. Manning,*
> *"Inspiring Students to Excel"*

Let me illustrate. Outstanding teachers grasp the importance of the first classroom meeting. They realize that by the time day one is over, most students have already formed opinions about a teacher's interest in teaching them, whether the teacher wants to be there, if the instructor has passion for his or her field, and whether the teacher likes students. So extraordinary teachers seize the opportunity to set a positive tone for the whole course at the first class.

Another thing that extraordinary teachers do is manage classrooms skillfully, taking full responsibility for what takes place in their teaching environments. They are effective leaders, not "control freaks," who have what it takes to get students to "share the vision" and cooperate. Students in turn see their teachers as confident, competent individuals. One key is talking with, not at, students. Top teachers see themselves as facilitators of learning, as opposed to conduits of knowledge, that is, people oriented to passing on what they know to students. Many think of themselves as coaches or tour guides keeping students on the track toward becoming educated. As Lief Carter states in "Teaching Tricks," ". . . authority is out of favor. The days of John Houseman in *Paper Chase* are gone."

Where do "basics" fit into the picture? Top teachers do all the basics of teaching well. They do not walk into class and "wing it" but instead try to give serious thought and effort to what they desire to accomplish each day. Their classes are run in an organized fashion. But they believe that doing the basics does not define great teaching. For instance, they think *all* teachers should have sufficient

---

Good teaching involves devoting endless hours to grading papers, designing and redesigning courses, preparing materials related to the objectives of each course, and, of course, talking with students. It requires one to move beyond the cubicle called your office and the borders of your campus in order to seek out knowledge in your field. Good teaching reflects a lifelong commitment to learning.

Sharon J. Price, "What I Wish

Someone Had Told Me: Advice to New Teachers"

knowledge of their subjects and competence in their fields before they stand in front of students. This is a minimum requirement of teaching. But they also recognize a window of learning opportunity and do not hesitate to digress from the teaching plan when it makes sense to do so.

> I found that teaching a course where humor is welcomed created a climate in which students knew and liked each other, felt free to express diverse opinions, shared anecdotes that added important dimensions, conducted research they really cared about, asked each other questions, taught me things I didn't know, and laughed whenever they felt like it.
>
> *Genelle G. Morain,*
> *"'Laughter Holding Both His Sides': Humor as a Welcome Guest in the Classroom"*

It probably won't surprise anyone if I state that most top teachers are cheerful individuals. They are. Moreover, a large number of the book's authors also are skilled entertainers. The classroom is their stage, and they relish the opportunity to perform before their students. What I am talking about is not performing just for laughs or popularity but rather using the classroom stage to excite a student response toward accelerated learning.

The importance of humor is not to be trivialized. Many extraordinary teachers use humor extremely well to induce learning. The objective is to create a more relaxed, open-minded classroom atmosphere and to make learning enjoyable rather than punishing. Humor has saved many a teacher's career from burnout. "Lightening up" and simply having fun at what you do can have a powerful impact on teaching results.

> Years ago, I asked my son, Joey, what he wanted to do when he grew up. Joey, who was four years old at the time, said, "Dad, I want to be a *professor* and a *comedian* just like you!"
>
> *Josef M. Broder, "Creating an Environment for Teaching and Learning"*

Characteristic 4: Extraordinary Teachers Connect Exceptionally Well with Students

The fourth characteristic that distinguishes extraordinary teachers is their exceptional ability to connect with students. What does this mean? First, they get students to trust them, to be more receptive to their advice, and to believe in what they are trying to accomplish. The goal is to create a bond, an educational partnership of learning, where students willingly work *with* teachers, not against them. It also means crossing the threshold where students take responsibility for their education and where students are as motivated toward learning as their instructors are. According to John Granrose, author of "Life's Meaning," the teacher and the students connect with each other, the teacher helps the students connect with the subject matter at hand, and the teacher also helps the students connect with each other.

Extraordinary teachers believe that mutual respect is vital to successful connections, and many indicate that nothing is more crucial to building student trust and respect than a teacher's caring and kindness. Perhaps this explains why top teachers tend to be student-centered, unselfish, and focused on fulfilling students' needs. They know that understanding, acceptance, compassion, and fairness carry much weight with students. And they comprehend the importance of a teacher's character and credibility and try to be good role models.

How else do extraordinary teachers reach students? They are strong communicators. Directions and course expectations are unambiguous, and lessons and points are clearly presented and understood. Using anecdotes and analogies, top teachers explain and demonstrate

> ...the most important component of teaching is having a sincere interest in the total well-being of your students. In short, I believe the teacher who really makes a difference in a student's life is one who is in touch with the student's heart as well as the student's mind.
>
> **Keith J. Karnok, "Thoughts on College Teaching"**

> As I have looked back over the years in preparing this essay, I have been over-whelmed with thoughts of the devotion and time dedication of a few teachers and mentors, including the three who were singled out. But on a negative note, I am even more amazed (and perhaps discouraged) about how few of these there were.
>
> *States M. McCarter, "What My Mentors Taught Me about Teaching"*

well, helping students grasp ideas and concepts. Most important, they teach at the right level—not over their students' heads or beneath their expertise levels. Other valued traits of extraordinary teachers are their attentiveness and above-average listening skills.

With few exceptions, extraordinary teachers are extroverted people. Can an introverted teacher win the trust of students? Yes, but most top teachers have excellent interpersonal skills and are people-oriented individuals. Not only do they like students, they willingly help, counsel, and guide them. Extraordinary teachers engage students not just inside the classroom but outside as well. They are available and accessible and make extra efforts to get to know their students as individuals.

Characteristic 5: Extraordinary Teachers Challenge Students to Reach Their Full Potential

One of the biggest misconceptions about highly rated teachers is that they are easy. Far from it—extraordinary teachers are demanding instructors who teach rigorous courses. Students are worked hard and held responsible for finishing assignments on time and delivering quality performances. Extraordinary teachers have high standards, which are not compromised. Their motto seems to be, "I welcome any and all to my classes, but don't sign up unless you are serious about learning." They intend to make students live up to, and fulfill, their potential.

Why such high expectations? Extraordinary teachers see potential in students that others miss. Furthermore, they are convinced, because they have succeeded so many times before, that they can coach students to meet these rigorous standards of achievement. One thing that these master teachers learned long ago is that students have to want an education more than their instructors want them to get one. The only way to fulfill this learning responsibility is for students to assume the lead role in their educational pursuits. No teacher can give anyone an education. It has to be wanted and earned.

> The ability of children to learn implores great teachers to challenge them, and my son's best teachers were never "easy" ones.
>
> *Jeanne A. Barsanti, "Teachers: From a Parent's Viewpoint"*

One of the most interesting aspects of great teaching is that despite widespread knowledge of the rigors ahead, students flock to extraordinary teachers' classes. What motivates students to accept the challenge? Teacher reputation! Students know that these teachers will work with them and for them and that these extraordinary instructors know how to teach and run thought-provoking, fun classes. By taking these classes, students get their money's worth.

Exceptional teachers also believe that learning is a participative sport. The way students learn is by doing—practicing until learning becomes second nature to them. Very few extraordinary teachers are lecturers in the traditional sense of talking virtually nonstop while students copy each day's speech. To the contrary, extraordinary teachers have grasped the concept of engaging students in active learning. Utilizing Socratic teaching principles, they ask students questions, encourage discussion, dialogue, and debate, and expect students to think, reason, and communicate. The goal is to provide students ample opportunity to try, succeed, fail, improve, and learn. It is this approach that tells students that teachers value their

> The teacher must set a standard of high expectations and then help the class to live up to it. There is no greater incentive to learning than having an adult teacher tell you that you are capable of it.
>
> *Richard K. Hill, "Why I Teach"*

opinions and believe in their capabilities. There is an old saying that if you think they can, they will. With outstanding teachers, the saying becomes reality.

There is one last element to Characteristic 5 that should never be forgotten, and that is the dual responsibility that teachers have to give meaningful assignments and provide instructive feedback helpful to student improvement and learning. Top teachers make it a point to explain the intended benefits of these exercises, thereby motivating greater effort and more positive results.

The complement to this is the grading and evaluation process. Extraordinary teachers are known as tough but fair graders. They understand that there is no substitute for honest feedback from competent, respected mentors and that when students have faith in their teachers' abilities, they are more inclined to take instructors' suggestions to heart and improve. This is why extraordinary teachers spend considerable hours grading and offering constructive criticism. Furthermore, this explains why top teachers are known for assigning more papers, essays, projects, and reports than their counterparts. Grading is painstaking, frequently punishing, frustrating work for most teachers, but it is an essential, necessary part of outstanding teaching. So they do it patiently and well to help their students.

Characteristic 6: Extraordinary Teachers Get Extraordinary Results

The ultimate characteristic of extraordinary teachers is that they get results that far exceed the teaching norm. An obvious measure of teaching success is the long list of teaching awards and other honors that top teachers have received from students and colleagues over their careers. Another is consistently high student evaluations. Consistency over a long time is a noted trait of top teachers. Regardless of course, grade level, or teaching circumstance, there is very little fluctuation in an extraordinary teacher's performance.

But let's probe more deeply for evidence of success. Based on what I read in their essays, the real mark of extraordinary teachers is more subtle and less quantifiable. For instance, top teachers teach students many more things than less experienced teachers typically do, such as those shown in the long list in Exhibit 1 of this chapter. Professor O. Lee Reed, in his paper "Personal Teaching and Storytelling in the Large Class," has a wonderful quote from William Arthur Ward that says, "The mediocre teacher tells. The good teacher explains. The superior teacher demonstrates. The great teacher inspires." I believe this says a great deal about what distinguishes top teachers. Few instructors motivate students as they can. Many of the book's authors remark, with extreme gratitude, how teachers changed or shaped their lives. I believe that the power to help build people, to help them realize their full potential, is the greatest contribution of exceptional teachers.

Another thing outstanding teachers do is get through to a higher percentage of students. What greater gift can there be than helping students believe in themselves? Excellent teachers change the way students approach and value education. Students then question more intelligently and think with more cutting-edge precision. Extraordinary teachers open minds and hearts. They influence attitudes and behaviors. They plant the seeds and momentum for lifelong learning and personal growth. The best teachers help students find direction, meaning, and satisfaction in their lives.

One way they accomplish the latter is by very effectively passing on knowledge and preparing students for careers. Exceptional teachers teach the subject matter well, excite students to the discipline, motivate students to enter a field, and prepare students for subsequent courses.

What I remember about Dr. Hook was his wisdom, loyalty, and dignity. A humble man of great presence, Dr. Hook was a true gentleman. He taught me that the kind of person I am is central to the type of teacher I hope to become and to the mentor whom I want my students to know and remember. Teaching is very much about living an honorable life.

Frederick J. Stephenson, "My Teaching Philosophy
and the Teachers Who Shaped It"

> I still see students whom I taught twenty-five and more years ago. They often say to me, "You worked our tails off, but, you know, Dr. Ganschow, I still quote from you in my teaching, in my preaching, in my law work, in my profession. . . . I still remember how excited I was as I left your classroom, despite the work you required of us."
>
> *Thomas W. Ganschow, "Helping Students Find Joy in Learning during Thirty-five Years of Teaching"*

But there is one last important thing I learned from *Extraordinary Teachers* that is definitely worth mentioning. Students view outstanding teachers as highly appreciated, respected, admired, even revered mentors and role models. In their lives and work, students and alumni quote their favorite teachers' wisdom and repeat their practices. And it is to these trusted mentors that former students go for advice. For the teachers in this book, the ultimate honor and proof of achievement is this respect from former students they care so much about.

Demystifying Teaching

There are countless opinions and myths about teaching, but I believe the most erroneous ones are that teaching is easy and that anyone can do it well. No doubt, many people have the ability to teach, but doing it superbly is an entirely different matter. What this nation needs, what it is demanding, is exceptional teaching, not average performance, and few instructors are measuring up to this standard. To prove my point, how many of your former teachers are indelibly etched in your memory as being superb teachers? And how many teachers actually taught you? The fact is that if so many teachers are doing their jobs incredibly well, educational reform would not be such a high national priority nor would teachers be the targets of so much criticism. No, teaching is anything but easy, and teaching is far from optimal in the United States today. The citizens of this nation have every right to demand teaching excellence from preschool through graduate school.

This impatience for change comes at a time when the job of being a teacher is getting tougher. Today's teachers are dealing with changing student attitudes and priorities, less parental support, larger classes, and increased pressures and demands that prior generations of instructors rarely faced. Discipline problems, increased paperwork, standardized testing, and publication and grant pressures take big commitments of teachers' time and energy and can be incredibly unsettling. So if people want low-stress, high-paying jobs, forget teaching. Try something else. However, if someone wants to give something back to society, and fortunately many do, teaching is a very meaningful way to make a contribution.

In this chapter, I have defined six characteristics of extraordinary teachers. I won't repeat those now, but let me draw some key conclusions. First, exceptional teachers are motivated by a personal quest for excellence. These perfectionists will never accept being average or even good teachers. They want to master the craft of teaching. For this, America should be grateful. Another is that top teachers aren't easy, they don't run popularity contests, and they don't give grades away. Top teachers have high standards, work their students hard, and expect and demand quality results. And yet, students fight to enroll in their classes. I believe this says a great deal about the seriousness of many of our nation's future leaders and their capabilities to rise to the challenges before them.

I believe one of the book's most valuable findings is that no field, grade level, or school level excludes any teacher from achieving teaching excellence. No one is severely handicapped by his or her teaching circumstances. Teaching is largely a generic craft, and no academic discipline has a significant teaching advantage as in, "If I taught in your field, certainly my teaching evaluations would be higher." The authors of this book teach in twenty-nine different disciplines. Some teach graduate-level courses. Some teach freshmen. They teach business, math, elementary education, and history. They teach introductory and advanced courses, seminars, and mass sections, classes of hundreds of students. The common denominator is that each author has achieved teaching excellence. Passion, determination, and patience, not fields or circumstances, determine teaching success.

Another significant finding is that great teaching is primarily learned. I cannot adequately stress the importance of this finding, because if I had discovered from the papers that teaching excellence really is genetically derived, then what hope of improvement would most people have? Because teaching is primarily a learned set of skills, *anyone committed to learning has the potential to improve.* What better proof can I offer than the fact that virtually all of the book's authors began their careers as poorly trained instructors? That, however, did not stop them from succeeding.

The crucial issues in *Extraordinary Teachers* are these. If people are motivated to learn to teach better, they can, and this book can show them how. No one has to reinvent teaching. Individuals are free, even challenged, to borrow from the successful practices of The University of Georgia's most distinguished teachers. The authors have given readers their trade secrets, and the only thing that will disappoint them is if people don't put their advice into practice. Also, parents must focus on their child's learning, not on grades or any other lesser objectives, and they must take greater responsibility for their child's education. Teachers, even great ones, can't do the job without parental commitment to educational excellence and parents' hard work assisting this learning process at home. *Extraordinary Teachers* will give parents the tools to evaluate teachers and school quality, but they must use them to motivate improved teaching and learning.

The essence of teaching is sharing one's passion for learning and discovery with students and sharing one's knowledge of teaching with teachers. It is all about mentoring unselfishly and well. This book's authors can't change anyone's past, but hopefully they can change attitudes and policies and can jump-start people's teaching careers. *Extraordinary Teachers* is our effort to try to help.

In closing, remember the teachers who made differences in your lives. Think of the impact that a mere 10 percent improvement in teaching would mean to society and realize that so much more is possible. Take the initiative. Much is at stake.

CRUCIAL LESSONS I HAVE LEARNED FROM MY LEAST AND MY MOST INSPIRING INSTRUCTORS

David R. Shaffer

You have absolutely no imagination.

Although you write in complete sentences, you cannot seem to combine them to construct a coherent theme.

I've seen enough to detect a pattern; you simply cannot write. I hope that you have other career options in mind.

THESE ARE VERBATIM comments that I received from Mr. Y., my teacher for senior English composition in high school and freshman English composition during my first year of junior college. Though I had no illusions of becoming the next Ernest Hemingway any time soon, I disagreed with Mr. Y.'s totally negative assessments of my budding attempts at creative writing and was particularly bothered by the dismissive tone of his comments. Where were the suggestions for improvement? Even the slightest bit of encouragement might have gone a long way toward inspiring the kind of writing he sought.

About midway through my freshman comp class, I mentioned my plight to an older associate of mine, a published novelist for whom I was working as a yardman. She offered to provide a critique of my next short-story assignment before I handed it in and proceeded to do just that for three drafts, until she said it was "pretty darn good." Thinking I'd produced a masterpiece, I was dismayed to receive a grade of C+ (my high-water mark in this course). In desperation, I made an appointment with Mr. Y., seeking suggestions for improving my writing. What resulted was the shortest one-on-one meeting I ever had with a college faculty member over the eight and one-half years of my undergraduate and graduate training. Mr. Y. informed me not to take his comments personally, but that I was simply "one of the 99 percent of Americans whose talent for communicating via the written word is virtually nil." In so many words, he implied that constructive commentary would be wasted on a person who lacked any ability to nurture, and he then made a statement I will never forget: "If you [Mr. Shaffer] ever make a dollar via a written communication of any kind, document it, send the documentation to me, and I'll take you to dinner at the restaurant of your choice."

Many thoughts went through my mind as I trudged away from Mr. Y.'s office. "He doesn't like me" was primary, but the one that came to dominate was "Maybe I have no writing ability, so why should I try?" I did subsequently devote less effort to his class, accepted my gentleman's C (which I took to indicate that he didn't dislike me, for I expected a D), and then avoided English classes throughout the remainder of my undergraduate career. My response was precisely that which research in the psychology of motivation would anticipate: when students truly believe that they have little ability in an academic (or any other) domain, they tend to assume that this deficiency is stable over time and largely unchangeable. They are then inclined to stop trying and to give up—a phenomenon known as *learned helplessness*. Had I been an aspiring writer or English major, the feedback I received could have been devastating. Fortunately, I then hoped to become a dentist and viewed my experiences with Mr. Y. as largely inconsequential to my future career.

I was wrong. Given the subsequent chain of events that conspired to make me a professor of psychology, the lessons I learned from Mr. Y. turned out to be a cornerstone of my own approach to teaching. Having become acquainted with the psychology of motivation and the harmful consequences of a learned helplessness orientation, I realized that a teacher's job is to make the best of the hand he or she is dealt, striving to improve the performance of each and every student—in short to *teach*. Today, I encounter many students who perform miserably on tests, not because they lack ability, but simply because they cannot successfully extract the wheat from the chaff when reading texts and listening to lectures or other presentations. I routinely encourage such students to make appointments with me, during which I help them to analyze their learning difficulties. I also stress that they would not have reached this point in their academic careers if they lacked talent and were incapable of overcoming their deficiencies by changing their approach to processing information.

Of course, not all students who founder seek such guidance. But of those who do, about three in four show solid improvements in their test performance. Indeed, one of the greatest satisfactions I glean from teaching is to observe the smiles of a student who has worked diligently at overcoming his/her shortcomings and has been reinforced for doing so by a noticeable improvement in performance. In these cases, I know that I am fulfilling my role as a "teacher." There may be an occasional student whom instructors can spur to new heights by making derisive comments, but the vast majority of students at all ability levels are more inclined to respond favorably to instruction that motivates and assists them to direct whatever abilities they do display along fruitful and productive pathways.

This brings me to a second set of lessons I learned about effective instruction from the teacher who perhaps did more than anyone else to alter my career plans. Dr. McNelis taught Speech for Teachers, a small remedial class in the College of Education for students who had failed the "speech test" then required of candidates seeking certification as a teacher in my state of residence. Although I was *not* an aspiring teacher at that time, I needed upper-division hours to graduate and had obtained permission to substitute this class for the lower-division speech course required of freshman and sophomores. As there were only six of us in the class, I was given the opportunity to give eight to ten speeches over the course of the semester, rather than the three to four I would have given in freshman speech. This prospect terrified me, for I probably displayed the most visible signs of stage fright of anyone I knew—a deficiency that kept me from asking questions or otherwise speaking up in my other classes, even when I thought I might have something meaningful to contribute.

The first month of that speech course was sheer hell! Throughout the first three assignments, I was visibly shaken at having to talk to an audience and had once even tossed my lunch in anticipation of speaking in that early afternoon class. The experience was tolerable (barely) only because Dr. McNelis was extremely supportive and made many constructive comments. What helped, too, was noting that my classmates seemed every bit as anxious and as "awful" as I was. Dr. McNelis was a master at helping us put together coherent talks (through the kind of feedback that would have helped Mr. Y. to become a more effective teacher of English composition). The breakthrough for me came as we began to move from message structure to message delivery in the fifth week of the semester.

Our assignment for that week was to prepare a twenty- to twenty-five-minute talk on a topic for which we would be the "expert" and our classmates the novices—subjects that we knew well but that might be sufficiently novel to hold the audience's attention. I chose: "How One Builds a Surfboard." First I gathered all the materials . . . the Styrofoam, resin, fiberglass, wood, etc., necessary to construct a miniature surfboard. I also prepared a stack of thirty-two index cards on which I outlined in exhaustive detail the steps one takes in building a surfboard. Boy, was I ready! All I had to do was read the cards as I worked with these props.

This is precisely what I attempted to do while giving my talk. Of course, it was quite distracting to try to read, mix chemicals, and build at the same time. As my talk began to founder, Dr. McNelis stood up, signaled "time-out," approached the speaker's table, snatched my index cards, and said, "Okay, Mr. Expert, *teach* us how to build a surfboard." After staring at him with a dumbfounded expression as I experienced gut-wrenching waves of nausea, I turned back to my props and proceeded to build that sucker, becoming progressively more animated and more confident as I went along. I found myself talking *to* rather than at my audience, and I began to feel that I was in command and that my classmates were actually interested in what I had to say. At the conclusion of my talk, Dr. McNelis asked a technical question about how the process differed when surfboards were mass-produced, and I sheepishly admitted that *I didn't know.* He then smiled at me and began his critique.

Dr. McNelis first noted the profound difference in the quality of my talk before and after he had taken my index cards. He then told my class, "You are going to be teachers—relative experts in your subject matter. If you hope for the lights to come on in your students, you had better learn to act like an expert. By simply reading what you already know from a text or from notes, you will communicate little more than that you know how to read and will probably bore your pupils to tears. But by talking *to*, rather than at, them, by making eye contact and searching for signs of puzzlement or enlightenment, you will communicate a sense of enthusiasm, expertise, and sensitivity that will make your students sit up and take notice." Dr. McNelis went on to say that the most noticeable aspect of my talk was the change in my enthusiasm as I was forced to quit reading and to trust what I already knew. He then made a statement that has stuck with me over the years: "You can hardly expect any student to be very enthusiastic about any subject matter if the teacher is not."

Dr. McNelis made a final point that I have never forgotten, saying that my "I don't know" response to his technical question was clearly the appropriate response for an expert to give if he or she doesn't know the answer. He went on to say that even high school students can often tell when a teacher is "BS-ing" in response to a meaningful question—a tactic that he claimed would detract from, rather than enhance, one's credibility. He then criticized my "I don't know" answer, saying that it might have been improved by the addendum "*. . . but I'll see if I can find out.*"

From that day on, I had little trouble with my speech class. In fact, I actually came to enjoy preparing and delivering talks and began to seriously consider the prospect of pursuing both my interest in the field of psychology and becoming a college professor. The key, I learned, to effective public speaking is to always *be prepared* and to communicate what I know with the sense of *enthusiasm* that Dr. McNelis thought so important. Over the next few years as a graduate teaching assistant, I learned how to build a sense of enthusiasm into my lectures by asking the kinds of questions (in a semi-rhetorical fashion) that capture student attention and start the gears turning. These devices are invaluable, for they help to compensate for those days when, for one reason or another, you might not be feeling all that enthusiastic as you step up to the podium. I also learned from Dr. McNelis that one needs not (and should not) rely on copious notes to deliver a lecture. Yes, I still take notes to class and even put an outline of the day's lecture on the board. However, I virtually never *read* from those notes, choosing instead to talk to my students and to encourage them to think about, and even challenge, what I am saying. I have learned to take student questions and challenges as indications that I am reaching them, and I rarely, if ever, attempt to provide an authoritative answer to a question for which my own knowledge is shaky. I have learned over and over again that Dr. McNelis was right: students generally respect an instructor who takes their questions seriously and who offers to seek answers for those queries that he or she cannot answer on the spot. In my academic discipline, many such questions have turned out to be researchable issues that my student collaborators and I have addressed empirically through the vehicle of independent study. And in many such cases, both the student and I have had an opportunity to grow from our collective lack of knowledge.

Here, then, are some important lessons I have learned from one of the very least and one of the very most inspiring teachers I've ever encountered. Effective instructors recognize that *all* students have ability and that *teaching* involves finding ways to nurture these talents; Mr. Y. taught me this truth by failing to embody it. To dismiss a student as incapable is to undermine his/her motivation and to foster the self-fulfilling prophecy of academic underachievement. Dr. McNelis, my stellar speech teacher, not only assumed that all students had the ability to become effective speakers but he also taught me that being well-prepared, enthusiastic, and open to new experiences was important for effective speaking (and instruction) in any discipline. Clearly, I have received many other pointers about effective instruction from many other teachers and colleagues over the years. But perhaps none of these lessons has served me as well as those I took from my experiences with Mr. Y. and Dr. McNelis.

Postscript

Many years later I had contact with both of the instructors mentioned in this essay. In 1979, Mr. Y. happened to see a story in the campus newspaper announcing the publication of a former student's first book (mine). He graciously penned a note of congratulations that also included an invitation, whenever I was in the area, to the dinner he had promised if I ever became a gainfully published author. Mr. Y. died shortly after I received his note. (Hopefully, the shock of my accomplishment had nothing to do with his passing.)

In 1981, I gave an informal research colloquium at my alma mater. As a couple of my former professors and I were relaxing after the talk over a pitcher of beer, Dr. McNelis approached and congratulated me on a presentation that he described as "much, much better than your lecture on building surfboards." I was flabbergasted that he remembered that fourteen-year-old talk but nonetheless managed to communicate why that experience and his guidance had represented a true turning point in my life. He then chuckled and said, "That sounds like it is worth a beer to me," as he pulled up a chair to our table.

◆   ◆   ◆

David R. Shaffer, a professor of psychology and chair of the undergraduate program in Psychology at The University of Georgia, has taught social psychology and developmental psychology courses to UGA undergraduate and graduate students for the past twenty-eight years. Dr. Shaffer's signature courses focus on socialization and personality development. His textbook *Social and Personality*

Development, the first of its kind and now in its fourth edition, has been translated into Chinese and Spanish and is widely used around the world. Dr. Shaffer has also authored a text entitled *Developmental Psychology: Childhood and Adolescence*, now in its sixth edition, and two editions of *Life-span Human Development* (with Carol K. Sigelman). He won the Meigs Award in 1990.

Dr. Shaffer is equally at ease teaching in either a lecture or a seminar format. Regardless of format, he strives to make his presentations "interactive" by frequently posing questions and using student responses as springboards for class discussions. Dr. Shaffer also enjoys working one-on-one as a research mentor, investigating interests that he and his students share in such topics as the influence of stereotypes on social judgments, maintenance of close interpersonal relationships, family caregiving and elder abuse, and social psychology and the law. Sixty-five percent of his one hundred scientific articles and chapters in scholarly volumes include graduate and/or undergraduate students as co-authors, and his charges have won many national, regional, and local awards for the quality of their research.

Dr. Shaffer enjoys all kinds of outdoor activities, ranging from leisurely strolls in the countryside to whitewater kayaking. His quests for outdoor adventure have taken him from Peru to Alaska, and he intends to continue his explorations after retiring from the university.

Helping Students Find Joy in Learning During Thirty-Five Years of Teaching

Thomas W. Ganschow

As I come nearer to the close of my formal teaching career, I have had more time and occasions to reflect back as a professional teacher on the joy teaching has brought me and, hopefully, my students. In fact, colleagues recently have asked me why I was thinking of retiring in my early sixties, since it seems as though I enjoy teaching so much. I replied, "That is exactly the reason! I want to retire while teaching is still such a joy to me!" After having been fortunate to be in a profession when day after day, month after month, and year after year, I truly have enjoyed my students and our wonderful interchange in the classroom, while being rewarded with about a dozen teaching awards in my career, I want to retire before all of that might slip away. And, hopefully, some fresh, enthusiastic teacher will step into my position and will have a joy-filled teaching career as I have had.

You might ask, what are the factors that have led to this feeling after thirty-five years of teaching—what is it that makes teaching such a pleasure for oneself and how does one succeed in making it a pleasure for the students? And I could, of course, immediately reply that it is not always pleasurable, and it is full of hard work and some frustrations. But I then would also list such things as the many wonderful colleagues I have worked with over the years, most of whom have encouraged my passion to teach; the excitement of researching new materials for the scholarship of teaching and the scholarship of publishing, though equating both teaching with publishing is still a dream unfulfilled in most colleges and universities; the satisfaction of seeing so many wonderful students reach success in their careers after their graduation, and believing, if too boldly, that I have contributed a little to their success; the challenge of being involved with colleagues in national and international projects over the years, realizing that there are many wonderful teachers all over this nation; and even the simple delight of having students come to me after I have worked with their writing, reading, and thinking process over an academic quarter or semester, to say "thank you," even though I embarrassingly knew that this was merely my job. All of these and more accumulate into the "joy of teaching." But none of these would have been possible, none of these would have been achievable without the underlying base of them all: the great challenge, joy, and excitement of engaging my students year after year in the classroom in the study of Chinese history and culture. Without the conviction that what I have been trying to teach to them through all of these years is vitally important; that it is as interesting as anything they and I will ever do; and that they themselves might someday be involved with China through travel, work, business, religion, or education, and, therefore, that it really is important that they study its history and culture, I honestly believe I could not write and think about the "joy of teaching" as I am doing now.

Students and colleagues have often asked me, "How did you get into Chinese studies?" After describing to them some of my background—small-town Wisconsin boy, growing up in a rural, rather isolated community, and whose only international experience was seeing an Indian snake charmer at the Minnesota state fair—I add that it was an accumulation of good teachers in grade school and high school and then a particularly wonderful teacher in college who turned me on to China and East Asia. Those early teachers taught me the value of working hard, the skills of studying, and the importance of believing in myself, and they showed infinite patience in their teaching, even when I did not immediately respond well as a student. The latter teacher taught me the value of the mind and the love of Chinese history.

Dr. George Gilkey, European history teacher extraordinary at Lacrosse State College (now the University of Wisconsin-Lacrosse), knew little about Asia but a lot about teaching a great class. He later told me that he had entered a faculty meeting a semester or two earlier, and when the department chairman asked if any of the faculty members had ever taken a class on Asia, Dr. Gilkey raised his hand, and he was then informed that he would be teaching East Asian history (then called the Far East) that fall semester. The fact that he was a specialist in Italian history and taught European surveys made no difference to the department. My guess is that Dr. Gilkey's reputation as a great teacher led the department chairman to pick him to "take care of Far Eastern history." And did he ever, with lots of reading, much writing, and many doses of humor, and now I know many Italian pronunciations of Chinese and Japanese names and terms.

Due largely to the inspiration of elementary and high school teachers, I knew I wanted to teach history, but it was due to Dr. Gilkey's sincere effort to convince us students that East Asian history was both interesting and important that I chose to teach that area of the world. After this class, I received a Ford Foundation grant to study Chinese and Chinese history and culture at Indiana University; embarked three years later on a twenty-five-day non-stop trip on a Chinese freighter to Taiwan; began a three-year teaching stint at Ching Yi Liberal Arts College in Taichung, Taiwan; spent another year in Hong Kong and Japan on a Fulbright research fellowship; and came back to the University of California and Stanford, and, then, Indiana University, where I married a wonderful Chinese girl whom I had met in Taiwan. Then I arrived at The University of Georgia, where I am about to finish a thirty-two-year teaching career, teaching Chinese history and culture. What a ride! What a pleasure!

And it really has been the classroom that has made it so worthwhile. Starting out in the usual way, I stuck close behind the speaker's rostrum, reading my notes, and somewhat afraid to let students speak, lest I not know the answer to their questions and thus embarrass myself. But it did not take me long to realize that that approach to teaching was neither natural nor comfortable for me, nor was it very satisfying to the students who candidly informed me of this in their student evaluations. And then there was the subject material! How could I stay behind the rostrum, how could I not involve the students as we talked about Confucius, one of the most influential philosophers who has ever walked on this earth; discussed the beauty and the candidness of the Chinese *Book of Poems*, whose songs reach back several thousand years and touch the soul of teenagers and elders alike; studied the "Columbus of China," who sailed down the east coast of Africa in the early 1400s in ships four times the size of Columbus's vessels and with a total of 25,000 crewmen; covered the western impact on China, as the Chinese tried to save their crumbling empire, while trying at the same time to enter the modern world; talked about reform, revolution, warlords, world wars, and the collapse of the Nationalist government and the rise of the Communists in twentieth-century China. And then to ask the students about China's future: if the Chinese people were allowed the freedom to create, invent, innovate, and "reach beyond their Great Wall," what would they be able to accomplish in the future? For me this has been a lot of pleasurable, hard work. And over the years the students have responded, dare I say, with a lot of "pleasurable," hard work of their own.

I still see students whom I taught twenty-five and more years ago. They often say to me, "You worked our tails off, but, you know, Dr. Ganschow, I still quote from you in my teaching, in my preaching, in my law work, in my profession. I still remember you falling over the wastepaper basket as you scampered around the front of the room, I still remember you flipping your chalk halfway to the back of the classroom as you tried to make a point about Confucius's view of human love, I still remember how excited I was as I left your classroom, despite the work you required of us. And I still read about China today, and I remember that you said China is *not* a mystery, if you are willing to study its history and culture. And I still remember how you laughed with us and not at us as we struggled to pronounce Chinese names and to absorb this ancient and wonderful culture of China."

And so, if I can say to the younger faculty who are in their early years of teaching, keep learning new things about your subject and adding them to your new teaching notes, involve the students in discussion and let them know when they have to do better (they can handle it), and celebrate with them when they do well (they need this). Work on new forms of teaching that will make learning more effective, hopefully moving from the straight lecture approach, which has its moments of effectiveness, to discussion and group activities and make use of the many resources both in and outside the classroom—compelling films, documentaries, individuals in the community, museums, and rich sources on the Internet. And know that teaching is hard work and exhausting, even if it is very exhilarating and satisfying!

Finally, keep in mind that for every student who may not live up to his/her potential and your standards, there are literally dozens who will and do. If you will engage your students in the importance of your teaching, they will often respond with the immeasurable joy of learning. And for every day you as a teacher may fail to succeed in your goals, there will be many, many days that you will succeed and that your students will have learned the joy of learning, at least in part, from your joy of teaching. Thank you, students, for giving me such joy.

◆   ◆   ◆

Thomas W. Ganschow recently retired from the Department of History in the Franklin College of Arts and Sciences at The University of Georgia. After finishing his Ph.D. course work in Chinese history and culture at Indiana University, he spent the next three years in Taiwan, where he taught at Ching Yi Liberal Arts College and where he completed work on his dissertation, "Dr. Sun Yat-sen and the United States." Dr. Ganschow held a Fulbright research award in Hong Kong and Japan, lived and did research in China, and published in his special area of modern China. He also read papers in Taiwan and in mainland China.

Dr. Ganschow taught Chinese and East Asian history at The University of Georgia for thirty-two years and for a decade served as the codirector for the Center for Asian Studies. He was also an adviser to the Taiwan, Hong Kong, and Students for a Free Tibet clubs at various times at UGA. But he is most proud to have received twelve teaching awards in his career at The University of Georgia, including the Joseph Meigs Award for Excellence in Teaching, Sandy Beaver Excellence in Teaching Awards, and seven Honors Teaching Awards. For the last sixteen years at UGA, Dr. Ganschow greatly enjoyed teaching the class "Teaching History in the University and College" to the history graduate students, and he observed dozens of classes that the graduate students taught in order to encourage them and to help them improve their skills in teaching. In spring 1998, Dr. Ganschow was invited to give the graduation address to the honors graduates, where he spoke about thanking their former teachers from elementary through college years.

Through all of these wonder years of teaching, Dr. Ganschow's wife, Lisa, and their children, Lesley and Erwin, have always encouraged his interest in teaching, even when it used up most of his evenings and weekends. For this he is most thankful to them.

Teachers: From a Parent's Viewpoint

Jeanne A. Barsanti

I WAS A STUDENT of teachers for twenty two years and a teacher of students for ten years before my son entered the world. With no formal education in pedagogy, I had modeled my teaching on that of the teachers I had, plus that of my mentors. However, my son's interactions with his teachers provided an entirely new way of looking at teachers. As a parent, one is outside the interaction, and yet, one has a very protective interest in one member of that interaction. When you are a parent who is also a teacher, it is often tempting to critique your child's teachers. To avoid this as much as possible, I decided to apply the training I have learned as a clinical scientist. I observed the stimulus (the teacher) and the response (my son's attitude and learning) by maintaining an active interest in what was happening while striving not to interfere with their interaction. What I've learned has had a profound influence on my own teaching.

The attitudes of my son's teachers have markedly influenced his performance in the classroom. Enthusiasm for the subject material is readily transferred to the students. Even teachers who seemed shy or reticent at parent conferences came alive when teaching their subjects in the classroom. Many different methods were used successfully to convey this enthusiasm: voice, facial expressions, props, and actions. Voice and facial expressions flow naturally from a teacher's enthusiasm and cannot be mimicked by a nonenthusiastic teacher. In contrast, props and actions require thought and become part of the lore of that teacher. One of my son's most effective teachers used a large ruler called Big Red, which would fall unpredictably to emphasize important points or to smack the desks of students who were not applying themselves to the task at hand. Big Red had a personality of its own (an attitude), which the teacher used to great advantage to augment her own enthusiasm.

My son's teachers also profoundly influenced his learning by emphasizing that all students have the ability to succeed in the subject if they try. The best teachers worked with the students who were a bit slower in that subject to point out their strengths while correcting their weaknesses. My son, for example, had come to believe he was good in math and science but not as good in English. Then he ran into a seventh-grade English teacher who had never heard of anyone not so good in English. Within a few months of applying himself to meet her expectations, and with her support, he learned that he could be good in English. Since then, English has been one of his strongest subjects. As his parent, I notice that he has to work much harder to do well in this area than in math and science, but he does not seem to notice or mind this, and I do not point it out to him.

Just as a teacher can motivate students to improve in areas that the students thought were difficult for them, so can a teacher take a gifted student in a particular area to unexpected heights. One of my son's teachers recognized his ability in math and taught him to multiply using an abacus when he was five years old. This teacher recognized his ability and challenged him with a tool geared to his age.

The ability of children to learn implores great teachers to challenge them, and my son's best teachers were never "easy" ones. They helped him jump each bar, but they always raised it again. Similarly, parents want children to reach their potential, but the parents' naturally protective attitudes sometimes interfere with teachers' efforts to challenge students. Parents have to guard against criticizing teachers for setting the bar too high. Sometimes the reason our children miss the bar is that they do not try to jump it but merely run through it.

My son had a particularly demanding math teacher one year, and knowing how well he had done in the past, I had a difficult time watching him struggle. I was inclined to believe that this was not a very good teacher, yet I chose to support the teacher to my son. During the next year, my son had to write an essay on what constituted the best and the worst experiences of the prior school year. His answer was that that particular math teacher was responsible for both his worst and best experiences. The experience was bad because the class had been difficult and he had not enjoyed the work required. At the same time, he recognized that the experience had been good, because he learned that he had to work in math in order to succeed at the higher level that his current class required. As a result, he came to appreciate this math teacher because he realized that his hard work the year before had paved the way for his success during the current year, even though a higher level of math was before him. When I read his essay, I was grateful that I had never given voice to my concerns about the teacher.

I learned through my son the immense impact that a teacher's care for his or her students has on their attitudes toward school and learning. Teachers who tried to know my son as an individual won his highest efforts, although this caring was expressed differently by teachers depending on my son's age and the teacher's personality. Each worked effectively, from the kiss planted firmly on the forehead of the birthday child (always complained about but secretly appreciated) to the moments of one-on-one serious discussion to the weekly breakfast as a homeroom class. When a teacher cared about my son, he cared about being in school and striving to learn.

One of the most difficult aspects for my son's teachers has been the challenge to see all that is going on in a child's world at school. The best teachers strove to ascertain whether the school environment itself was contributing to any difficulties my son experienced. While good teachers did not always recognize problems initially, they were willing to adjust in response to either my son's or our expressed concerns. One of the few times we became advocates for our son was when other students caused him to be blamed for misbehavior. The teacher did not believe him, but we did. Consequently, we asked the teacher to observe the situation more carefully. She agreed and within a few days called us to say that we were correct. With the help of the principal, she used counseling to address the problems for all those involved. Interestingly, my son learned that his tormentors had their own serious problems (for example, one was dealing with his parents' divorce). From this our child learned that people sometimes act negatively toward you not because of the way you are, but because of the way they are. That year went from the worst for my son to one of his best, all because the teacher listened and observed and then knew what to do.

My son's best teachers likewise allowed their students to have feelings of ownership for the subject, the classroom, and the school itself. These teachers assigned the students tasks important to the functioning of the classroom, expected these tasks to be done as well as the child's age allowed, and recognized the importance of these labors. My son learned from these teachers responsibility and the importance that all work should be done well for the good of the whole.

The best teachers were not only enthusiastic talkers but also enthusiastic listeners. I found some of my son's best teachers to be highly opinionated (or at least not hesitant to express their views); however, these teachers did not demand that these opinions be memorized. Rather, they used them to encourage debate. Although this method of teaching has become more utilized now that my son is in high school, one of his most effective teachers used it in the second grade! I have also learned from reviewing my son's tests with him that the questions asked are often difficult to decipher. My son's best teachers allowed student input on why questions were missed, searching for misinterpretation of the question rather than lack of knowledge.

When teachers understand the normal behavior and abilities of children of the age they teach, they can put the student's performance in perspective for both the child and the parents. A teacher's reassurances that your child's actions are typical of the age group allow you to interact appropriately with your child. This was especially important to us as our son became an adolescent. Because teachers have seen many students go through this difficult period, they can provide appropriate advice to parents on how to respond to particular problems in school.

Good teachers are important role models. I find this increasingly true for my son in high school. He has no desire to be a teacher, so the role his teachers model is one of appropriate behavior. They show that those in authority can be friendly, fair, ethical, slow to anger, responsible, willing to listen, and caring. Sometimes they can even be fun to be with. My son is calmer, more responsible, and more caring because of these teachers.

So, what have I, a teacher of veterinary students, learned from my son's teachers and molded into my own teaching? First, if I maintain my enthusiasm for my subject, I have a chance to teach well. If I lose that enthusiasm, then I need to discontinue teaching and channel my efforts elsewhere. Also, I try to take each student from his or her knowledge base and ability and build from there. Challenging each student to higher levels of performance is very important. It is more difficult to do this in a lecture class of eighty than in a clinic group of twelve, but it must be attempted regardless. The fact that a veterinary student expresses more interest in cows than dogs may be related to a lack of confidence in dealing with dogs, but this is not a reason for her to do poorly with dogs. This student must be challenged and helped to learn about dogs.

Today, I try to use more props while teaching, and I even try to incorporate some weird behavior at times to maintain attention and make a point. I try, without being judgmental, to search for the reason that a student might not be performing optimally. I am deliberately more open to the different ways that students learn and also use a wider variety of instruments to assess their abilities. Regularly, I review tests with students and listen to the reasons why they missed questions. I further encourage them to debate my opinions, especially when they find references to support their views. By doing my best with sick pets and their distraught owners, I try to model being a caring veterinarian. On occasion, I take time to eat breakfast with the students and bring in snacks when I know they have been working especially hard. It is important that I try to learn what they think their future holds and what their goals are, for I realize more than ever that what they are today is only a stop on the way to what they will become.

Finally, as a parent, I've learned to look at each student as someone else's child (even though my students are adults) and try to treat that student as I want my son's teachers to treat him. This variation of the "golden rule" should never lead me astray.

◆　　◆　　◆

Jeanne A. Barsanti, DVM, MS, Diplomate of the American College of Veterinary Internal Medicine (Specialty of Internal Medicine), is Professor and Chief, Small Animal Medicine Section, Department of Small Animal Medicine in The University of Georgia College of Veterinary Medicine. She won the Meigs Award in 1998.

Dr. Barsanti began teaching in 1974 upon completion of her DVM degree program at Cornell. Her first position was as an intern in small animal medicine and surgery at the Veterinary College at Auburn University. She spent two years at Auburn as a neophyte teacher, entirely in the Teaching Hospital with fourth-year students. Quickly she learned that what she loved most was teaching, writing, and clinical internal medicine and so committed herself to an academic career, rather than private practice. In 1976, she came to Georgia. Today Dr. Barsanti primarily teaches in the fourth-year clinical program using a problem-oriented approach on pets presented to the Teaching Hospital for diagnosis and therapy. She also teaches a large lecture class of eighty second-year students. In addition to veterinary students, she assists in training graduate veterinarians, principally interns and internal medicine residents.

Outside of work, her family operates a small farm raising goats and cattle (just can't get enough of animals!). Her son has no interest in veterinary medicine, teaching, or farming but looks forward to success in the business world.

FOSTERING CRITICAL THINKING: MAKING LEARNING FUN

Anne L. Sweaney

WHEN I HEAR the term *critical thinking*, I am reminded of my son, Christopher, who came home from first grade excited but exhausted. I said, "Christopher, what in the world did you do today to make you so tired?" He replied, "Mrs. Newton made us think all day long." Not thinking, I said, "Oh, that's too bad." Christopher quickly responded, a little miffed that I had missed the point, "No, Mom, thinking is fun!"

Today's world is hungry for people who can think. Where traditionally students in our educational institutions were offered little opportunity to "think outside the box," the careers that university graduates now pursue require skills beyond facts and figures learned by rote and repeated from memory. For these reasons, I have made it my personal mission to give students freedom to think critically. Since the very first day I stepped into the classroom, I have felt the need to make sure students have an opportunity to think on their feet and for themselves.

Meeting the challenges of preparing students for life in the twenty-first century has resulted in some serious reevaluation of our educational methodologies. The general public, parents, politicians, and professional educators all seem poised to implement several new approaches for educating the next generation. Foremost among the required changes in educational methodologies is a new emphasis on the teaching of critical thinking skills. The ability to think and use information is fundamental to the creative, flexible, and independent thought that will be essential for students to compete in life after completing formal schooling.

Like all skills, critical thinking requires practice, not just for students but for teachers as well. Students need the opportunity to try new approaches and repeat and modify techniques until they gain proficiency. And it is a teacher's responsibility to create an environment more conducive to learning. Teachers have to be willing to let go of some control, and black-and-white questions and answers must give way to occasional gray and even purple. Providing students with activities that foster critical thinking takes time and requires that teachers engage in their own critical thinking. This in turn forces decisions and, perhaps, shifts in faculty priorities that aren't always easy. Professors already have many demands on their time while striving for tenure and promotion, like research agendas, advising, outreach activities, and university service. In addition, since many professors have not had formal training in teaching methods, they must learn the skills. Time and imagination limit their abilities to develop learning activities that require the use of critical thinking. Still, I think we have no choice but to shift our teaching in this direction because of the potential benefits to students.

During my many years of interviewing and working with employers, I have learned that the number-one characteristic employers hunger for in new employees is their ability to solve problems and think critically and creatively. Employers are not looking for people with random access memory. They can buy a CD that will hold more of that type of information, they don't have to pay benefits to a CD, and CDs are very dependable and don't complain. What employers need is people who can use information to solve problems. Higher-order thinking is the one skill that humans possess that computers still don't, despite the new advances in fuzzy logic and artificial intelligence.

During the last half of the twentieth century, we have experienced a "knowledge explosion." There is so much information available, and because it is growing geometrically, we can no longer teach students everything that they will need to know. This adds urgency to the need for faculty to teach students how to organize information so that they can access it more efficiently. Critical thinking skills actually help students learn ways to process facts and information and use them to evaluate, analyze, and synthesize solutions to problems. The rapid rate of change likewise means that traditional solutions to problems are quickly becoming outdated. Thus, there will be an increasingly critical need for people who are mentally quick and ready to find new solutions to old as well as new problems.

What can teachers do to give students practice while tapping their critical thinking potential? Here are a few suggestions:

1. Let go of traditional lecture-only sessions. Encourage activities such as group problem solving, independent data gathering, and analysis of current events to force more active, participant learning.

2. Use case studies and problem sets to give the students an opportunity to apply their thinking skills to real-life situations. Case studies involve using situations germane to one's discipline that students analyze from beginning to end, evaluating the progression of events and what they would have done differently had they been key players. Case studies and brainstorming in groups or as a class teach students how the flow of events culminates in particular outcomes while prompting them to think. Problem sets tend to be shorter, more focused exercises, such as addressing situations currently receiving attention in the media that can help give students a sense of relevancy in their efforts. Cases and problem sets engage students in active class participation to develop their critical thinking skills and also serve as "dress rehearsals" for their futures.

3. Encourage students to use the world and the community as a classroom. Study-tour classes, where teachers and students learn from on-site visits, are often mentioned by students as their greatest college learning experience. A community as well as the university campus can serve in this role.

4. Create projects that have an end use and that contribute to society. Projects that produce tangible results show students the importance of developing skills, rather than just memorizing facts. These tangible results can also be used by students to show potential employers their skills and experience. In fact, more employers today are asking for a portfolio of work, as well as writing samples.

5. Develop objective as well as subjective assessments that test for critical thinking. Not only is assessment of student learning an essential component of instruction but if we are to have a rich and effective instructional program, it must be supported by an assessment program of equal quality. Traditional approaches (multiple choice, short-answer, essay, and other paper-and-pencil tests) served us well when we stressed knowledge and comprehension skills. They provided educators with reliable and reasonably valid information with a minimum of cost in time or money. But they aren't sufficient today. Although carefully constructed multiple choice and other paper-and-pencil test items *can* measure critical thinking skills, successful teaching of higher-order thinking necessitates adding the dimension of performance (doing rather than knowing) to the instructional program. Including subjective assessments also helps to develop critical thinking skills in constrained time situations. Demand for improved performance in general and the acquisition of higher-order thinking skills in particular require educators to introduce new and varied instructional methodologies into the classroom. These new techniques extend to the assessment component of instruction as well. The challenge is to develop teaching assessment programs (often called "performance assessments") that support and enhance the instruction of critical thinking.

6. Reward critical thinking by stressing its benefits on the syllabus and by pointing out how those skills will impact student grades through the various projects and assignments that are planned.

7. Make thinking and learning fun!

This last point may be one of the most important ways to encourage students to develop their critical thinking skills and become lifelong learners. While some may feel that "making thinking and learning fun" is pandering to generations who have become accustomed to instant gratification and a weakened work ethic, I have found quite the opposite to be true. Using teaching techniques that develop interest, activity, and passion sparks the internal fire for knowledge that encourages students to look for that which inspires thought and action in future situations they encounter, both inside and outside the classroom. The fact of the matter is, making learning fun is important for all of us, students or not. Just think about the seminars and workshops you have attended as a professional. Which ones did you retain more from—those where you listened passively or those with more engaging (i.e., fun) activities?

But how do we make thinking and learning fun while still conveying adequate information about the subject? And how do we achieve all of our teaching goals within the limitations of our resources? One of the simplest ways is to encourage (and require) group activities both for in-class and out-of-class assignments. Students enjoy feeling part of the classroom community and will be exposed to new ideas by their peers. These activities can also foster a healthy sense of competition, which also encourages critical thinking skills.

While it may seem contradictory to use "critical thinking skills" and "fun" in the same sentence, it is actually imperative that we begin to tap into the potential of both concepts in our teaching to produce the very best learning outcomes possible. Making learning fun increases the potential to teach critical thinking skills to students. It also has the side benefits of improved class attendance and motivating students to engage in class participation. Students will begin working on the learning process together, sharing ideas and inspiring one another. Additionally, encouraging students through "fun" activities that involve active participation helps them develop their communication skills, which are an essential companion to critical thinking skills.

We know, in our experiences as both instructors and students, that active, engaging teaching methods are one of the best ways to entice students to learn. Students who are taught in creative, innovative ways also learn to be creative and innovative themselves. The ability to be innovative and creative thinkers, in addition to being critical thinkers, provides students with an invaluable edge in life.

◆   ◆   ◆

Anne L. Sweaney is a professor in the Department of Housing and Consumer Economics in the College of Family and Consumer Sciences at The University of Georgia, where she serves as Undergraduate Coordinator and Director of the Housing and Demographics Research Center. She teaches undergraduate and graduate courses in housing and household technology and specializes in student internship placement, especially where former students can serve as supervisors and mentors. Dr. Sweaney was instrumental in the development of the Ph.D. program in the department, while also directing nineteen Master of Science students and serving as a member of twenty-four thesis committees. She won the Meigs Award in 1999.

Her award-winning teaching includes developing off-campus learning experiences, including the College of Family and Consumer Sciences' Legislative/Congressional Aide Program and the Department of Housing and Consumer Economics' study tours to Washington, D.C. She also coordinated and taught the first session of the college's study-abroad program. Dr. Sweaney is a leader in using learning technology and developed a Web site for teaching policy research and analysis.

Before coming to Georgia, Dr. Sweaney taught at the University of Alabama and was a Housing Specialist for the Cooperative Extension Service at North Carolina State University in Raleigh. She was born in India to a Norwegian missionary father and Norwegian-American missionary nurse mother. Following the death of her father, two-year-old Anne and her mother moved to a farm in Iowa where her ninety-four-year-old mother still resides. Dr. Sweaney is married to David Sweaney, a consultant with American College Testing. They have four children: Kirsten, twenty-seven; Sean, twenty-five; Heather, twenty-two; and Christopher, twenty. Her passions include connecting with people, collecting flow blue china and Coke glasses, traveling, and spending time with her family. She loves teaching and learning creatively.

WHY I TEACH

Richard K. Hill

*From a very early age, perhaps the age of five or six, I knew
that when I grew up I should be a writer. Between the ages of
about seventeen and twenty four I tried to abandon this idea,
but I did so with the consciousness that I was outraging my
true nature and that sooner or later I should have to settle
down to write books.*

George Orwell, "Why I Write," 1947[7]

MOST OF US are fortunate if we *ever* discover our "true nature" and
even luckier if we can manage to spend a large part of our adult
lives nourishing, rather than outraging, it. I certainly had no inkling
before the age of twenty-four of becoming a teacher. At the time I
entered college, I thought I might like to become a writer and had
been strongly attracted to Orwell and his books of powerful essays,
particularly "Reflections on Gandhi," with its impassioned arguments for humanism.[8] But my childhood had been dominated by the
Depression and the importance of having a steady job, and I was
easily persuaded to aim for a more practical career in science.

Yet I have been around fine teachers all my life. During the thir-
ties my mother had provided room and board to the out-of-town
young women who taught in our rural school. All through high
school and college a succession of kind teachers, from science and
math professors to debate coaches, befriended and educated me.

Dean Frank Whitmore, a world-famous organic chemist, taught a class to all four hundred Penn State freshmen physical science majors, nominally on atomic structure but actually on how to study, and another to all sophomore chemistry majors on what use chemists were to the world. (I was too young to be surprised that a dean would teach beginners, let alone teach at all.) He made chemistry come alive, and I knew then that I wanted to be part of it.

When it came time to leave graduate school and actually get a job, many of us who aspired to a serious scientific career were attracted to teaching positions in universities not because we had any particular calling or teaching ability (certainly no *training* in teaching) but because of our conviction that only in academia, not in industry, would we have the freedom to work on our own ideas or whatever observation aroused our curiosity. The irony, as time has passed, is that academic research has become just as goal-driven as industrial research, and the vision of freedom to pursue one's own ideas has largely vanished for most of today's young scientists, who must choose research projects that the government considers to be in the national interest.

Would the public be surprised to learn that most university faculty did not choose their careers for the rewards of teaching? I suspect not, for many have a dim view of the teaching that goes on today in research universities. The shift in emphasis from teaching to research, documented so thoroughly by historian Roger L. Geiger in his 1986 book *To Advance Knowledge: The Growth of American Research Universities*, has clearly brought tremendous advances in science and medicine, but the downside is the diminished emphasis on teaching undergraduates and the lower status of teachers.[9] Critics are legion, both from within and outside the ivory towers. Professors Robert and Jon Solomon, in *Up the University*, point out, "The mission of the university is to teach undergraduates . . . And yet it is fair to say that virtually no other institution or organization, public or private, has as bad a record for neglecting, ignoring, or denying its basic mission."[10] And to cite the most recently publicized investigation (the 1998 Boyer Commission Report, *Reinventing Undergraduate Education*), "The research universities have too often failed, and continue to fail, their undergraduate populations."[11]

The fault, I believe, lies only partly with the faculty, most of whom are serious and dedicated educators, and primarily with the underlying emphasis throughout the university on prestige, publications, and especially bringing in money.

Universities are not benevolent institutions, and for those at a research university who value teaching, academic life can be studded with disillusionment. Today's college students take most of their classes in groups of 250 to 400 ("Stack 'em deep, teach 'em cheap," as one of my colleagues put it), and a course with only 100 students is described as "an intimate learning experience." The material perks—promotion, salary increases, travel, computers, lighter teaching loads—go to those who bring in the bucks. *The Chronicle of Higher Education* has repeatedly reported statistics showing that the less time faculty spend teaching, the higher their salaries. One of my department heads once warned us, "Every hour spent in the classroom is a wasted hour." Joab Thomas (president of both the University of Alabama and Penn State) said in a 1991 speech at UGA, "The faculty, not the administrators, are the true custodians of the university," and on many occasions, we teachers felt we were treated indeed like custodians.

I must admit that these inequities rarely bothered me early on. I always enjoyed the excitement and rewards of research and was successful for most of my career in publishing and attracting research support. But I also relished teaching and worked hard to do a good job. In midlife, offered a research professorship at UGA, I passed it up for a regular teaching appointment, reasoning that I had received a valuable education at a state university and had the responsibility of giving young people like myself the same opportunity.

As time passed, it became more clear that, for me at least, the best aspects of an academic life were the opportunities to work with bright students in the lab and in the classroom. A watershed experience for me was the opportunity, as a UGA Senior Teaching Fellow, to learn about theories of learning that had not been part of my previous education. Serving on the UGA team in the American Association of Higher Education's (AAHE's) "Peer Review of Teaching" project introduced me to a host of strategies for assessing and improving teaching.

One may wonder just what it is that keeps teachers going at a university that emphasizes research. To me, teaching is the next best thing to raising children, without most of the discipline problems. The most important duty of anyone who becomes a parent is to raise his/her children well, and the state of Georgia has entrusted us teachers to do this not just with our own children but with everyone's. In my view, it is a sacred trust. Besides, what more life-affirming job is there than the opportunity to help shape the lives of creative, energetic, irrepressible young people?

What does it take to become a good teacher at a research university? On one level, not that much: a genuine interest in students as people, a willingness to spend precious time with them, and pride in doing a good job. Some falter because good teaching is hard work, and those who have not done it or have not tried to do it well have little idea of how much effort it really takes. The principles of good teaching have to be learned, just like anything else, but they are no mystery; the AAHE and UGA's Office of Instructional Support and Development (OISD) have published lists. My own list would include the following:

1. Students respond better when they understand that a teacher's interest and concern are genuine. I have made it a point to learn every student's name (even in classes of 180) and to spend time in the labs getting to know them.

2. The teacher must be scrupulously fair and treat students with respect. After all, if young people don't encounter fairness from adults on a university campus, where in society can they expect it? This does not require that teachers be wimpy. My freshman English teacher good-naturedly hurled chalk at students who made egregious errors, and he deducted a letter grade for each misspelled word (leading to occasional grades of "K" or "L"), but I came out of his class a confirmed proofreader.

3. The teacher must set a standard of high expectations and then help the class to live up to it. There is no greater incentive to learning than having an adult teacher tell you that you are capable of it. Carefully designing a course so that students gain confidence

by passing a series of hurdles of gradually increasing difficulty is a hallmark of good teaching.

4. We scientists are typically good lecturers, in that we can deliver facts and explanations clearly, but less often are we good teachers; we tend to focus on ourselves as transmitters and ignore the receivers. A real teacher points out patterns and relationships, links ideas and facts to previous knowledge, and teaches students to reason and analyze.

5. Studies show, not surprisingly, that the most effective teachers are those who somehow persuade their students to spend more "time on task." Writing assignments, homework, labs, group exercises, etc., may be unpopular but are indispensable to learning.

6. The best teachers know that the teacher is, like it or not, a role model, for good or bad, and that the act of teaching consciously or unconsciously imparts the values of the instructor.

Many more entries could be added to this list. My advice to those who wish to improve their teaching technique is to put yourselves in the student's place, literally. The best way to force yourself to think about your teaching methods and their effectiveness is to sit in on other teachers, good, bad, and ordinary, and reflect on what they are doing well or poorly. My teaching improved in my fifties as a result of taking a beginning Japanese class, partly because of the wonderfully patient and good-natured Mr. Honda and partly because I could easily put myself in the place of a student facing a mysterious subject like organic chemistry for the first time and think about what kind of reassurance, guidance, and feedback I would require.

So while I greatly admire the outstanding scientists whom I have known and worked with, the authors of the essays in this book and the teachers like them are my real heroes, and I feel lucky to be included among them and to know most of them personally. They exemplify the finest aspects of the academic world: intellectual curiosity, a spirit of free inquiry, critical and objective assessment of issues and ideas, and a lifelong interest in learning. To the names in this book should be added that of Keith Osborn, who received the Meigs Award in 1987 but did not live to contribute to this collection.

First educational director of Head Start and one of the founding fathers of *Sesame Street*, Keith was a true giant of American education, and a bench in his memory appropriately sits outside Aderhold Hall at The University of Georgia.

Looking back, I realize that nearly all the adult endeavors on which I made a conscious effort to achieve "success" (tennis, chess, piano playing, and even chemical research) met with very modest results. At the same time, the two areas of my life that have given me the greatest joy are those I did almost instinctively: helping Joan to raise four daughters and teaching for forty years.

I wish now that I had been better prepared for both enterprises and known more about what I was doing, but that does not diminish the enormous pleasure and satisfaction I have received from sharing our daughters' lives as they grew up and from interacting with bright, motivated students. Though it now seems inevitable that my life should have taken this turn, it took me decades longer than Orwell to realize my "true nature." I was very lucky that it proved to be the teaching career that I had fortuitously chosen.

Acknowledgments

I am grateful to Ron Simpson and Bill Jackson of the UGA Office of Instructional Support and Development for the chance to participate in the Senior Teaching Fellow program. Now in its fourteenth year, the program gives eight senior faculty members each year the chance to focus on undergraduate instruction, share ideas about teaching, and work on a project to strengthen teaching in their home departments. Through this and the Lilly Fellows program, which has similar goals for ten to twelve young faculty members each year, Ron and Bill are building a broad base of outstanding teachers who will serve the university well for decades to come. I also want to express my thanks to Bill Prokasy, who led UGA into the "Peer Review of Teaching" project and supported teaching improvement vigorously during his ten years as Vice President for Academic Affairs.

◆   ◆   ◆

Richard K. Hill, Professor Emeritus of Chemistry, grew up in north-western Pennsylvania and earned a chemistry degree from Penn State. He was a high school and college debater, and his wife accuses him of still being too argumentative for his own good. After receiving his Ph.D. from Harvard in 1953, Dr. Hill taught at Princeton for fifteen years before moving to The University of Georgia in 1968. He served as Acting Head of the UGA Chemistry Department for two two-year terms.

Dr. Hill's chemical research has focused on organic synthesis, stereochemistry, and natural products, and he has taught both undergraduate and graduate courses in these subjects. He has published over 120 papers, was awarded research fellowships from the Alfred P. Sloan Foundation, the National Science Foundation, and NATO, and was elected a Fellow of the American Association for the Advancement of Science for his research on the stereochemistry of enzymatic reactions. He supervised a total of forty-four Ph.D. students and ten MS students, and has taught thousands of undergraduates. He held visiting appointments at the National Heart Institute and the universities of Maine and New Hampshire and has consulted for several pharmaceutical companies.

Professor Hill was selected three times as Outstanding Teacher by the UGA chemistry majors and, in 1978, was one of the first group of General Beaver Teaching Chair appointees. He shared the 1987 Meigs Award with Keith Osborn. Since his retirement in 1993, he continues to conduct the organic chemistry review in the UGA preparation course for the Medical College Admission Test.

Dr. Hill and his wife, Joan, have four daughters and six grandchildren. He swims regularly and is struggling to learn to play the piano.

ELEMENTS OF EFFECTIVE TEACHING

Loch K. Johnson

Over the years I have frequently asked colleagues and students what they thought were the keys to more effective teaching. This essay attempts to sum up the insights derived from these conversations, melded with some of my own thoughts based on thirty years of classroom experience.

Subject Mastery

Mastery of one's subject is the starting point for effective teaching. This expertise doesn't come overnight, of course. Those who teach at the university level have had years of training in their disciplines already, yet we understand that learning is an ongoing process. We realize we have mastered only a fraction of what we would like to know, so we keep studying, researching, going to conferences, discussing our fields with others, reading the scholarly journals, and—based on all of this—revising our lecture and discussion notes to keep them current. This effort to continue learning has a revitalizing effect and keeps us interested in our subjects. The resulting enthusiasm inevitably spills over into the classroom.

Course Considerations

We also recognize that effective teaching requires organization. After all, what good is it to be a subject master if we fail to present our thoughts clearly? A first step is the crafting of a detailed course syllabus, one that outlines for the student precisely what the reading assignments are and when they are due. The syllabus should also spell out what the written assignments for the class will be and any other expectations the instructor has for the successful completion of the course. A student needs a road map at the beginning of his classroom journey. Spontaneity also has its place, though, and the instructor should feel free to modify plans along the way.

Other course considerations deserve advance attention. Among them are the kinds of tests you intend to use. Have the ambiguities been weeded out as much as possible? Have you considered trying oral exams in your smaller classes—those that still exist? What are the research experiences you want your students to have? Are they meaningful to students, or merely sterile exercises they must endure? What are the logical connections that lead your lectures from one topic to another? What types of visual aids do you intend to use?

This matter of visual aids is particularly important, I think, as we try to reach the MTV generation. Those of you who are William Jennings Bryans may be able to rely on oratory alone, but most of us could use some extra help. Today, universities have many first-rate films, videos, and documentaries available for classroom use. Some of the best instructors I have known integrate their lectures with overheads and slide presentations.

"Show and Tell" works beyond grade school, too. Bring interesting exhibits to class, say, a whale and an elephant humerus (if you are teaching zoology) to demonstrate aquatic and columnar adaptations among mammals. Once a physics colleague brought to my class on War and Peace in the Nuclear Age an elaborate model he had constructed from Ping-Pong balls and mousetraps, all encased in a large Plexiglas cage. He used it to demonstrate a nuclear chain reaction. The students watched from the edge of their chairs as he explained the principles behind an A-bomb, then released the first

Ping-Pong ball to start his own chain reaction. The visual depiction made the theory vivid, understandable, and unforgettable.

Drama has its place as well. I reenact in class a well-documented murder attempt by the Central Intelligence Agency (CIA) against an African leader during the earlier 1960s (Patrice Lumumba of the Congo). The props include rubber gloves, a gauze mask, a hypodermic needle, and a vial of poison. The room becomes quiet as I fill the needle with poison (water actually) and inject the fluid into an orange, all ready for Mr. Lumumba's lunch. This enactment is followed by a lively discussion about what place, if any, assassination plots have in America's foreign policy. This, in turn, leads to the question of the proper balance between morality and realpolitik in the nation's relations with other countries. I have heard of one professor who dresses up like Charles Darwin, then discusses "his" journey on the H.M.S. *Beagle* and the theory of evolution.

I am not arguing for an "Entertainment Hour" approach to learning. Most of the classroom period ought to be devoted to a serious examination of the central findings in one's discipline, but, when feasible, a visual display of the theories, concepts, and empirical findings holds great appeal to the student and assists the learning process.

Passion

The instructor should try to be interesting (Ernest Hemingway's first principle of good writing). Animation is a valuable attribute for any teacher. In contrast, the professor with a low, monotone voice who remains frozen behind the lectern will soon find enrollments plummeting, and rightly so; if the instructor feels no zeal for his topic, why should the student? Posture, facial expressions, tone of voice, intensity—in a word, the joy that one brings to the classroom—set the mood. If that mood is upbeat, the student is more likely to take an interest in the subject. One instructor I know in the Business School has a marvelous voice and, now and then, will even sing a few bars of his lecture!

Celebrate your academic discipline in the classroom: tell students about its history and its heroes, how the science or art is practiced, why it is important. I find that my students are especially fascinated

by the personalities of political figures, so, in and around the theoretical concepts and conceptual definitions I want them to learn, I
tell them about J. Edgar Hoover and why he had a phobia about
making left turns in his limo (and refused to do so). I also discuss
where Senator Joseph McCarthy obtained his counterfeit list of "57
Communists in the State Department," talk about John Maynard
Keynes's vivid impressions of Woodrow Wilson at the Versailles
Peace Conference, and tell how a few snowflakes on Edmund
Muskie's cheeks drove him from the 1972 presidential elections.

Rapport

The best instructors I know take time to develop rapport with their
students. Some come to class early for informal chats with them before
the lecture begins. Others go out of their way to encourage office visits or to invite small groups of students for a Dutch-treat lunch (standard practice at Harvard Law School). Field trips provide a wonderful
opportunity for more informal dialogue with students. One instructor I know recently took a group of undergraduates to the Carter Center and later reported that, on the bus ride, he got to know several of
them better than he would have in just a classroom setting.

I once asked a friend, F. A. O. Schwarz, Jr., a successful New
York trial attorney (and grandson of the toy manufacturer), how he
always seemed to win his cases. "Eye contact with the jury" was his
immediate reply. In the classroom, nothing so improves rapport with
students as eye contact; conversely, nothing so quickly loses students
than an instructor who stares at his lecture notes the whole period.
Move around a little, ask some questions, and look into the faces of
those whom you are trying to reach.

Listening

Good teachers are invariably good listeners. Unfortunately, many
instructors tend to dominate the classroom, talking without listening very much. We should obviously play the leading role, since pre-
sumably students are there to learn from our expertise. Still, students
should not be viewed merely as empty vessels that we are supposed

to fill up with information. They become more interested in what we have to say, paradoxically, when we take more interest in what they have to say. Besides, part of their education ought to be learning to speak more effectively before groups, a skill that requires practice. If our undergraduates go on to pursue MBA or law degrees, or other advanced graduate training, a premium will be placed on their oral presentations. To prepare them, we need to do a better job at drawing our students out in the classroom—not in a harsh Socratic method used in some law schools (a dubious approach to learning, in my view), but with encouragement and practice.

Rigor

Great teachers demand much of their students, challenging them to seek new levels of excellence. Students may grumble about all the reading, the research papers, and the tough quizzes, but I find that most of them are eventually pleased to be taken seriously and to be urged toward higher achievement. I reject the cynical conclusion of some that the easy teachers get the highest evaluations from students. I doubt this is true—certainly not with the Meigs professors whom I know at The University of Georgia.

Relevance

The most effective teachers seem to have a knack for making their subjects relevant to the student. Where does the student fit into the academic material; what do our lectures mean for him or her personally? How does our topic connect to broader ideas and values in our society? One way that provides a valuable means for showing students the ties that exist between their textbooks and the real world the authors are trying to capture is internships. So are field trips and guest lectures by practitioners. The involvement of students in our work, as research assistants and coauthors, can also provide rich lessons from hands-on experience.

Many of the best instructors I know have taken time off from academia to labor in the outside world, where they have been able to examine their disciplines from a more practical vantage point.

With this experience, they have integrated the theories in their disciplines with their own sense of "ground truth." Their scholarly lectures are seasoned with anecdotes from this "external laboratory" (where most of our students will end up).

Networking

Effective teachers build alliances, on and off campus, with other individuals interested in the instructional mission. Have you tried team teaching? This collegial approach to the classroom has proved to be an exciting experience for many instructors. It is usually a boon to students as well, because it gives them more than one perspective on a subject. Also, cross-disciplinary classes can be especially valuable in stimulating fresh cerebral connections. One of my favorite classes to teach is the one I mentioned earlier on War and Peace in the Nuclear Age. I invite into my classroom a succession of over twenty instructors from various disciplines (physics, religion, philosophy, history, ROTC, political science, law, education, and psychology), as well as off-campus experts from Atlanta, Washington, and elsewhere, to discuss the causes and prevention of international violence. Membership in instructional support groups can be a valuable experience, too. If you don't already belong to a group of individuals who meet to discuss their classroom experiences, why not form one? This is a great way to reinforce one's commitment to teaching while learning new pedagogical approaches.

Self-improvement

WALL ST. LAYS AN EGG, the newspaper *Variety* succinctly summed up Black Tuesday in October 1929. Every instructor similarly lays an egg at one time or another. The joke bombs, the discussion topic goes nowhere, the lab experiment fizzles. By weeding out the approaches that have failed, though, one makes the presentation better next time. I find that formal student evaluations can be insightful for improving one's classes, especially the written portions of the evaluation form. Less formally, once you know your students, the best of them will tell you candidly what they think about your course, from the texts to the tests. Each term, I modify much of what I do in the classroom based on the constructive criticism of students.

Enjoyment

We tend to take ourselves too seriously, huddled over word processors in our separate academic caves. Come out. Relax. Enjoy your students. Try some humor in your lectures. Don't be a drone: go on a hike, take an hour off for mountain biking, buy those roller blades. Be engaged in stimulating research. If you're not enjoying yourself in the classroom, seek counsel from some of the successful teachers in your department—or seriously consider a career change.

Commitment

The best teachers make a lifetime commitment to classroom excellence. Unlike Olympic sprinters, good teachers are not born with the talents necessary to succeed. Good teaching is a process of trial and error, of learning over a long period of time. One practical way to improve our teaching is to observe the lectures and seminars of outstanding instructors in our own departments and across campus. Find out where the Meigs recipients (and other instructional award winners) are teaching and ask if you can sit in occasionally.

Finally

Here, then, are some elements of effective teaching; this book is a rich lode of other examples. One thing is certain to me: those of us who have entered the teaching profession have chosen well. In our daily opportunities to serve as mentors to the young, we are given a rich reward—the satisfaction of seeing our students prepare themselves for their life's work. Over the years I have heard faculty members comment time and again on how this experience has been of more enduring satisfaction to them than any other aspect of their academic careers. I stand happily among their ranks.

◆   ◆   ◆

Loch K. Johnson is Regents Professor of Political Science, in the School of Arts and Sciences at The University of Georgia. He was born in Auckland, New Zealand, and educated at the University of California. He has taught large undergraduate courses such as the Introduction of American Government, as well as more specialized courses, like the U.S. Presidency and a course on American foreign policy. At the graduate level he has conducted seminars like the U.S. Presidency and War and Peace in the Nuclear Age. He also teaches seminars on U.S. intelligence policy and American foreign policy. Dr. Johnson likes the mixture of teaching experiences that a succession of large and small classes allows. In each class, he varies his presentation with a blend of lecture material, visual presentations, and open discussion. He won the Meigs Award in 1988.

Before joining the faculty at The University of Georgia, Professor Johnson taught at the University of California, Riverside campus; the University of North Carolina, Chapel Hill; and Ohio University. He has also served as a White House staff aide in the Carter and Clinton administrations and has been a staff member of four congressional committees: Foreign Relations and Intelligence in the U.S. Senate, and Foreign Affairs and Intelligence in the U.S. House. He has served as the staff director of the Subcommittee on Oversight for the House Intelligence Committee. In Georgia, he is a member of the Georgia State Board of Elections. Professor Johnson is the author of several books on foreign policy, national security, and American politics, including *A Season of Inquiry* (1987), *Decisions of the Highest Order* (1989, with Karl F. Inderfurth), *America's Secret Power* (1989), *Runoff Elections in the United States* (1992, with Charles S. Bullock III), and *Secret Agencies* (1996). His hobbies include distance running, drawing, and various civic activities. Dr. Johnson's daughter, Kristin, is an economics major at Amherst College in Massachusetts, and his wife, Leena, is an administrator for the Public Administration program in the Department of Political Science at The University of Georgia. All three are avid Alpine skiers and travelers.

LIFE'S MEANING

John Granrose

TEACHING IS IMPORTANT business. At least that's how it seems to me. For those of us who take teaching seriously, it can be one of the things that gives life its meaning. Two stories might help explain what I mean.

First story: when I was an undergraduate I once confided to a favorite professor that I was interested in becoming a college teacher. He *immediately* responded, "And if you lose your passion for it, make a change. Promise?" I promised.

Second story: many years later, when I was just beginning my teaching career in the UGA Philosophy Department, I was startled by a colleague's challenge: "Would you give your life for philosophy?" We had, as I recall, been discussing Socrates's choice to accept death rather than escape from prison. Still, the question surprised me. My colleague continued: "You know, if you spend your whole life teaching philosophy and then you die without having done anything else, you have given your life for philosophy."

The question has remained with me to this day. "Would you give your life for . . . ?" Well, what *is* worth dying for, anyway? As I have reflected on this question over the years, my own conclusion has emerged: "persons." For me, it could only be persons and their well-being that could ultimately justify the giving of a life. Philosophy as such, a collection of theories and ideas, is not sufficiently "real" to justify the giving of one's life.

But wait a minute. *Teaching* philosophy makes a difference in people's lives. I know that from experience. It made a difference for me when I first encountered it as a student, and I could see that it made a difference in the lives of my students over all those years. *Teaching* involves *connecting*. The teacher and students connect with each other. The teacher helps the students connect with the subject matter at hand. And the teacher also helps the students connect with each other. These were the things that motivated me to spend a major part of my life teaching philosophy.

Teachers are different, of course. Not all of them are as energized by the idea of *connecting* as I was. Some are simply so fascinated by their particular subject matter, and so knowledgeable about it, that their excitement "rubs off" on their students. Others, including some of the most brilliant teachers I know, enjoy "performing" in front of an audience—"showing off" their abilities, as it were. But for me, I found the meaning of *my* teaching career in the experience of sharing with my students.

When I first joined the UGA faculty I was only a few years older than my students. Despite having earned a Ph.D. in philosophy, I wasn't very far ahead of them in knowledge either—especially when I was assigned courses in areas outside of my academic specialty. I recall, for example, teaching a course in aesthetics for the first time in 1966 and wondering if I would be able to keep ahead of my students and/or whether I would end up making a fool of myself. But somehow the importance of feeling "in this together" kept me going. I recall saying to one of these early classes, "The motto for this course is not 'Let me show you what I can do' but 'Let's see what we can do together.'" This became something of a leitmotiv during my UGA years.

I began teaching in the sixties, during a time when students in general, and philosophy students in particular, were often actively involved with the issues of war and peace and racial and sexual equality. The courses in ethics and in social and political philosophy that I taught were filled with debate about the practical implications of philosophy for such topics, a kind of connecting that seemed important to the students and to me as well.

It was also during the sixties that my three children were born and that I learned the value of family life, something I experienced as *enriching* my teaching career rather than *competing* with it. I frequently found "teaching stories" and useful examples of ethical dilemmas in my home life during those years. My children knew that and were proud of me when I received the Meigs Award in 1983.

During my early years of teaching, I also encountered the tension between the demands of teaching and of research. As a young assistant professor with a family, I was aware of the importance of earning tenure—and the necessity of academic publication to achieve this goal. So I did the relatively narrow research this required and wrote the necessary articles. What I discovered in doing so was that I loved to read, to learn from others, and to communicate to others what I had learned—but that I was more motivated to *teach* than to publish. The strong desire to learn and to share was there, but it focused on classroom teaching rather than on professional publication. Fortunately for me, my department head and my dean recognized the value of this, and I felt recognized and rewarded. I have sometimes described these years as the time when I "came out" as an *intellectual* rather than a researcher.

This is important, I suppose, because my own struggles to find my identity as a teacher, and to resist the temptation to shortchange my classroom responsibilities in favor of forcing myself to write for publication, served indirectly as something of a model for my students. I was trying to find my *own* path in life, my personal calling, and not simply conform to social expectations. I was trying to find and then to follow what some have called "the path with heart," the path that gives one energy. For me, this path required classroom teaching and the associated interactions with students. Personally, this is where I was "in my element." And the students, of course, noticed and appreciated this. They could tell that I loved my work—and *them*. And they returned the favor. One of my favorite comments on a course evaluation form was, "I'm 'more myself' now than before I took this course."

During the 1960s and 1970s, I devoted much energy to learning the more or less "standard" material of academic philosophy and sharing it with my classes. In the 1980s, however, I noticed that my interests were shifting somewhat. During this period I became more interested in the kind of philosophy that shaded into psychology, religion, and even mythology. I began reading authors like Carl Jung and Joseph Campbell, and I felt "called" somehow. For the most part, especially at first, I kept these new interests separate from my classroom teaching. Eventually, however, I offered an undergraduate seminar on Philosophy and Mythology and received a warm response. At the conclusion of the seminar, I confessed to the class that I also wanted to offer a seminar on the philosophical and personal implications of Grimms' fairy tales, a topic I had discovered through my developing interest in Carl Jung, but that I was concerned that my academic colleagues would consider the theme "silly" (or worse). The students in the seminar encouraged me to go ahead. I did so, we "connected" even more than before, and all of us enjoyed and benefited from the experience. It became clear to me that both folk tales and myths, in their own mysterious ways, could contain deep philosophical and psychological insights, insights that our contemporary culture sometimes overlooked.

Then I remembered what my undergraduate professor had made me promise. Somehow my passion had migrated from academic philosophy to these new areas of psychology, mythology, and the like. The passion for teaching, in the sense of "connecting," remained. But the subject that now energized me was new. As a result, and after much reflection, I decided to give up teaching philosophy as such and devote the remainder of my life to working in these new areas. It seemed to me that many persons were suffering from a hunger for more meaning in their lives and that there might be something that could help.

To have the time to devote to my new interests, I retired from the UGA Philosophy Department in 1993 and moved to Zurich, Switzerland, to study at the C. G. Jung Institute for Analytical Psychology. The psychological training offered by the Jung Institute includes attention to comparative religion, mythology, dream and fairy tale interpretation, in addition to standard psychiatric topics. It was a difficult decision to give up my philosophy teaching career and The University of Georgia, both of which I had greatly enjoyed for so many years, but I felt that I had to do so if I was to remain true to myself. So I did it. Somehow, for me, it was connected with my life's meaning—and I remembered the promise I had made.

Now, some years later, having received my diploma from the Zurich Jung Institute and having had a private practice as a psychoanalyst since then, I have returned to teaching and added "academic administration" to my career. I am now Director of Studies at the C. G. Jung Institute Zurich. As such, I am responsible for arranging the courses taught to our over three hundred students, who come from a variety of professional backgrounds and from over forty different countries. All of them have found themselves "called," as I was, to learn more about that special area where psychology, philosophy, religion, mythology, and the like overlap. And in addition to my administrative duties, I get to *teach* again—to *connect* with a new generation of students and with a subject matter that is close to my heart.

Interestingly enough, I find many aspects of my administrative duties exciting. I have contact with Jungian psychoanalysts and other experts worldwide and get to encourage them in their work with our students. So my influence reaches beyond my personal classroom. On the other hand, as I experienced with my earlier research efforts, I am sometimes frustrated and dissatisfied with the sorts of activities administration requires: the frequent committee meetings are the best example. Still, I am experiencing, and mostly enjoying, this new form of connecting. On the whole, I feel "in my element" once again. But if I should lose my passion for this new life, well, perhaps you can guess the answer. In my view, openness to new experiences and a willingness to change give life its rich meaning. The *details* of this meaning are different for each of us, but the core is the same: find what you love to do—and do it with all your heart. That is my prayer for those of you reading these words.

◆   ◆   ◆

John Granrose was born in Miami, Florida, and attended the University of Miami as an undergraduate, where he had a double major in philosophy and psychology. After a year as a U.S. Fulbright Grantee in Heidelberg, Germany, he attended the University of Michigan, receiving his Ph.D. in 1966. That same year, he joined the faculty of The University of Georgia, where he remained until his retirement in 1993. At UGA, Dr. Granrose taught courses in ethics, aesthetics, and social and political philosophy, as well as the usual introductory courses in philosophy and in logic. While he sometimes taught lecture courses with as many as 250 students, his preference was seminars, especially those in the Honors Program. Professor Granrose also enjoyed working with graduate students and directing theses and dissertations. Currently, he is Professor Emeritus of Philosophy.

Professor Granrose says his years at The University of Georgia were good ones and that he will always be grateful to his former students and colleagues. Besides the Meigs Award, which he won in 1983, he received a number of other signs that his teaching was appreciated, including the Honors Program's Honoratus medal and the Franklin College's General Sandy Beaver Teaching Professorship.

After retiring from UGA, he moved to Switzerland to study at the C. G. Jung Institute and received his Diploma in Analytical Psychology in 1996. At that point, he returned to Athens and established a private practice for Jungian psychoanalysis. In 1998, he accepted his present position as Director of Studies at the C. G. Jung Institute in Zurich, Switzerland, where he now resides.

Dr. Granrose has three grown children and five grandchildren. His interests include magic, music, and computers, and he is a member of an a cappella singing group, the Gentlemen Songsters of Zurich.

Responsibilities of a College Teacher

Dean G. Rojek

As I LOOK back at my twenty-five years of teaching, I am painfully aware that much of what I have been doing in the classroom was nothing more than on-the-job training. I had no courses in how to teach; I had no mentors to guide me through my first classes; I attended no workshops on how to be an effective college teacher. Unfortunately, I see no evidence to suggest that our most recent cohorts of newly minted Ph.D.s who are marching into their classrooms have any more experience or guidance than I had. It is amazing how we devote so much time and energy into producing first-rate researchers, but teaching simply becomes an add-on. We assume that good researchers will eventually be good or at least adequate teachers. It seems that teaching has become a do-it-yourself enterprise that we muddle through in our early years as college instructors, and eventually we acquire our classroom survival skills through trial and error. Many survive this boot-camp experience, but it can exact a terrible toll on early careers and on students. For others, the art of teaching does not come with simple experience, and life in the classroom experience becomes a chore or an irritant. However, teaching ought to be more pleasurable, more stimulating, and more rewarding.

I believe that our first responsibility as college teachers is to pass on to the next generation of college teachers what we have learned in the classroom. Conversely, I think that new college instructors should be required to sit in on classes and see firsthand what front-line action is all about. We need some way to convey to the next generation of college instructors what works and what does not work. But there seems to be the perennial reinvention of the wheel on every college campus every time a new instructor is hired. We need to fling the doors of our classrooms open and have not only new faculty but also the veteran instructors as well sit in on our classes. We desperately need more collegial exchanges, formal and informal, about classroom techniques and teaching strategies. I am embarrassed to say that I have visited very few classes taught by my colleagues, and very few of my colleagues have ever visited my classroom. There is little sharing of teaching methods, and yet teaching is our profession. Unlike any other occupational endeavor, the life of an academic is cloaked in academic freedom, but at times this becomes a cocoon where we live, teach, and conduct research. The life of a college professor can be a very insulated and isolated experience. We are not supervised, tutored, monitored, or made to respond to any time clock. It is a most unusual existence, terribly liberating but yet potentially debilitating. The very essence of teaching is sharing, and yet we share so little information about teaching with our colleagues. It strikes me that most of the more successful teaching techniques that I have utilized in the classroom were actually borrowed from other college professors.

There is no question that teaching is an art form, and as with any artistic endeavor, there needs to be a basic talent or ability, diligent preparation, monitoring or guidance, and a certain reckless abandon to attempt new techniques at reaching our audience. Teaching invites a constant trial and error, innovative techniques, and an honest reassessment and rebooting. It is easy to march into the classroom and lecture, but it is far more difficult to engage in an intellectual dialogue. I can remember my first year of teaching and struggling with the realization that some students were not interested in the material. I was tossing out every thought and idea that I could conjure up, but I was afraid to ask them why we were not connecting. It took me many years to realize that being a good instructor is not being a gifted orator or a brilliant researcher but having a certain element of compassion and openness. I really did not know my audience. I was still functioning in the rarefied air of graduate school and never realized that many undergraduates are not going to be brilliant academics, but they might become competent and successful real estate agents, law enforcement officers, sales personnel, or perhaps even automotive mechanics. My course was one of many courses that students take, and I needed to gear my teaching to a much more pragmatic audience than future Ph.D.s. Thus, I believe that a key responsibility of a college instructor is to try to reach out to every student, to allow feedback, and to implement change in the classroom. It is so easy to preach to the choir but so much more difficult to reach out to those who are not shouting the "amens."

I just finished reading my course evaluations for the past term. They were good, but I know they could be better. I lost touch with a few students; I said things carelessly in class that a few misunderstood; I failed to explain a few topics clearly. My first reaction is a bit of anger and hurt that some students did not feel this was the most exciting course they ever took. Each time I read course evaluations, I skip over the laudatory ones and then focus on the less than flattering ones. I am always amazed how thin-skinned I become whenever I read a negative reaction. But after a few days, the wounds heal, and I try to devise strategies for improving the course. There is a sort of a rebirth with the start of each term. I can start fresh and try new approaches, try to clarify certain topics, and try to relate more effectively with a new audience. I find it exciting and challenging to start over and to move from course to course. I think of my nonacademic friends who deal with the same clientele over and over again, and who work on the same issues day in and day out. Teaching at the university level can be terribly energizing because you can make dramatic alterations in your subject matter, interact with a new audience, and test out new approaches and new ideas. It strikes me that a key responsibility of a college instructor is never to grow old in spirit. We need to stay in touch with our students, with our discipline, and with the world. In order to stay connected, we need to jettison some material and bring in new thoughts and new ideas. We need to really converse with our students and pick the minds of our consumers in evaluating courses and classroom strategies.

One of the most difficult aspects of college teaching for me has been listening. It is easy to lecture, to prepare transparencies, or to prepare and grade examinations. But I have a far more difficult time listening to my students, understanding their position, and giving credence to their thoughts and ideas. I interact with racists, born-again Christians, staunch conservatives, wide-eyed liberals, students who cannot spell, students who sleep in class, exceptionally bright students, and some students who just want to get through the course. I like to impose reality on my students, but there are times that I realize that my view of reality may not coincide with the views of my students. It has been at times a challenge for me to accept their views or even tolerate the suggestion that there may be other perspectives. However, the most successful class for me is when I can connect with the views of my students. I try to respect their perspective but show them that there could be other ways of viewing reality. It is easy to cram concepts down their throats but far more difficult to convince them that there are other ways of looking at the world. Rather than bringing the sledgehammer to class and demolishing the student's world, it seems to be more effective to renovate or perhaps put on an addition, or better yet, add a skylight.

I developed a nasty habit of lecturing to that bored, zombie-like student who stares out the window in the back of the room. There was a period of several years when I became so focused on those less than scintillating students that I would overlook the rest of the class. It became a challenge for me to motivate, energize, and excite these glazed-over students. I would define the success or failure of each class by the reaction I got from some of those few disinterested students. Teaching became a battle between those students who appeared to be anesthetized and me. But I gradually began to realize that I cannot excite every student and I was not a failure because every student did not smile when I cracked a joke. More important, I learned that some very capable students sit in the back of the class and my judgment about their abilities or interest was often in error.

Finally, after years of teaching, I came to the conclusion that not every successful student earns an A and not every student finds my material of vital interest. But over the course of the semester, I could reach most students and add some bit of wisdom to their intellectual storage bin. I sincerely believe that every student is educable, but some are simply not as intellectually gifted as others are. I have also come to appreciate the very average student who works extremely hard, struggles through every examination, never makes the dean's list, but is diligent and conscientious. We have to make a place for average students, and many times, they are the most rewarding students to work with.

My objective is to make students think, to challenge them to take a position, and to force them to defend their position. It disturbs me that students can go through my course, know the material very well, but not internalize this material to the point that it influences their outlook on life. In all of my courses I require students to submit position papers or reaction papers. I want them to take an issue, look at it from their perspective, and write clearly and succinctly how they would address the issue. I find that college students take too many notes and read a wealth of material, but it bothers me that for many the essence of the course does not become part of their worldview. We allow the classroom to become too comfortable for our students. They can reiterate someone else's view, but they have a difficult time explicating their own position. Worse yet, I find students who are fearful of taking a position because it does not coincide with the perspective of the instructor, and these students feel that their own views are worthless. Perhaps the most difficult task in the classroom is to build a certain sense of self-esteem and mutual respect. I understand the position of someone else, I can endorse or reject that position, but most important, I can explain why I accept or reject that position. I try not to brainwash students as much as to expose them to ideas and let them build their own philosophy of life. A critical responsibility is to empower our students to think, to take positions, and to have the ability to defend those positions.

The sacred aura of office hours has long lost its luster. Most of the time I forget when my office hours are scheduled, and they simply become filler on the syllabus. I have found that the advent of e-mail is a simple but effective way of encouraging direct contact with students. The "respond" key is easy to hit and students seem to appreciate any response. My students appear to be intrigued with Web pages, and I am experimenting with Web pages for each class, and inviting them to look over the links that I provide to other related material. I encourage my students to prepare a "legal brief" on any exam item that they feel deserves full or partial credit. They submit these appeals via e-mail, and it takes only a few minutes to read and evaluate these appeals. In point of fact, I routinely give some credit to any student who attempts to conjure up a reasonable explanation for why he or she responded to an examination question. My goal is to encourage my students to think independently, to introduce them to the world of research and scientific evaluation, and to invite them to challenge me on any point I bring up in class.

In sum, teaching ought to be a collective enterprise. We need to share our thoughts, teaching techniques, and philosophies of education with our colleagues. We ought to visit classrooms to learn and to offer constructive criticism. New faculty members ought to be given guidance and regular feedback on their classroom strategies to get them started. Similarly, established college instructors ought to invite colleagues to the classrooms to encourage positive feedback. But just as important, we need to incorporate our students into our classroom agenda. I found that by having a class critique early in the semester, I can respond to specific requests and make midpoint corrections in the course. We need to learn more about our students, why they take a course, previous courses they already have taken, and what it is that they are expecting out of a course. Thus, the primary responsibility of effective teaching is the ability to connect with our students, and getting connected means that we as instructors need to first plug in not only our microphones but also our hearing aids.

◆   ◆   ◆

Dean G. Rojek is an associate professor in the Department of Sociology at The University of Georgia. He received his Ph.D. from the

University of Wisconsin in 1975. Initially he intended to get a law degree and minor in sociology, but he reversed his priorities. Prior to coming to The University of Georgia, he taught at the University of Arizona. His primary interests are in the areas of juvenile delinquency and the sociology of law. He won the Meigs Award in 1998.

Professor Rojek has visited China on several occasions and has written on Chinese social control strategies. Presently he is gathering data on homicides in Atlanta and is writing a book on the causes and correlates of homicide. He teaches courses in juvenile delinquency, social problems, sociology of law, and selected topics in criminology.

His research interests allow him to work with community groups on specific issues. He has administered self-report surveys to sixth- through twelfth-grade students throughout Georgia on drug use and abuse. This has led to numerous presentations to parents, school boards, and students on the issue of drugs in American society. Similarly, his interest in homicide has led to numerous presentations to law enforcement agencies on the causes and prevention of homicide.

A number of years ago Dr. Rojek became interested in being a track official, and he is currently certified in U.S.A. Track & Field at the national level. He helped run a training facility for the 1996 Atlanta Olympics and obtained track shoes for a team from the Comoros who had neither track shoes nor any uniforms. Later, he officiated at the 1996 Paralympics, working with blind and disabled athletes. He routinely officiates at track meets at Clemson, Emory, The University of Georgia, and various high schools.

Creating an Environment for Teaching and Learning[12]

Josef M. Broder

Teaching is a messy, indeterminate, inscrutable, often intimidating, and highly uncertain task.

Richard Elmore

I WOULD LIKE to share with you some insights from my teaching experience, which began when I was a graduate teaching assistant and continues today in my role as Assistant Dean for Academic Affairs in our college. Throughout my teaching career I have sought to create an environment that will promote and reward teaching and learning. Thus, this paper is devoted to creating effective teaching and learning environments.

Graduate Teaching Experience

One of the more fundamental and strategic periods for learning how to create teaching and learning environments is during one's graduate education. Graduate school can, and should, provide opportunities to teach professors how to teach. But on this subject, Richard Elmore writes (p. xi):

> Professors spend most of their graduate education preparing to conduct research; their only preparation for teaching is their own, largely unexamined, experience as students. In the peculiar world of universities, one is expected to know how to teach as a condition of employment, but the practical problems of teaching are almost never discussed.

Unlike teachers in primary and secondary education, college teachers seldom receive formal training on how to teach. In a survey of teaching evaluations, William Taylor and I found almost no involvement by graduate students in the teaching programs (Broder and Taylor). Granted, faculty do more than teach, but because the potential impact of our teaching efforts is immense, it seems very shortsighted that graduate students receive so little teaching guidance and encouragement. This lack of involvement by graduate students is a disservice to young would-be teachers, their students, and the university.

I was more fortunate than most because I was given the opportunity to teach classes as a graduate student. My experience was invaluable and left me with a profound and lasting impression of what it means to be a professor, a scholar, and a member of the university community. On this basis, I advise future professors to get involved in teaching while in graduate school. Don't wait until you receive your faculty appointment and are struggling to publish and develop new research projects. Graduate teaching assistants also tend to do far better on their oral exams and defenses than their counterparts. Learning from and being comfortable with academic discourse are valuable assets in our profession. Believe me, I've watched some of our top graduate students fail oral exams because they lack experience expressing their knowledge verbally. Teaching would have helped them.

Teaching Experience

While graduate school training can initially prepare individuals for college teaching, hands-on classroom experience as a faculty member is critical to developing effective teaching and learning environments. I've watched many young, and some not-so-young, faculty struggle in the classroom. Not only have they suffered but their students also suffered and ultimately complained to me as the department's undergraduate coordinator. When on occasion I was asked to diagnose the problem, I found most often that students became hostile or uninterested when faculty changed or violated the student contract, i.e., course expectations. Changing the rules of the game defined in the syllabus, being too dogmatic and inflexible, and not giving students any benefit of the doubt all ask for trouble. To avoid these pitfalls, my advice to young teachers is that they not try to solve these problems on their own. Instead, recognize

1. that you are not the only teacher in the department,
2. that others have probably taught your course,
3. that others have more experience in teaching than you, and
4. your colleagues are more than glad to help.

Seek help. Don't worry about losing control or feeling inadequate. Second opinions can give you some amazing insights into solving teaching dilemmas. However, you don't have to duplicate exactly what other teachers do. Recognize that teaching styles are unique to individual personalities. Identify and adopt a teaching style that is comfortable and seems natural to you.

Because student evaluations are another valuable source of data to diagnose your teaching performance, I strongly encourage faculty to regularly survey students and use the information to improve your teaching. Ask colleagues to help you interpret your evaluations. Don't focus on the outliers, i.e., extreme comments, but focus on means or trends. If possible, gain access to the raw data and generate a richer set of statistics. If you are having problems teaching, try to identify which groups of students are being the most critical and why. Try to identify who is your audience, or which audiences you have been ignoring. Of course, bear in mind that overall student evaluations may be largely determined by a few teacher and course characteristics (Broder and Dorfman).

Beyond Lecture

Teaching styles and methods shape the teaching and learning environment. A common mistake in many classrooms is the overuse of lectures to the exclusion of other teaching techniques. Many of us were taught in lectures, and we continue to use this technique to a fault. My major professor in graduate school, Al Schmid, had some keen insights about the lecture method. He said that lectures were artifacts of the Middle Ages, before there were printing presses. Without printed materials, students merely transcribed the teachers' or speakers' comments. This was not learning but transcription. Yet today, the practice continues almost unabated, while learning suffers and students become transcribers, and inefficient ones at that. The next time you lecture, take a moment to read some of the notes your students are taking. You'll be surprised at the inaccuracies and gaps in their note-taking.

My advice to young teachers is to vary your style. Lectures are effective to a point, but fifteen minutes into the lecture, you may lose half of your class. Add some variety and diversity in your delivery. Ask questions, have students write and react, be quiet, have students speak, show a video, or use visual aids. Recognize that students get tired of any one teaching technique and tend to learn more if they are exposed to an idea through different mediums.

Engage Students

Experience has taught me that teaching and learning are interactive processes. Teaching and learning environments are affected by the extent to which students are actively involved in the process. Yet, many of us are overly concerned with the delivery of factual content. A number of studies have found that when lecturing is the dominant mode of teaching, students forget up to 50 percent of course content within a few months (Garvin, p. 4). Elmore writes (p. xii), "We have knowledge, only as we actively participate in its construction." Students learn by engaging with other students and with the teacher in a process of inquiry, critical discourse, and problem-solving. When teachers fail to engage students, the entire class experience suffers from a lack of *class energy* (White).

The teaching and learning process can also suffer from a lack of ownership. Teachers deliver factual materials, students transcribe notes, and no one claims ownership or responsibility for the process or outcome. A classic problem of common property, lack of ownership results in a lack of responsibility. Students learn from being actively involved in the learning process and not from memorizing facts and figures presented in soon-to-be-forgotten lectures. Active learning begins with the premise that faculty members don't own knowledge nor is the knowledge that students might gain restricted in any way by the course syllabus. The latter is merely a guide to some of the things students could learn in the course. Elmore adds (p. xvi), "The main value that students take away from our classes is not their knowledge of the subject, but a predisposition to learn." My colleague, Steve Turner, has long argued that to instill in students the predisposition to learn, we should teach them the capacity to learn by having them conduct independent research (Turner).

In practical terms, I advise you to engage your students, make them partners in the education process, and share with them the responsibility for learning. Listen to what students have to say, give students a voice in the learning process, and don't assume that knowledge is a one-way affair. Let me give you an example. We had a bright instructor who was struggling in the classroom. Class morale had deteriorated to the point where one student publicly berated the teacher in class for a long list of shortcomings. The teacher was devastated and the class was in turmoil. He was advised to deal with the crisis and shift the burden of learning to the students. In response, he incorporated some marketing games that engaged the students, the students enjoyed the experience, and his teacher ratings improved drastically—not so much for what the teacher had done, but because of what the students had done.

Civility

Interpersonal relationships between students and faculty also affect the teaching and learning process. Students are more inclined to accept the responsibilities of learning if the class environment is open and based on mutual respect. Unknowingly, some faculty members lose empathy for students who are confused or slow to comprehend. Some use teaching methods that rely heavily on fear, intimidation, and anxiety. While the last approach may work for basic training in the military, I have serious reservations about its usefulness in college education. Negative techniques may have short-term positive effects on class attendance (i.e., too many absences and students fail the course), but classes that use negative techniques are often unpleasant for both the teacher and students.

Positive techniques, in contrast, afford students a measure of respect and trust. When faculty treat students with respect, the latter are more likely to direct their energies toward learning than in hostility toward teachers, the text, the course, or the university. By "respect," I don't mean (1) that teachers should avoid hard choices, (2) that every student will pass the course, or (3) that faculty defer to the whims of the class. My point is that faculty should treat students like equal partners in the educational experience.

I use a number of techniques to enhance mutual respect in my classes. First, I routinely take class photographs and make an honest effort to learn my students' names. Class photographs extend the contract beyond the class period and give a sense of permanence to the teaching experience. Second, I replaced pop quizzes, which seem rather punitive, with asking students what they learned today and what confused them. Third, I routinely ask students about their study habits and run regression models that explain their exam scores (Broder and Wetzstein). The objective is to show how exam scores are affected by absences, prerequisites, study habits, grade-point averages, and other factors. Fourth, I make an effort to write a brief note to the parents of my top students, congratulating them on their child's performance in my class. The parents and students truly appreciate this gesture. Follow-up letters from these parents have been some of the most rewarding mementos of my teaching career.

Faculty Renewal

Faculty renewal is critical for sustaining effective teaching and learning environments, especially for faculty members with heavy teaching loads. Renewal activities range from periods away from the classroom, to attending workshops, to sabbatical leaves. These activities help faculty generate new ideas, fight teacher burnout, and reinvigorate one's passion for teaching. Attending teaching workshops and participating in peer dialogues on teaching can be most rewarding. On occasion, we should seek workshops outside our profession. While each discipline has something to say about teaching, the interaction with other disciplines can provide a valuable source of new teaching ideas and techniques. One of my most memorable experiences as a faculty member at The University of Georgia was participating in the Senior Teaching Fellows program.

Sense of Humor

Finally, faculty attitudes and perceptions contribute to the teaching and learning environment. Years ago, I asked my son, Joey, what he wanted to do when he grew up. Joey, who was four years old at the time, said, "Dad, I want to be a *professor* and a *comedian* just like you!" While I make no claims of being a classroom comedian, I have always appreciated humor in the classroom, whether coincidental or intentional. However, those who want to introduce humor in their classrooms should distinguish between *delivering humor* and *developing a sense of humor* (Berk). I think a key element of effective teaching is for teachers to develop a sense of humor that goes beyond telling an occasional joke, which has become dangerous in this age of political sensitivity. By a sense of humor, I mean a state of mind that recognizes the limitations of ourselves and our knowledge. Humor is a relief from dogma, which students find to be tedious. Humor and irony can be powerful teaching tools when used to challenge, and present, conflicting points of view. Teachers with a sense of humor appear more human and, perhaps, more believable. Without a sense of humor, it would be difficult to survive the rigors of teaching at a research university.

In closing I leave you with the thought that humor is not exclusive to faculty. Elements of humor are found in some of the more common questions asked by students. My top-ten list of (unintended) humorous questions and remarks by students is given below, with all due respect to my past, current, and future students.

10. *"Do we have to buy the book?"*

9. *"Do you grade on a curve?"*

8. *"Can we drop a grade?"*

7. *"Do we have to take the final exam?"*

6. *"I knew the material. I just couldn't give it back to you on the exam."*

5. *"Is this going to be on the test?"*

4. *"I can't be in class tomorrow. I have to register for classes."*

3. *"I got the exact same answer as my classmate, but she got a higher grade."*

2. *"Is this score on my exam the number wrong or the number right?"*

1. *"I can't be in class tomorrow. Will you be talking about anything important?"*

References

Berk, Ron (1999). *Professors Are from Mars, Students Are from Snickers*. Madison, Wis.: Mendota Press.

Broder, Josef M. (1994). "Empiricism and the Art of Teaching." *Journal of Agricultural and Applied Economics* vol. 26, no. 1:1–18.

Broder, Josef M., and Jeffrey H. Dorfman (1994). "Determinants of Teaching Quality: What's Important to Students." *Research in Higher Education* vol. 35, no. 2:235–49.

Broder, Josef M., and William J. Taylor (1994). "Teaching Evaluation in Agricultural Economics and Related Departments." *American Journal of Agricultural Economics* vol. 76, no. 1:153–62.

Broder, Josef M., and Michael E. Wetzstein (1983). "Improving Student Performance in Economics Classes Through Diagnostic Information." *Midsouth Journal of Economics* vol. 7:491–98.

Elmore, Richard R. (1991). "Foreword." *Education for Judgment.* C. Roland Christensen, David A. Garvin, and Ann Sweet, eds. Boston: Harvard Business School Press, pp. ix–xix.

Garvin, David A. (1991). "Barriers and Gateways to Learning" in *Education for Judgment.* C. Roland Christensen, David A. Garvin, and Ann Sweet, eds. Boston: Harvard Business School Press, pp. 3–13.

Turner, Steven C. (July 1993). "Morale and Faculty Development in Agricultural Economics. Discussion." *Journal of Agricultural and Applied Economics* vol. 25, no. 1:24–26.

White, Fred C. (December 1992). "Enhancing Class Attendance." *National Association of College Teachers in Agriculture Journal* vol. 36, no. 4:13–15.

◆　　◆　　◆

Josef M. Broder is Assistant Dean for Academic Affairs in the College of Agricultural and Environmental Sciences and D. W. Brooks Distinguished Professor of Agricultural and Applied Economics at The University of Georgia. He taught in the Department of Agricultural and Applied Economics from 1977 to 1997. He was a 1996–97 Senior Teaching Fellow at The University of Georgia and now leads the UGA Teaching Academy.

Dr. Broder received the Josiah Meigs Award for Excellence in Teaching in 1989. He also received the Golden Key Outstanding Teacher Award, the D. W. Brooks Distinguished Teaching Award, the Gamma Sigma Delta Outstanding Teaching Award, and the Agricultural Alumni Award for Distinguished Teaching. In 1993 he received the National Award for Excellence for Outstanding Teachers in Food and Agricultural Sciences sponsored by the U.S. Department of Agriculture.

Dr. Broder is best known for promoting the scholarship of teaching through publications on pedagogy, faculty development, and student affairs. He has developed and used case studies for classroom instruction and professional development.

He is married to Diane Brownlee, an outstanding teacher who has taught special education in Georgia's public schools for most of her professional career. They have three children, Elizabeth, Josef, and Michael, all of whom he says are smarter than their father. Dr. Broder is a native of Switzerland. His parents immigrated to the United States in the early 1950s. He was one of eight children and was raised on a dairy farm. Seven of the Broder children graduated from The University of Georgia, a school record for a single-generation family.

TEACHING AS A
VOCATION

Susette M. Talarico

WHY TEACH? THERE are probably as many answers to this question as there are members of the professoriate. Possible motives include, but are not limited to, the love of a particular subject, the desire to perform, the flexibility of the work schedule, the opportunity to lead a life of scholarship, and the chance to shape the minds and lives of young people. While effective teachers can, and do, work from a variety of motives—good things can come, after all, from varied intentions, it is rare that college and university faculty conceptualize their work in terms of a vocation. In short, few would assert that in teaching they were responding to a call.

In some respects, this is not surprising, as the term "vocation" is commonly associated with a more explicitly spiritual or religious endeavor. Priests, ministers, rabbis, and religious people of one kind or another frequently speak of being called with the implicit assumption that the resulting vocation was initiated by some higher or divine being. Increasingly, however, writers like Parker Palmer talk about education as a spiritual journey and emphasize that teaching must involve intellect, emotion, spirit, and the will to be effective. It is, certainly, these and similar conceptions that are illustrated in

Mitch Albom's *Tuesdays with Morrie* and that have helped to make that book a best-seller.

Whether one considers teaching as a spiritual exercise or not, it is clear that thinking about it in terms of a vocation can be instructive. To demonstrate this point, consider some of the essential attributes of a vocation and then apply them to higher education.

Religious and spiritual writers have much to say about vocation, but underlying the related discussion are certain characteristics or attributes. These include the importance of listening, the requirement of a commitment, and the prevalence of grace. In a vocation, listening is essential as one has to be quiet to hear and then to respond. If one hears some kind of call or experiences a specific attraction to a given line of work, then commitment is essential. Decisions are lived, not made, and it is the explicit promise to carry out a plan and to fulfill related obligations that distinguishes a vocation from just a job. Finally, one cannot understand a vocation without some recognition of grace. In distinctly spiritual terms, grace can be understood as the unmerited favor bestowed by a divinity. In more secular fashion, it can be understood as the capacity to affect others beyond one's obvious or human efforts. Many of those who consider their line of work or career in vocational terms admit that at the outset they were not sure if they were up to the challenge or task. Similarly, many acknowledge that oftentimes their labors bear fruit in excess of their actual or identifiable contributions.

How can this brief, and admittedly cursory, understanding of vocation be applied to higher education? How do listening, commitment, and grace play out in the corridors of academe? How can college and university teaching be understood in terms of vocation?

Listening plays an important, though often unheralded, role in higher education. Simply put, one cannot teach if one does not listen. Here, listening means more than just hearing. To be sure, there is a sense where no one can teach effectively without listening to students. But listening as understood in the context of vocation means something more. Simply put, listening means that one is engaged, that one has accepted one's work and is content to do it. In the contemporary academy, many teach but don't like to. Rather, they teach because this work gives them the opportunity to pursue scholarly endeavors, to read, and to enjoy the benefits of a flexible schedule. In the context of a vocation, however, and in the specific terms of listening, teaching is an engagement with students. This means that one teaches because one accepts the work on its own terms and not simply as a means to something else. As Frederick Buechner puts it, it is the place "where your deep gladness and the world's deep hunger meet."

In the context of higher education, one of the most important dimensions of listening is the acceptance of the person talking. Acceptance here does not mean that each opinion, assessment, work, or even excuse should be well regarded. There is, after all, varied quality in all of these. But it does require that we take the person as she/he is, i.e., with the abilities and knowledge that she/he has.

Oftentimes, faculty complain that the quality of students is not very high and that they would be better teachers if only the admissions process was more selective. Interestingly, former Georgia governor Lester Maddox advanced a similar theory about the state's prisons when he observed that there was nothing wrong with the Georgia Department of Corrections that a better class of inmates couldn't cure!

For teaching, then, listening requires that we accept students as they are and that we work to move them from that place. It also requires that we sustain this openness by incorporating some kind of conversation or dialogue into our teaching, that we give a careful, though not always agreeable, ear to student concerns, and that we make an effort to put their work in some kind of perspective. All of this does not imply that standards should be forsaken and grades gratuitously given. But honest assessments cannot be made if one ignores where students start and continues to ignore them during the learning process.

Of the three vocational attributes, commitment is the one that is most easily applied to higher education. In the most basic sense, college and university faculty demonstrate substantial commitment before they enter any classroom. Doctoral programs typically require considerable time, money, and energy. But commitment to one's discipline and to one's own intellectual development is a necessary, though by no means sufficient, condition for successful teaching. Higher education requires more than an interest in, and passion for, a subject. Without students, few college or university teachers would have jobs, regardless of their disciplinary authority and expertise. In this most basic sense, then, faculty appointments require a commitment to students.

In many institutions and departments, this commitment is ignored as faculty focus almost exclusively on their own intellectual and professional development. In some circumstances, even, release from teaching is a sought-after reward. Clearly, though, commitment requires that faculty appreciate the challenge of teaching, that they take the obligation of students seriously, and that they act on that obligation. To embrace higher education only because one is passionate about a particular subject of study, because one is enthralled with research and writing, and because one enjoys the flexible lifestyle of a scholar is to cut one's faculty commitment short.

It is hard to imagine an effective teacher in any college or university who is not passionate about the subject, who has abandoned intellectual pursuits, or who takes advantage of flexible work schedules to avoid students and related obligations. Commitment to one's discipline and the general scholarly enterprise is, in the final analysis, necessary but not sufficient. Higher education demands that faculty bear and demonstrate a commitment to teaching, i.e., to the development of our students' minds and lives.

Although less obvious than commitment, grace plays an important role in higher education. If one agrees with Palmer that "we teach who we are" and that teaching takes place where the public and personal interact, then it is clear that there is room for, and need of, grace. All of us come to higher education with our own distinct limitations and flaws. Some of these will diminish over time in the authentic acquisition of wisdom and experience while others will simply be better recognized or controlled. As teachers, and as human beings, we will always bear some limitation. What is amazing about teaching is the fact that these limitations do not bar substantial and often lifelong positive results. When I was first teaching, I had considerable difficulty and made many glaring errors. These errors arose from the structure and content of my courses as well as from the way I responded to specific students and problems. It is amazing, then, when a student from this particular stage of my career writes to say that I had a substantial effect on his or her life. How could I have affected anyone, I wonder, when I was doing such a terrible job?

I can only surmise that there was something about that experience that I was unaware of and which impacted this and perhaps other students. Here is where personal honesty, identity, and integrity come into play, as I suspect that students learn more from how we live than from what we say. As I struggled with a beginning teacher's typical inexperience, some personal concern, discomfort, or effort must have been evident to students. This limited success can only be attributed to a power beyond myself. For those with a religious inclination, that power can be understood in divine terms. For those of a more humanistic bent, perhaps it was the mutual sensitivity of the student or a communality of experience. However conceived, the effect was clearly beyond my actual contributions, something that can be understood in terms of grace.

Few if any faculty will admit to hearing a call when starting a career in college and university teaching. In my own case, it often seems that I fell into teaching, that it was the natural result of a fascination with both politics and crime, that it was what one did with a Ph.D. Yet, however teaching is initially embraced, it can be effectively carried out only with listening, commitment, and grace. These vocational attributes have considerable relevance in our contemporary system of higher education, a system that is increasingly conducted as a business and that oftentimes rewards those who do not listen to students, who do not give students much time or effort, or who assume that there is little they can do to affect students' minds and lives. Teaching must be a vocation if it is to be done justly and well.

References

Albom, Mitch (1997). *Tuesdays with Morrie*. New York: Doubleday.

Buechner, Frederick (1992). *Listening to Your Life*. San Francisco: Harper.

Palmer, Parker (1998). *The Courage to Teach: Exploring the Inner Landscape of a Teacher's Life*. San Francisco: Jossey-Bass.

♦   ♦   ♦

Susette M. Talarico is Professor of Political Science and Director of Criminal Justice Studies, an interdisciplinary instructional program at The University of Georgia. She received her Ph.D. from the University of Connecticut in 1976 and taught at St. Michael's College in northern Vermont from 1975 to 1977. In September of 1977, she joined the UGA faculty, where she has taught ever since. She is a two-time recipient of the Meigs Award, 1986 and 1990.

Dr. Talarico teaches a wide range of courses in political science at the undergraduate and graduate level. These include Criminal Justice Administration, Criminal Law, Law Enforcement, Research Methods, and Judicial Politics. Every year, she also teaches a seminar on Criminal Sentencing at the UGA School of Law. During the fall 2000 term, she taught a freshmen seminar on Crime and Literature, something she has wanted to do for many years.

In addition to the aforementioned courses and seminars, Dr. Talarico has directed several doctoral dissertations in political science and public administration. One of these, Bradley Chilton's study of institutional reform litigation, was awarded the 1988 Outstanding Dissertation Award from the National Association of Schools of Public Affairs and Administration. She has also presented and published several research papers with graduate students, including several from a current study of tort litigation in Georgia.

Married to Rodger Carroll and the mother of teenager Robert, Dr. Talarico likes to travel, read, sing, cook, and golf. She and her family have visited Europe several times and traveled throughout the U.S.A. They hope to see Australia and New Zealand before long. An avid reader, Dr. Talarico is particularly fond of murder mysteries and other crime stories while she also enjoys singing with the Athens Master Chorale, a local choral group. Although a better cook than golfer, she enjoys both regularly, the former more than the latter!

Teachers Who Meant the Most to Me as a Student

James Walters

As a UNIVERSITY professor, my entire adult life has been filled with learning experiences. In the great maze of individuals who have been directly involved in teaching me, why do a few stand out so clearly in my mind? Perhaps because they cared as much about me as they did the subjects they were teaching and in the process of informing me, they helped me.

A Teacher Who Helped Me Plan My Future

Like many students, I was uncertain what I would do when I completed my undergraduate degree. Dr. Tran Collier, a psychology professor of mine with whom I had several courses, asked me on several occasions what my future plans were. I was evasive because I was unsure. One day he said, "A month from today I want you to tell me what decision you have made about your future. If you decide to go to graduate school, I would like to help you obtain a graduate assistantship."

Previously, I had a course with Dr. Sybil Escalona, a child psychologist at the Menninger Psychiatric Foundation, and subsequently I obtained a position as a recreational therapist at the Southard School, a residential treatment center for emotionally disturbed children at the Menninger Psychiatric Foundation. Also, I had seen an educational film that featured Dr. Arnold Gesell, Director of the Yale Laboratory of Child Development, and I had read Benjamin Spock's popular book, *Baby and Child Care*. I could imagine myself as a teacher of child development and in a career that permitted me to write material for parents.

The library at the university I attended, Washburn University in Topeka, Kansas, was very limited, so on several Saturdays I got on a Greyhound bus to travel to the University of Kansas to review material on child development. It was there that I learned about the Iowa Child Welfare Research Station, a leading research center at the University of Iowa.

On the scheduled day, I told Dr. Collier that I would like to study at the Iowa Child Welfare Research Station. At his own expense, he traveled over four hundred miles to the University of Iowa to convince the director of the station that I deserved to be considered for a research assistantship. He succeeded, and the assistantship paid me $75 per month in exchange for twenty hours of work a week. Because I had taken several courses in creative writing and journalism as an undergraduate, by the beginning of the second year my assistantship duties consisted of writing and delivering a weekly fifteen-minute radio show for parents.

Had it not been for Dr. Collier, who guided me through the process of career selection, I would never have gone to graduate school. Each time I have assisted a student through the process of career selection, I have thought of this undergraduate teacher who was determined to help me. It was not just me whom he helped; the year I entered the University of Iowa there were two other students in different fields who were there because of the efforts of this teacher.

A Teacher Who Was Serious About Writing

In 1952 I obtained a leave of absence from Oklahoma A&M College to undertake advanced study. When I arrived at the Florida State

University to study for a Ph.D. in Child Development, the head of the department, Dr. Ruth Connor, asked me to identify some of the skills I wished to acquire. I told her that if she had research underway in the areas of child development and family relationships, I would like to have access to the data and work with faculty in preparing drafts of manuscripts that might be considered for publication.

Such data were available, and I prepared several drafts of three manuscripts the first year, which were subsequently published. I was the junior author. Her guidance provided exactly the kind of experience I desired. She had me prepare drafts over and over, and each time the drafts got better and better. Because of my teacher's guidance, I have had an array of opportunities: writing research and professional articles for a wide variety of journals, serving as an editor of a professional journal, and serving as coauthor of a text on marriage that survived three editions before my retirement.

Upon my graduation, the faculty requested that I return as a member of the faculty. Much of the credit belongs to my major professor, who was as excited as I was about writing for publication.

A Teacher Who Helped Me Appreciate Being One of the "Least Awful"

One of the difficult tasks faced by teachers is to encourage students to persist in spite of failure. In my own case, one of the most formidable requirements I faced was passing examinations in two foreign languages. Many years ago during the era when two languages were required for a Ph.D.—an era during which many students never received their Ph.D. because of their failure to pass the language examinations—I faced my second language examination. As I reviewed the test, I recognized that it was beyond my level of competence. Turning in my examination and leaving the room crossed my mind; however, I stayed believing that it would increase the chances of someone else's passing. I gave the assignment my best effort, though it was humbling.

About a week later, several students approached me, telling me that the results were posted and that of the roomful of students who had taken the examination, I was the only one who had passed. I ran to see the results, believing that it was too good to be true. As I approached the posted list, I saw beside my name the word *passed*. All of the others had failed. Just then the head of the language department passed by, and I expressed to her that I was surprised to find that I was good enough to pass. The teacher very kindly indicated that my test wasn't really good but that my examination was the least awful: the members of the committee believed that they should pass someone. I was so relieved that I burst out laughing and she laughed, too. Through the years, I have remembered the valuable lesson—sometimes being one of the "least awful" can be more reasonable in life than trying to be the best.

A Teacher Who Helped Me Accept Myself

About the same time, I was taking a class from Dr. Mildred Morgan, a former president of the National Council on Family Relations, the leading professional organization of family specialists in the nation. One day in class when we were talking about achieving success in our profession and attaining professional recognition, I reflected on the fact that she was one of those rare teachers who created an atmosphere in class that was sheer magic. I asked her, "How do we learn to become a Mildred Morgan? How do we ever learn to be like you?" She responded, "Jim, you don't need to become a Mildred Morgan—you need to become the best Jim Walters that you can be." Many years later when I received the Osborne Award given annually to the outstanding teacher of the year in the field of family science, and was then named editor of *Family Relations*, one of the leading professional family journals in the United States, and then afterward when I was elected president of the National Council on Family Relations, I thought of the many teachers who provided me with the encouragement to be the best that *I* could be. More important, I had many teachers who provided me—through *their* encouragement—with the desire to create an educational climate in which students are motivated to do *their* best.

A Teacher Who Taught Me I Could Face Great Odds and Succeed

One of the teachers who had a tremendous impact on her students was Dr. Helen Cate, former head of the Department of Foods and Nutrition at the Florida State University. As a candidate for a Ph.D. in Child Development, I was required to take a graduate class in child nutrition. After several class sessions, Dr. Cate asked, "Jim, did you complete a course in biochemistry before enrolling in this class?" A course in biochemistry was a prerequisite for entering the class, but I had not known this when my major professor enrolled me in the class. "No," I responded, "I haven't had a class in biochemistry." I had not had a beginning course in chemistry either, but I thought it better not to mention it. "Is there anyone else in the class who hasn't had biochemistry?" she asked. Everyone else had completed the prerequisite. She asked me to remain after class at which time she could not have been nicer. "We've got a lot of work to do," she said. "I've got several books that I believe you'll find really useful." Then she identified chapters I should read and areas of knowledge with which I should become familiar. Dr. Cate made me feel that she had no intention of abandoning me but that we were in this together and that she was going to play an active role in my learning process. And she often worked with me after class. I couldn't believe how interesting the class was, and I was very pleased that I was learning about an area that was so important in the development of children.

Although Dr. Cate was a demanding teacher and the class in child nutrition remained difficult for me, the psychological support she provided not just to me but also to each member of the class stimulated the best efforts of everyone. She was truly a gifted teacher. At the end of the course, I said good-bye to her. Instead of reminding me of how little I knew at the beginning of the class, she said, "Jim, you are truly a wonderful student, and I am so glad that you were in my class."

Upon completing my course work at Florida State, I returned to my teaching in Oklahoma. Within a few weeks of the beginning of the term, a young man who was in my marriage class made an appointment to see me in my office. When he arrived, he said, "Mr. Walters, I feel very uncomfortable about asking this, but I am going to be married in a few weeks, and I have never had sexual intercourse. I know a lot of facts that I have read in books, but I am not sure how to do it." I thought he might be a pledge in a fraternity and that his fraternity friends were making him do this. On the other hand, I thought maybe he was truly unsure of himself. I thought of the challenge my nutrition teacher had faced in teaching me nutrition, and I responded, "I'm glad you came to see me, and I believe that I can be of some help to you." I realize that few people reading this can imagine facing such a challenge with a student of university age, but back in the old days the world really was different. Several months after his marriage, the young man stopped by and told me how deeply he appreciated my kindness and my instruction. I thought of my nutrition teacher, who faced unbelievable odds in introducing me to a new world that was completely foreign to me, yet Dr. Cate was persistent in her efforts.

Not long ago Dr. Cate passed away, but her relentless persistence and kindness to thousands of students throughout her career are remembered. Kindness is something we don't talk about much in education, but I suspect that a great deal of the influence teachers have on students is dependent on their kindness. Many of us who have encountered trouble spots in our lives and were fortunate enough to be guided by a kind teacher believe that we were truly blessed.

Teachers Who Helped Me Learn That Men Can Become as Good as Women—Almost

Upon the completion of my master's degree, I was the first male in the United States to be appointed as a child and family specialist in the Cooperative Extension Service. My appointment was at Rutgers

University in New Jersey. Because the field of child and family studies was considered to be the province of women, the title of my position was Specialist in Human Relations. I worked with parents' groups that included many men.

I had a choice of being housed with the agricultural specialists, all of whom were men who labored in tiny, bleak offices, or with the home economists, all of whom were women who labored in a magnificent building with huge offices, beautiful furniture, hardwood floors, and very large windows that overlooked a lake in which there were ducks. I believed that I clearly belonged with the women. They appreciated my support by joining them, and the men believed I was fearless.

All of the home economists were specialists whose support and encouragement contributed greatly to my success. They provided excellent feedback on my work at every step of the way. I had no doubt in my mind that my colleagues, all of whom were women, were superior to me.

Later, when I joined the faculty in the School of Home Economics at Oklahoma A&M College, I was the only male in home economics among seventy women faculty. Here, again, I was cordially welcomed, and, again, I encountered a quality of scholarship that challenged my own. Any illusion I had left about men outperforming women was corrected by the women faculty at UGA.

Finally

Teaching is more than the transmission of information. Teachers we remember are teachers who build people. If we look at studies of the learning process, we might conclude that teachers who are remembered would be those who used good teaching strategies, those who demanded the best from their students, and those who were the most knowledgeable in their subject matter. Unquestionably, these are important attributes of good teachers, but they are not the qualities that make us remember teachers. Those who are imprinted positively, indelibly, in our memories are those who cared about us as individuals and joined with us in this important growth process.

◆   ◆   ◆

James Walters is Professor Emeritus, Department of Child and Family Development, The University of Georgia. Over a period of forty years, he served as an extension specialist, a teacher, a researcher, a text writer, and a department head. Because there were relatively few persons who held the doctorate in the early years of Home Economics, Dr. Walters directed dissertations in the areas of child development, family relationships, home economics education, housing and interior design, and family economics. His other academic appointments were at Rutgers University, Oklahoma A&M College (Oklahoma State University), and the Florida State University. He won the Meigs Award in 1984.

Among his national contributions, Dr. Walters served as a member of the President's Commission for Planning the White House Conference on Children and Youth. In the Department of Agriculture he served as a consultant to the Deputy Director for Cooperative Research. In the National Science Foundation, in the United States Department of Education, and in the National Foundation for the March of Dimes, he served as an evaluator of research proposals. In the American Home Economics Association, he served as a member of the Council for Professional Development, as a member of the Home Economics Defined Committee, as a member of the Board of Directors, as a chair of the Section on Child and Family Development, and on the editorial board of the *Journal of Home Economics*. In the National Council on Family Relations, he served as a member of the Board of Directors and as an associate editor of *The Family Coordinator* and the *Journal of Marriage and the Family*. Following his six years as editor of *Family Relations*, he was elected president of the National Council on Family Relations.

Dr. Walters is married to Lynda Henley Walters, Professor of Child and Family Development at The University of Georgia. He is the father of Dr. Connor Walters, Associate Professor of Child Development at the Florida State University; Dr. Anna Morgan, a licensed psychologist in private practice in Watkinsville, Georgia; and Christopher Walters, a businessman who resides in Orlando, Florida. He and Lynda are the grandparents of five remarkable grandchildren.

Tough Love in the Classroom

Conrad C. Fink

I'D ALWAYS STRUCTURED my teaching on tough love, but doubts constantly nagged: Was the love too tough?

And here was another chance to doubt—a letter from a former student, one of those many splendid young people who stay in touch even years after leaving the Grady College of Journalism.

"I thought I was in hell for that first week or so of [your] class," she wrote.

I read quickly, wondering how she looked back on her many classroom hours with me and, yes, I admit, searching intently for clues on whether she now regarded my teaching as helpful, instructive, memorable.

Most important: Was she unhappy today with what she learned then? Did my classroom technique need adjusting?

Apparently not. Her letter, in fact, thanked me for leading rigorous courses, for forcing students to focus, and for requiring classroom performance that, at minimum, is at semi-pro levels.

The woman wrote that her considerable professional success, with a major West Coast newspaper company, was due in large measure to my teaching.

"Just thought you should know how much I benefited from your classes," she concluded. "Bravo!"

And that's how my mail runs—that's what they write in student evaluations and say in person when they revisit UGA. They strongly endorse my technique of laying heavy obligations on all students and demanding from each a performance that meets a standard of expected excellence I tailor for each.

The key here is *responsibility*—theirs and, even more important, mine.

It all begins with rumor—yes, rumor, which I encourage, on the student network. It's extremely active, you know, and, in my experience, accurate in its assessment of teachers and their effectiveness. According to informants (as we say in journalism), the word on me is: Fink is one tough old bird; he'll work you hard, *but* you'll get, in return, more than your money's worth.

Now, why would I encourage such talk? Because I teach at a major research university. Substandard work cannot be accepted here. I teach in a *professional* college, and my subject matter is free, ethical, responsible journalism, created by a vigorous and financially strong (and, thus, independent) press. As a journalist and media executive for twenty-five years and now, since 1982, as a teacher of journalism, I've devoted my life to the people's right and need to know, an ever-threatened blessing crucial to the continued viability of our democracy.

That is, I am a serious man who teaches a serious subject—and only serious students need apply to share the enthusiasm, experience, and hard work I put into teaching it.

Is this educational triage? Do I cruelly reject the crippled and dying and admit to my educational tent only those easily saved?

Not really. Of all vital signs normally checked in higher education, I require just two—enthusiasm and willingness to learn. And that is on the student network, too. However bright or dim your lightbulb, commit to learning and the man will work, *hard,* to help you get where you want to go.

So, if you're keeping a list, head it with two attitudes that fundamentally drive my teaching:

• I am dealing with adults, not children, in intellectual endeavors of first-rank importance, and I thus have a *right* to demand hard work and a manifest willingness to learn.

- I have an *obligation*, therefore, to work very hard to keep my side of the bargain.

And I *do* work very hard at teaching. Indeed, after what I thought was a *really* hard career, in journalism, I am surprised constantly at just how hard it is to teach effectively.

And I don't mean just the obvious: maintaining an open-door policy and being easily available, or painstakingly editing student writing and providing personalized critiques of overall performance.

They're crucial to effective teaching, of course. And they are a drain on the finite physical, emotional, and intellectual assets any teacher can bring to the job.

- A weekday open-door policy *does* devour the clock and *does* force to the evenings and weekends (*your* time) your research and writing.

- Painstaking editing of thirty, forty, or more term papers *is* physically demanding.

- Investing time and energy to get to know each student, required if you try to tailor your teaching, *does* drain you intellectually.

However, the real challenge comes in structuring and simultaneously executing a two-dimensional approach—call it the "macro and micro" approach—to teaching.

The macro dimension involves developing a wider process, creating yourself as a *personality*, around which you can build a larger program. And yes, we're talking here about more than a wee bit of showmanship.

The micro dimension requires extraordinarily close attention to the subtle nuts and nuanced bolts of effective course structures, pace of material, lecture delivery, and so forth.

Your Personality, Your Program, Your Macro Effort

We teachers live in the world of ideas and ultimately are judged on the merit of our ideas.

Such, of course, was the case with Albert Einstein. His ideas changed the world.

But remember those turtleneck sweaters? The pipe, the mustache? The wonderfully wild white hair?

What? Am I suggesting Einstein was a bit of a showman? In the parlance of my native Upper Midwest, you betcha.

I'm also suggesting that you, whoever you are, can create, one way or another, a *presence*. For most of us, this cannot be something physical. Wild white hair is unfashionable; the tweed jacket with leather elbow patches is what *Hollywood* thinks professorial presence to be. And even if we wanted to, few of us could make it as classroom comedians or song-and-dance performers.

But each of us has *something*.

For one of my colleagues, that something is a deliberately underplayed presence—a sort of quiet self-confidence that draws student attention precisely because, in this era of the big oversell, he is quiet and underplayed. Students flock to this colleague, sensing that when he does speak, wisdom flows.

For another very successful colleague, the "it" is a lively, almost electric wit coupled with a habit of challenging all comers to a one-on-one and sometimes almost vicious bout on the basketball court.

For me, "it" is an attempt at *studied professionalism*, a total immersion in journalism, its history, obligations, and daily practices. I position myself as the "newspaper guy." My office is filled with newspapers, books about newspapers, articles I've written, and articles I wish I'd written. It's where students go to talk about reporting, writing, ethics, media management, and careers.

And on that niche presence I've built a wider program that extends far beyond a fifty-minute class period *but which is essential to effective use of those fifty minutes*. Components of my wider program include:

• A Publications Management emphasis, which is a journalism degree that, in turn, is a strong liberal arts program with a top dressing of journalism courses. This gives students the *career orientation* so many seek (and deserve) as part of their broader educational program.

• A Media Management Club, which gives students a social as well as professional rallying point. Leading newspaper executives nationwide are our guests for luncheons and dinners, plus hours of newspaper talk.

• Newspaper management internships, which, unlike traditional newsroom internships, give students eight-week overall views of all dimensions of newspaper strategy.

• What I'm told is called "Fink's Career Service." There's free assistance on résumés, job applications, interview techniques, and even career counseling long after graduation.

• High visibility. I write textbooks that are used in my college. I'm in debates, workshops, discussion groups—and, thus, so is my ongoing dialogue about newspaper reporting, ethics, management, and the stuff of my classroom presence. Students hear the importance of my classroom subjects, and they see the wider dimension of my effort.

Does that build *authority and credibility* for my teaching effort? I believe it does.

In the Classroom: Your Micro Effort

We say in newspapering that 90 percent of a successful career is in reporting, 10 percent in writing.

Can it be that 90 percent of successful classroom performance is in life experience and career preparation *before* you even step in front of a blackboard?

That is, do successful teachers build the essential bridge of credibility to student minds during—or before—the lecture? Both, of course. But the most stellar lecture technique falls short unless built on that wider macro effort in research, industry involvement, and careful planning.

Students are far too intelligent to buy into a classroom presentation, that while facile and fast-moving, merely skips a chapter ahead in the assigned reading.

What, then, are the components of a successful "micro" teaching technique based on tough love?

Recognize Student Individuality

My first several class sessions are spent talking about the students, where they're from, where they're trying to go. I can *feel* the class warm up as I ask about their career goals and how I can tailor my course to meet their educational needs. Only *after* that do I give them a brief sketch of my background.

Lay Down a Contract

My syllabi are detailed, sometimes running to seven or eight pages, laying out precisely what students must do to meet course requirements and, in equal detail and precision, *what I will do.* Attendance is mandatory (only a sucking chest wound is an acceptable excuse), and term paper dates are firm. I add, "If you don't want to, or cannot, commit to this contract, please withdraw . . . and no hard feelings. There are easier ways to get five credits, just down the hall."

Negotiate Each Individual's Objectives

All students submit, in writing, proposals for their course objectives: story ideas in reporting classes; term paper outlines in ethics and management courses. Within the broad course contract and its objectives, each student is permitted to tailor individual objectives to meet his or her own educational and career goals. These are discussed in my office during the many individual conferences I have during each teaching term.

Evaluate Progress

I keep detailed records of student performance in research and reporting, writing clarity, analytical ability, and persuasive logic—all the factors that count so much in principled, authoritative journalism. *And* I evaluate, constantly, classroom participation and what I want to learn from it: Can the student gather his or her thoughts quickly if challenged or questioned without warning? Can the student perform professionally and coolly, with balance, as we must do under fire in journalism every day?

Adjust Performance

In my advanced reporting class, a student will receive from me at least fifty pieces of edited writing. I edit line by line, heavily, and on a professional basis—there's no slack for the amateur status of my young writers; all must come up to entry-level performance that is expected in professional newsrooms. In larger lecture classes, I edit for each student three term paper proposals and three lengthy papers. Adjustment of class participation is constant: duck your head in my class and drop your eyes, and you're *certain* to be asked questions.

Grade Hard but Fairly

I very rarely get a complaint about grades. I believe that is because students can see, in my editing, evidence of my care with their work and my grasp of its quality. Indeed, I would feel I have failed if I did get a complaint, because that would mean I had not *evaluated* the student's work properly throughout the course and had not *adjusted* his or her performance. To sharpen the point: if a student gets a bad grade and is surprised by it, I haven't been working properly with that student.

Make It Enjoyable

Lordy, life can be dull! So, I feel challenged personally to make it fun, in addition to informative, enjoyable, as well as educational. I've found even a corny joke lightens the burden, if told with vigor, and war stories about running through Southeast Asia's rice paddies can drive home a teaching point.

Finally

Well, it's graduation time. What now? Is it over? Happily no.

If you've taken my courses, you've won a friend for life. Scores of students have gotten their first job—even the second or third—off telephone calls I make to newspaper colleagues throughout the country. My helping hand is extended long after graduation, and I am touched by how many former students reach for it.

And *that* word is out on the student rumor network, too!

♦   ♦   ♦

During a twenty-five-year career in the media, Conrad C. Fink was a reporter, editor, and foreign correspondent in many parts of the world. He was vice president of The Associated Press and a media executive involved in managing newspapers and broadcast stations.

Fink joined the UGA faculty in 1982 as head of the media management program in the Henry W. Grady College of Journalism and Mass Communication.

He was appointed, in 1990, director of the James M. Cox, Jr., Institute for Newspaper Management Studies and in 1995 was named William S. Morris Professor of Newspaper Strategy and Management.

Fink teaches in the university's honors program and has been a University Senior Foundation Fellow since 1996. All his courses offer honors options.

Fink is the author of seven books on journalism and a number of case studies used in management and strategy courses.

Fink won the Grady College's "Superior Teaching" award four times and, in 1992, the university's Josiah Meigs Award for Excellence in Teaching.

THE JOYS OF TEACHING ENGLISH

William G. Provost

THE JOY WE find in any of life's undertakings is linked to the sense we have of the realness and validity, the coherence and wholeness in that undertaking. In order to describe and convey the particular kinds of pleasure experienced in teaching English, therefore, it's necessary first to confirm the real integrity of this activity. And this integrity is not always immediately obvious. Much of what we deal with in our profession seems either merely conventional—e.g., style, literary genres, rules of grammar; or subjective—e.g., critical commentary, evaluation; or self-contained—e.g., a freshman composition course or a doctoral-level seminar on theory. But the integrity is there, and good teaching of English at any level, as well as the joy inherent in it, comes about when we are aware of that integrity. So, conveying the joys of teaching English can begin with describing good teaching. Trying to do this leads easily to either pomposity or simplemindedness. Opting for the latter, I would suggest that three kinds of "things" are essential to good teaching: eschewing excess technicality, I'll call them the little things, the middle-sized things, and the big things.

By the "little things," I mean the basics, the everyday things, the nuts and bolts of what we do. An example of what I'm talking about is the simple matter of rereading the poems, stories, and essays we teach each time we present them. I've taught Book II of *Paradise Lost* at least fifty times. I've got one of those set jokes of the sort we all use, about how the exchange there between Moloch, Belial, Mammon, and Beelzebub is a lot like a faculty meeting. The joke is usually good for a chuckle, and the chuckle often has the effect of grabbing a couple of those "middle attentions": not the students who are already attentive, and not those three or four who are asleep, but a few of the ones in between. The last time I taught this work in a sophomore literature survey course, I used the joke as always. *But* that week I was trying hard to get a committee report done and a set of papers for another course graded, and I didn't reread Book II. I used the joke, and it did get a small chuckle, but it didn't work. I'd simply forgotten that the specific place the joke makes the most sense, and thus the place where it may help focus the students' attentions successfully is just when you get to Belial's response to Moloch, where he says in effect, "I agree perfectly with my strong-minded colleague, but . . ." [that knife-in-the-back "but" we all recognize]. Instead, I used the joke in my introduction to Book II, simply because I didn't have the whole thing really fresh in mind. The presentation was flat—not just because of a poorly timed joke, but because my sense of the work was flat.

Other examples of such "little things" include the comments we make on papers, and the things we say in student conferences. It takes a long time, and serious thought, to figure out exactly what might help this particular student at this particular time read and think and write better. It's easy to make the generalizing comment, and on occasion it may even help. But doing so does not constitute the careful attention to nuts and bolts that good teaching of English requires. It does not affirm the integrity of our profession, and it thus does not partake of the pleasure that integrity underpins.

By the "middle-sized" things I mean attending to the developing shape of what we do as we continue to learn and teach: that is, thinking not only about what our most recent rereading of a story or poem has given us but also about the research we've been doing or reading and the ways in which it shapes our reactions to the literature. We remind ourselves simultaneously of both particularity—this particular class, this particular assignment, this particular passage—and of the larger evolving process of knowing and teaching language. Reading and rereading Book II of *Paradise Lost* is partly to refresh our acquaintance with something timeless and perfect, but it also is—it also *must be*—an experience that is alive, and thus one that grows, changes, and, it is to be hoped, improves. Reading about and assimilating a new historical slant on the ideas and effects of Chaucer's General Prologue to *The Canterbury Tales* is not more important than, nor does it obviate, the need to remind ourselves of the exact meanings of his words or how his use of the subjunctive is marked. But it's not less important either. It requires a different level and kind of attention and thought than the nuts and bolts do, in something of the same way as raising a family is different from washing the windows. This kind of attention and thought reminds us of the shaped and shaping things that the nuts and bolts hold together. It is thought about measuring and proportion and design and change. And it also is part of the integrity of what we do.

And of course by the "big things" I mean our ongoing attention to the entire structure: to what it is that we are ultimately about, and to why that is important. In this regard, I think many of us would agree that a feeling of being beleaguered is shared by many teachers of language and literature these days. It's a feeling that can be evoked, for example, in the response we've all had from a new acquaintance who has just learned that we teach English: "Oh, English! That was always my worst subject, ha ha!" (subtext: "And it hasn't mattered a bit. I make three times what you do.") Or it may be brought out by an attitude we occasionally discern in a non-literature-teaching friend: something like, "Why haven't you all made more progress yet? You don't know for sure what *Hamlet* is all about; you can't tell me in a simple, definite way whether I ought to say '*It's me*' or '*It is I*'; you haven't even pinned down a good rhyme for *orange*." Our extradisciplinary friends and even colleagues sometimes seem to assume that we ought to have the specialized, rigidly demarcated goal orientation—with accompanying policy statements, procedural manuals, and timetables—so common and essential in so many other contemporary professions.

Maybe we should simply abandon the term *professional*. It would be a shame to do so, since it is etymologically a most precise description of what we ultimately do. But in many ways we do not measure up to the significations the term ordinarily bears these days. We can't, because we teach language. We study and perform and analyze and demonstrate the power, precision, range, meaning, and beauty of language as it struggles to embody and convey human thought and belief and feeling. And language is essentially unspecializable; is essentially process, not achieved goal; is gloriously fluid and remarkable, not rigid and demarcable. We know these "big things," but they are the sorts of things that are sometimes difficult to explain, and they are also easy to lose track of.

We teach our first-year students the tools of language, showing them that they are exceedingly powerful tools, and that like all such they require care, practice, and painstakingly acquired skill to be used well (and, of course, that they are capable of doing much harm when misused). As the composition sequence melds into a sequence of literary survey courses, we begin to show them the extraordinary economy of literary language: the subtlety and range found therein, and the implications of such for the educated person. As our students advance into the more specialized undergraduate and graduate courses, the particular mix of theory, method, history, and strategies we show them becomes more complex. At all these stages, we have to attend constantly to the immediate nuts and bolts and to the shaping process of which they are a part. But the center of all we do at all these levels is constant.

I try to keep as the center for all my teaching the fact of language: not as a thing to be fully mastered or even as a discrete end in itself, but rather as an essential and intimate feature of our humanness, and one thus participating in all the paradoxical variety of that humanness: in the glory, jest, and riddle that we think, feel, and are. Our reverence for, fascination with, and love of language are at the heart of our teaching and its joys. When we teach well—attending to little, middle-sized, and big things—we on occasion may even change an "Oh, English," to an "Ah, English!"

◆   ◆   ◆

William G. Provost is General Sandy Beaver Associate Professor of English. He has taught in the English Department of the Franklin College of Arts and Sciences at The University of Georgia since 1969. His areas of specialization are medieval literature with an emphasis on Chaucer, and historical linguistics. Dr. Provost has taught undergraduate and graduate courses in these areas as well as English composition, world literature, British literature, American literature survey courses, both regular and honors sections, and fantasy literature. He has done large lecture sections of the survey courses, regular discussion/lecture sections of all, and small honors or graduate seminars. Also, he has supervised directed readings at both the undergraduate honors and graduate levels in many topics related to medieval literature and linguistics, and also in Old English, Old Norse, Gothic, and modern fantasy writers. He won the Meigs Award in 1993.

Dr. Provost's hobbies are reading (of course), drama, and flying. He has five children, only one of whom shows even the slightest inclination toward becoming an English teacher.

THE PSYCHOLOGY OF TEACHING

Shawn M. Glynn

FOR MORE THAN two decades, it's been my good fortune to teach in the College of Education of The University of Georgia. Over that time, I've been guided by a straightforward philosophy of teaching. I simply want to become the best teacher I can be, and I want to help my students—who are themselves teachers—to do the same. I enjoy the process of improving my teaching and the process of enhancing others' teaching. It is my belief that teaching is both an art and a science. The artistic side taps creativity and motivation, whereas the scientific side taps technical knowledge and methods. My metaphor for good teaching, the kind of teaching to which I aspire, is that it is a craft—an honorable, ancient craft, like that of a potter. A potter must be a good technician to create functional pottery, but there's much more to the craft than this. There's the artistry, or the potential for artistry, in the creation. That's what distinguishes expertise, be one a potter or a teacher. A teacher should integrate the art and science of teaching, resulting in an effective and distinctly unique style.

The Characteristics of Highly Effective Teachers

Highly effective teachers are knowledgeable. It's important to be knowledgeable, just as it's important to be challenging, organized, clear, and fair. Without question, these are characteristics that are possessed by effective teachers. These are also the characteristics that are immediately mentioned when academics discuss and intellectualize the nature of effective teaching. But there are other characteristics that are just as important. These other characteristics are less well understood and receive less attention because they are emotionally charged and psychological in nature.

I, like many others, have found that psychology plays a fundamentally important role in the development of teaching ability. There are key psychological characteristics that are shared by highly effective teachers regardless of the disciplines they are teaching. Over the course of my career, I've studied the characteristics of exemplary teachers and have endeavored to develop these characteristics in myself. Have I become as effective as those exemplary teachers I've studied? Unfortunately, no. But I'm not discouraged by that. Instead, I remind myself that becoming an effective teacher is a process. Even though I may not be as effective as those I admire, there is no question that studying them has helped me to become a better teacher.

In addition to being knowledgeable, challenging, organized, clear, and fair, the exemplary teachers that I've studied have possessed three psychological characteristics that have contributed significantly to their effectiveness. These characteristics are commitment, enthusiasm, and interpersonal warmth.

Commitment

Highly effective teachers are committed teachers. They believe in the basic and applied value of the discipline they are teaching. They also believe that they are making a valuable contribution to the discipline by teaching it effectively.

Effective teachers are committed to their students as well. They are role models for their students. Often, students choose to make a discipline their career because they admire their teachers and their commitment to the discipline. Effective teachers help their students learn not just the content of the discipline, but also attitudes toward the discipline as well. They are committed to helping their students become proficient in the discipline and develop a lifelong appreciation for it.

I tell my students why my discipline is important to me and why I decided to make it my career. I'm honest with them about times in my career when I found myself reexamining my commitment but emphasize that my commitment always became stronger as a result of these examinations. I also tell them about the satisfaction the discipline has brought me and how it has contributed to my appreciation of the world around me.

In addition to being committed to teaching, I'm committed to my research. I think of my teaching and research as being strongly connected. They are mutually enhancing activities. They are in effect two sides of the same coin, and that coin is "scholarship." True scholarship involves both research and teaching. Research is the creation of knowledge, and teaching is the sharing of that knowledge. Over time, teaching and research became seamless activities for me.

Enthusiasm

Highly effective teachers are enthusiastic about their discipline, about their teaching, and about their students. They constantly seek to inspire and motivate their students. They know they are building more than their students' knowledge of the discipline; they are building their students' attitudes as well. They are changing their students' lives and helping them to realize their potential.

Effective teachers are downright joyful in their teaching. For them, teaching is a performance art, and each class is a command performance. Regardless of whether they are teaching one student or five hundred students, effective teachers strive for peak performance. And they love doing it. For them, teaching is not a chore. On the contrary, it's an irresistible challenge to enrich their students' knowledge and appreciation of their discipline.

I'm often nervous or even scared when meeting a class for the first time. But, just the way an actor has learned to handle stage fright, I channel that energy into my teaching. And what a "rush" that can be. After all, teaching is a "live" performance—anything and everything can happen. I've come to enjoy this feeling of "working without a net." There's nothing quite like the thrill and terror of being in front of a large class of students on the first day, knowing that it's my responsibility to motivate them and shape their attitudes toward the discipline I love so much. For me, it doesn't get much better than that.

Interpersonal Warmth

Highly effective teachers usually have "warm" personalities that foster a positive classroom climate. They are empathetic and compassionate. They are not cold, stuffy, and aloof. They are not egocentric. They are humanitarians who are truly interested in the well-being of their students. They value their students and treat them with the kind of respect with which good businesses treat consumers, good lawyers treat clients, good physicians treat patients, etc.

Although effective teachers have interpersonal warmth, they are careful to avoid "dual relationships" with students. They do not try to become students' "friends." That would compromise the effectiveness, and perhaps the legitimacy, of the teacher-student relationship.

I've learned from effective teachers that it is important to address your students by their names. I believe that the most important word that anyone wishes to hear is his or her name, and when I address students by their names, it tells them that I care about them as individuals.

I get to class a half-hour early and stand outside the door of the classroom, so I can greet students as they arrive. This works well even with a large lecture class. After class, I immediately go the door and wish the students a nice day as they are leaving. Those who wish to talk with me about an issue I ask to wait until I've had a chance to wish the others a nice day. Then I set aside a half-hour or an hour after class to chat with the smaller group of students who remain.

Conclusion

In conclusion, highly effective teachers possess many important characteristics. It's essential to be knowledgeable. It's also important to be challenging, organized, clear, and fair. But it's just as important to be committed, enthusiastic, and interpersonally warm. The latter are more emotionally charged than the former and for that reason often receive less attention when academics intellectualize about what it means to be an effective teacher. These three psychological characteristics, however, contribute immensely to a teacher's success in establishing himself or herself as a role model who can help students learn about a discipline and develop positive attitudes toward it.

Sadly, ineffective teachers are often in a psychological state of "denial" regarding the importance of these characteristics. They believe that commitment, enthusiasm, and warmth are frills that have little to do with teaching quality (as defined by themselves, of course). Often, when ineffective teachers receive poor evaluations from their students, the ineffective teachers dismiss the evaluations as irrelevant because "the students only give good evaluations to the teachers they like." Well, "Hello, is anyone home?" That's exactly the point. Students appreciate teachers who are not only knowledgeable, but committed, enthusiastic, and warm as well. Teachers who wish to increase their effectiveness should strive to develop and refine these important psychological characteristics.

◆　　◆　　◆

Shawn M. Glynn is a professor in UGA's College of Education with appointments in the Department of Educational Psychology and the Department of Science Education. In the Department of Educational Psychology, he currently teaches graduate courses in the psychology of learning and instruction and undergraduate honors seminars in learning and development. He also serves as a major professor for doctoral and master's degree candidates. In the Department of Science Education, he currently teaches graduate courses on methods of teaching and evaluation. Dr. Glynn enjoys all styles of teaching, ranging from large group lecture to small seminar discussion. He incorporates technology into his teaching and believes that teaching should be a "show me" enterprise as well as a "tell me" one. He won the Meigs Award in 1998. Dr. Glynn is married to Denise Muth Glynn, a professor in the Department of Elementary Education at UGA. They share many hobbies such as running, scuba diving, bird watching, and home repair.

THOUGHTS ON COLLEGE TEACHING

Keith J. Karnok

MOST PH.D. STUDENTS specializing in the basic or applied sciences receive very little encouragement or opportunity to gain significant teaching experience. The total of my graduate teaching experience consisted of serving as instructor for two laboratory sections of a beginning course in our department. What I remember best from this experience was my sincere desire to have it end as soon as possible so I could get back to the research laboratory. I do remember receiving no instruction or guidance in regard to how I should approach this department-mandated assignment. I believe the basic thought presented to me was, "Here is the syllabus, go teach." Reflecting back, I pity the poor students who were subjected to my monotonous delivery style and total lack of creativity in preparing and presenting the various laboratory exercises. Frankly, at the time, I gave little thought to the entire situation since I was certain that I was going to secure a predominately research-weighted appointment following graduation.

It wasn't long after accepting my first faculty position, which included a 25 percent teaching appointment, that I realized how inept I was as a teacher. The students were inattentive and appeared to have little motivation to learn. Attendance was poor and the students were generally apathetic toward the course and me. Although I wanted to blame the students for their lack of interest and overall poor attitude, deep down, I knew they were simply reflecting their perception of my interest and attitude toward teaching and them. Little did they know that their perception was not based on fact. To the contrary, I was very concerned about doing a better job of teaching, and I certainly wanted to develop a better rapport with the students. I could clearly picture in my mind the kind of teacher I wanted to be and the desire for learning I wanted to instill in my students.

Unfortunately, I was at a loss as to how I could make enough improvement in my teaching that would result in the kind of change I knew was necessary. My desire to improve turned to a quiet desperation after I taught several courses and failed miserably. In other words, I was not making the necessary changes fast enough. It became very apparent that improvement was going to occur only if I took fast and immediate action.

After deciding to make a concerted effort to change, first I attended several lectures of the best teachers I knew. My purpose was to study and model their every move and see firsthand how they presented their lectures and interacted with their students. This was a very good exercise for me. It showed me that there was not a single universal style that guaranteed teaching effectiveness—but rather a variety of styles, each being unique to the personality of the teacher. Next, I attended as many seminars, workshops, and conferences on teaching as I could fit into my schedule. Since I was predominately on a research appointment, it was difficult to justify the time for these activities. Fortunately, I had a department head who understood and encouraged me. Although many of the sessions I attended seemed boring, I never failed to pick up one or two tips that I thought would help my teaching. In addition to the above, I subscribed to a well-known teaching journal in my field and read as many books and articles on teaching effectiveness as time would permit. Without question, all the effort I put into learning how to teach provided me with a very clear map to follow in becoming a good, and possibly even an excellent, teacher. Of course, it was one thing to know and understand the principles; it was another to put them into action. Unfortunately, I found no easy or short-cut method to improving my teaching. Basically it was (is) a trial-and-error process. I will say that from the beginning of my quest for teaching improvement until the present time, I continually conduct a self-evaluation. Another way to look at it might be taking an "inventory" or completing a "checklist" of myself considering those factors that I believe truly impact the teaching/learning process. And while I have come to realize over time that each component when considered alone is important and will affect the learning process, it is the combination of all the factors working together that forms a framework that helps to ensure success in the teaching profession. I would like to briefly review these points that I believe are integral to the teaching/learning process and share my views and approach to each.

First and foremost, a teacher owes it to his or her students to be as current as possible and have a broad and thorough understanding of the subject matter being taught. In addition, I believe it is essential that the teacher use real-world examples that students can relate to. Having even the strongest understanding of the subject matter will do little good if the teacher cannot explain it in terms, or on a level, that students can understand. Therefore, I try to have an example or illustration for every major point I make in lecture and try to draw from personal experiences whenever possible. Although at times the use of examples or illustrations appears to slow down the amount of material covered, I believe the increased level of comprehension by the student far outweighs this concern.

Certainly, students appreciate the teacher who is well organized and has an overall plan of instruction. I tell my students on the first day of class exactly what I expect of them and what they can expect from me. I list the overall course objectives and take a few minutes to explain the reasoning and importance of each. On the first day of class I also show my students exactly how the lecture material will be presented. This I do in outline form using the overhead projector. I also use this time to administer a "noncredit" pretest, which allows me to determine the overall background of the class in botany and as well as other related areas. At the same time, they get the opportunity to see how my exams are structured. In all aspects of my teaching, I try to eliminate as much of the guesswork by students as possible. I want them to concentrate their full attention on learning the course material and not trying to decipher my approach to teaching.

One of the most challenging aspects of good teaching for many teachers is developing effective delivery and communication skills. The ability to involve students in the learning process is something all teachers should strive for. Unfortunately, each of us has had the experience of being taught by those we knew were brilliant individuals but who were totally inadequate in communicating their mastery of the subject to us. Consequently, I spend as much time as possible trying to improve my communication skills, and although I utilize as many slides, videos, and other teaching aids as possible, I put most of my emphasis on verbal and nonverbal communication. Remember, the greatest teachers of all time (Jesus Christ, Socrates, Aristotle, Plato, etc.) relied on their innate communication skills to capture the minds of those who were fortunate enough to hear their teachings. In my own lectures, I concentrate on moving around the room and making eye contact with as many individual students as possible. I not only focus on students in the front of the room but also often stroll down the aisles to the back of the room and speak from there for several minutes. On occasion, I will find an empty seat in the back of the room where I will sit down and lecture for a while. This forces the students to turn their bodies, which breaks the pattern of passively sitting and possibly allowing their minds to drift. I also work hard on exaggerated voice inflection and hand gestures to emphasize a particularly important point.

I believe it is the teacher's responsibility to keep the students' attentiveness at a peak, something that is absolutely essential for learning to occur. My personality is such that humor is my strongest attribute to ensure student attentiveness, particularly during those lectures that are not as inherently exciting as I would like. It is my belief that a good hearty laugh relieves anxiety and shows students that I am just a regular, everyday person like they are. Although I rarely use jokes per se, I have found that impromptu jests directed at a point in the lecture or even current events work wonders in regaining class attention, particularly after twenty-five or thirty minutes of continuous lecture. Of course, I never make fun of or embarrass students; however, I have found that poking fun at myself shows that I am human and helps to establish rapport with the class. Admittedly, I had great apprehension when first using humor in the classroom. Without a doubt, on occasion you risk looking foolish. However, after much trial and error, you eventually understand what works and what doesn't, and it becomes a very natural and highly anticipated part of the learning experience. This may sound as though I put considerable emphasis on entertaining the student—and perhaps I do—but I see nothing wrong with making learning a fun-filled experience for both the student and the teacher. I also believe humor is the primary reason why after twenty-two years I have as much, or more, enthusiasm for teaching as I ever did. Without question, each time I walk into the classroom, it is the high point of my day regardless of how great that day may have already been.

In my opinion, mastery of the subject matter and staying current, having a teaching plan and being organized, and developing one's communication skills are the responsibility of *every* teacher. This is true whether a person teaches one class each year or several. These are components of effective teaching that teachers *owe* their students, and I believe they can be mastered by all teachers if adequate time and effort are spent. When the teacher takes the time to develop these things, he or she takes a significant stride toward becoming truly effective.

With all of the above being said, I believe that the most important component of teaching cannot be learned from books or articles on teaching. Neither can it be learned by observing master teachers. In fact, the most important aspect of teaching hasn't even been mentioned yet. In my opinion, the most important component of teaching is having a sincere interest in the total well-being of your students. In short, I believe the teacher who really makes a difference in a student's life is one who is in touch with the student's heart as well as the student's mind. The teacher who cares about the well-being of every student and does everything in his or her power to help students realize their full potential is the teacher who will have the most significant and long-lasting effect on students. This is something that cannot be learned from a book, a seminar, or even modeling superior teachers.

◆   ◆   ◆

Keith J. Karnok is Professor of Agronomy in the Department of Crop and Soil Sciences in the College of Agricultural and Environmental Sciences at The University of Georgia. He received his BS and MS degrees in Agronomy from the University of Arizona and his Ph.D. from Texas A&M University in Turfgrass Physiology. Dr. Karnok began his teaching career at Ohio State University, where he taught both beginning and advanced courses in turfgrass management. In 1983, he joined the faculty in the Department of Crop and Soil Sciences at The University of Georgia. Currently, he teaches three courses in turfgrass management as well as advises both undergraduate and graduate students specializing in turfgrass science. Dr. Karnok also advises a student club—the UGA Turf Club. In addition to his on-campus teaching, Dr. Karnok has adapted two of his courses to the independent study format. He also developed a continuing education (CEU) correspondence turfgrass management program in cooperation with the Professional Lawn Care Association of America. There have been more than two thousand students from all fifty states and twenty-one countries enrolled in this program.

Dr. Karnok's research interest is the study of those factors affecting turfgrass root growth. He conducts this research in a state-of-the-art rhizotron facility (underground root observation laboratory) that he designed on The University of Georgia campus. Dr. Karnok has over two hundred publications and has received fifteen teaching awards at the departmental, college, university, regional, and national levels. Among these honors are the highest awards given by The University of Georgia, the American Society of Agronomy, the Crop Science Society of America, and the National Association of Colleges and Teachers of Agriculture. He won the Meigs Award in 1996. Dr. Karnok and his wife, Melinda, have four children, Kristen, Kara, Keith, and Kortney, and two grandchildren, Carlie and Camron.

TEACHING TRICKS

Lief H. Carter

IT MAY SEEM a bit irreverent to refer to teaching as a form of trickery. "Tricks" in my title works as both a noun and a verb, and I intend both meanings here. As a noun, "tricks" means that good teaching and good learning involve many of the techniques and activities that we associate with magic and magicians. As a verb, it means that good teaching alters, i.e., tricks, the mind. Learning replaces the old with the new. To suspend our belief in the old involves the magician's trick of getting us to suspend our disbelief in the new.

Three characteristics of contemporary education very much heighten the need for magic. First, we no longer live in a political climate where the authority of the teacher alone changes minds. I recently asked a large group of college students to raise their hands if they had ever had teachers in grades K–12 who did not know the subject they were teaching. Most raised their hands and groaned as they did so. And quite apart from a decline in substantive skills, authority is out of favor. The days of John Houseman's Professor Kingsfield in *Paper Chase* are gone. Second, interpretive theory is in and seat-of-the-pants positivism is out. The world does not offer itself to us in obvious factual chunks anymore, which means that we cannot in good conscience stand before students and tell them what "is." (It really *does* depend on what "is" is!) We teachers need to persuade students why seeing a phenomenon in one way (or some ways) is better than seeing it in other ways. Our mere declaiming doesn't cut it.

These first two conditions of education today are, on balance, good things. At least they conform to my understanding of how education works in liberal democratic cultures. The third characteristic, however, is not desirable. It is now clear that the conventional classroom is a lousy learning environment. The studies of student retention rates of course materials X months after taking a class are very discouraging. The reason turns out to be quite clear. There is a patterned way that humans learn and retain what they learn, and sitting and listening and occasionally talking and taking notes isn't it. Human beings learn by role-modeling people who have mastered something. They do this through what we call "apprenticeships." (Note, *not* "internships.") Students choose, out of their own motivations, someone who has mastered the knowledge and skill that the student wants. They study with the master for hours a day for months or years, doing the skill as they learn it. And, whether it is learning a craft from a parent, or learning a musical instrument or a sport from a coach, these apprentices remember. Only something magical can transform a classroom full of students fulfilling a requirement into something even remotely like a self-motivated apprenticeship.[13]

So how do we do that? It turns out that the primary "trick" to effective teaching is the old cliché "love of the material." Our students *are* going to role-model us, or, to put it rudely, ape us (we are higher primates, after all). The trouble is, we do not actually do what we teach. We do not, in the undergraduate classroom, file appeals in death penalty cases, or fight Napoleonic campaigns, or discover new properties of primordial stem cells—the sorts of things masters would do in real apprenticeships (but which graduate research training comes closer to achieving). So what is left to apprentice to? Students apprentice to the thing the teacher does know and do, which is to love and master the subject. Learning (and it is learning, not teaching, that matters) happens when students want it, and they want it by role-modeling we teachers "wanting it." If I'm right about this, the classroom must engage and stimulate. It must be fun. Not fun in the gimmicky way that panders in order to win popularity contests, but fun in the sense of being unforgettably challenging, as in the film *Dead Poets Society*.

Trick One: Startle Early

Whenever I can figure out how to do it, I start my class with something that jogs the experience of *this* course out of the ordinary. My favorite (so far) happens in my course on political power. Before I hand out the syllabus or take roll, I announce that we will do an ice-breaking exercise. I tell the students to sit on the fronts of their desks or tables. I then get them to sing "Row, Row, Row Your Boat" in a round. They are inevitably terrible the first time around, so I tell them to stand on the desks and do it louder. I then stop and ask them how I, a mere political science professor, got them to stand on desks and sing. They don't always get it at first, so I tell them that power is getting people to do something they would not voluntarily do, or trade for, on their own. I have just exerted power over them. When we get to the next question, "What are the sources of a professor's power?" they jump in with both feet. They have learned by experience the basic definition of political power before they even have the syllabus. The tricks must be course-specific, but I cannot imagine a course where you can't begin with something fun. In basic math, for example, start out by taking bets that you can prove 3 + 4 = 12 and see how long it takes them to tumble onto base five.

Trick Two: Don't Be Too Nice in the Classroom

Magicians entertain us, but they entertain *because* they make fools of us. I have not found a way of maintaining my love of material without at the same time telling students who don't understand what I love that I think they are wrong. In substantive knowledge courses, I have never learned how to love and analyze a question by merely going around the circle asking what students (who, if they already knew the material, should not be in the course) think about it. But of course there are tricks for correcting students constructively. I teach quasi-Socratically, and my first line, when confronted with blatant student error, is usually to ask, "Does anyone disagree with this?" I sometimes pause and then add, *sotto voce*, "Besides me." For complex matters, we may spontaneously divide into sides—split down the middle of the room is easiest, gender next easiest, and alphabetically least so. Or students can count off and break into small groups.

Above all what makes fairly blunt correction work for me is that I make very clear in every course what my test of correctness is. My "speech" (and/or my syllabus) goes something like this:

> I will evaluate everything you do in this course this way: you must show me that you have mastered the material covered in *this* course. If you have learned something about the subject in another class or have thought long deep private philosophical thoughts about a problem in this class, that's great, but you still have to show me how it integrates with, or contradicts, material covered in the course. If you write a brilliant answer to an essay question, but it is an answer that intelligent students not in this class could write if I dragged them in out of the hall and sat them down, you will get no credit.

So, in correcting students, I ask them to justify their position in relation to course materials. If they cannot, I say that my correcting is my way of coaching them to get more points on exams and papers. It also helps to role-model that it is okay to be wrong. I do that sometimes by making a superficially plausible-sounding statement that I know to be wrong and asking them to challenge me. More often, sadly, I will in fact say something badly, or wrongly. It probably took a decade to learn it, but saying to the class, "Gee, I totally screwed up point X. Forget everything I said! I'm sorry. Let me start over," is very healthy.

Trick Three: Impress Them with Your Magic Powers

I can no longer do it for a class of eighty, but there was a younger time when I could memorize every name and face in a large class in its first day or two. The trick is, as you take first-day roll, to jot down something that the new student reminds you of—a friend, sibling, something about hair, height, weight. (I was always fearful that my roll sheet would fall into the wrong hands!) Then, immediately after class, you drill yourself on your key. Calling on people by name the second day of class says that you have a mind, but more important, it sends the message that you care about the students individually, that you care about the course, that you, the teacher, do mental work in this course, and expect them to do the same. A few other things fall into this category: Get exams and papers graded *fast*. Give exams on a Friday and get them back Monday morning. In addition, I always take my own tests. I hand the students my own "Sample A answers" when they turn in their exams. This actually reduces grading time, since you can write "See sample answer" in the margin of a bluebook rather than writing out an explanation of the same mistake over and over again.

Trick Four: "Look, There's Nothing Up My Sleeve."

While it is admittedly a bit of a stretch, fairness, both in fact and in appearance, is as essential to good teaching and learning as is the magician's appearance of "honesty." Here are some suggestions to maximize fairness.

1. Whenever possible, grade anonymously. All students have some ID number. Ask them to put it, not their name, on anything they write except assignments uniquely tailored to them, like individual paper topics.

2. Never allow extra-credit or makeup work to one student unless you can provide every student in the class the same opportunity. (I never allow it, period.)

3. If you must grade on "class participation," make this as minimalist and mechanical as possible, e.g., a measure of acceptable attendance. Grading on the quality of comments in class disfavors

the slowly thoughtful and leaves open a fudge factor that others may perceive as permitting favoritism.

4. Follow as simple a grading scale as possible, so students always know where they stand. I have always equated letter grades with numbers. That is, if a course has 500 total possible points in it, a student who gets 400 or more gets an A or (A−). If an essay question on an exam is worth 20 points, answers in the A range get somewhere between 16 and 20 points.

5. Finally, do not grade on a curve. I have told every class I've ever taught that I dream of the day when everyone will get an A. Abilities are distributed along the bell curve, and this golden day will probably never dawn, but it is immensely important that students believe that they compete with themselves for mastery of the material and not with each other.

Conclusion

I conclude with what I think is the hardest thing for undergraduate teachers to learn: like a magician, you are *not* teaching "the truth." Obviously I don't mean that you hide the truth and protect your secrets like a magician, but I do mean that undergraduate teachers must get comfortable with the notion that we start where our students are. Where they are can be simpleminded and/or downright incoherent. If we start out trying to teach the latest hot academic debates about the "real" truth of, say, internal coalition building on the Supreme Court, we will bore the pants off them. Better to start out, like a magician, with an illusion they understand and that challenges them to get behind and beyond it.

Readers may rightly note that I ignore here the great variety of students and student-learning styles. My response is only that there are also a great variety of teaching styles. My hunch is that a teaching institution maximizes achievement of both good teaching and meaningful learning by allowing teachers to teach in the most authentic ways they can, and letting students find the teaching styles that work for them. What I've written here is not "the truth." I simply hope that teachers like me find it helpful.

♦ ♦ ♦

Lief H. Carter is McHugh Family Distinguished Professor, Department of Political Science, Colorado College. He attended Harvard College (1962) and Harvard Law School (1965). During the Vietnam War, he served in a Peace Corps teaching program in Bolivia. On his return he earned a Ph.D. in political science at the University of California, Berkeley (1972), where he specialized in legal politics and organization theory. Dr. Carter's dissertation, on the organizational dynamics of a prosecuting attorney's office, won the American Political Science Association's Edward Corwin Award for the best doctoral dissertation in public law in 1972–73.

Professor Carter came to The University of Georgia in 1973. He taught legal process, constitutional law, administrative law, and legal theory courses at the undergraduate and graduate levels until he moved to Colorado in 1995. Periodically, he has served as a visiting professor at the University of Washington and at Brown University. Dr. Carter has adopted a modified version of the Socratic teaching style, from his days as a law student, which he employs in classes of all sizes. At The University of Georgia he won teaching awards at the departmental, college, and university-wide level. He was Georgia's first professor to win the Josiah Meigs Award twice, in 1984 and 1989.

Dr. Carter is a devotee of classical music. He has built a harpsichord and served as choir director at his church. For several years he organized and conducted the Athens Chamber Music Ensemble, a small chamber orchestra. He enjoys playing piano compositions for four hands with his wife, Dr. Marilyn Vickers. She maintains her clinical psychotherapy practice in Athens, Georgia, so he returns to Athens often.

"Laughter Holding Both His Sides"[14]: Humor as a Welcome Guest in the Classroom

Genelle G. Morain

I LANDED MY first teaching job fifty years ago and I was jubilant. The high school was in the northwest corner of Iowa—a daring distance from my hometown south of Des Moines—and my salary was an astronomical $2,300 for nine months! Eager to meet my new colleagues, I hurried into the first teachers' meeting, grinning indiscriminately at one and all. But Miss Karlson—matriarch of the English Department—lost no time in correcting this excess of bonhomie. Leaning across the cafeteria table, she caught my eye in a net of steel and whispered, "A word of advice to you, my dear. Don't . . . smile . . . until Christmas!" She meant it. A smile might lead to a giggle, which could trigger a chortle that would degenerate into a full-blown guffaw. And seasoned teachers knew that laughter, being contagious—like disease—would create chaos in the classroom. Studies show that the average child of five laughs over four hundred times per day—an adult only fifteen (Morreall, 1991): obviously, a triumph for Miss Karlson.

Our culture still relegates humor to a low rung on the intellectual ladder. Judging from the paucity of Nobel Prizes awarded to humorists, levity lacks luster in academe. Today's humor researchers usually present their results in a grim-jawed manner derived from earlier humor scholars: Kant, Goethe, Hobbes, and Freud. These were not merry men. Miss Karlson would have been proud of them.

Reinforcing our suspicion of anything pleasurable, we have learned that many of life's simple joys—staring at the TV, basking in the sun, eating something greasy and good—are dulling us, wrinkling us, clogging us. Fortunately, scientists now claim that something we enjoy—laughing—is truly good for us. Laughter, like exercise, increases the normal breathing rhythm. As muscular tension, blood pressure, and heart rate increase, so does the amount of oxygen in the blood. When laughter subsides, the resulting sense of relaxation helps combat depression, high blood pressure, and heart disease. Laughter also releases endorphins, which act to reduce pain. Finally, laughing increases the immunoglobulin A in saliva—which is more than you wanted to know—but this multisyllabic laughter-lover helps the immune system fight off disease.

Researchers have also found evidence of compelling social reasons for fostering humor. This comes as no surprise to the Navajo, who have long venerated the role of humor in life. From the moment of birth, Navajo infants are watched closely until they laugh for the first time. That is the moment, their parents believe, when a child is born as a social being (Crodkin, 1993).

As scholars remind us, humor fills a variety of roles in our lives. Some of us are "appreciators" of humor; we delight when others tell jokes, but we can never remember the punchlines ourselves. A second group, the "reproducers," are those who know a joke for every occasion and always get the punchline perfect. A third and gifted group creates the humor. They dream up the gags, write the comic sketches, and draw the cartoons. Then there is the enviable fourth group: they not only create the new jokes and receive the plaudits of the present; they also remember the old jokes and preserve the humor of the past. Unfortunately, there is a fifth group into which the "nonhumorous" fall. None of *us* belongs in this sorry category, but we all know someone who does. To be told "You have no sense of humor" is an insult to Americans. As the saying goes, "A person has two legs and one sense of humor. If you're faced with the choice, it's better to lose a leg!"

Humor helps us control our feelings of aggression. Every culture devises a few acceptable ways to release hostility. In our society, competitive sports are one way, and—as someone suggested—literary criticism is another. Perhaps the most widely practiced way to release aggression is humor. UGA Professor Charles Gruner (1978) supported the "derision theory" of seventeenth-century philosopher Thomas Hobbes as the most credible explanation for why we laugh. Hobbes insisted that for a situation to be humorous, the plight of the victim must occur suddenly and arouse an immediate feeling of "sudden glory" (superiority) in the viewer. Others, however, feel that "derision" is not the sole motivation for laughter. They would broaden the functions of humor, saying that it also enables us to derive vicarious pleasure from sexuality without incurring social censure. They point out, too, that in the form of satire, humor influences positive changes in society. Humor also serves as a defensive mechanism that helps us deal with our worst anxieties: fear of failure, tragedy, and death. By permitting us to laugh at things that frighten us, this "gallows humor" makes them less menacing. As Asimov (1971) put it, "One of the functions of the joke is to speak the unspeakable" (p. 311). And finally, humor simply brings us the pleasure of solving the intellectual puzzle posed by a good joke.

Scholars struggle to explain how we go about solving that puzzle. Central to most solutions is the "incongruity theory," which holds that in every humorous situation there are two elements that clash— two seemingly disparate "scripts" that do not belong cheek by jowl. It is when the brain suddenly discovers the connection between these two incongruous elements that we "get" a joke. Unless the sequence of initial bafflement, sudden insight, and resultant amusement takes place, the joke fails. Perhaps the teller structured the joke clumsily— timing it wrongly or mangling the punchline. Maybe the presentation was flawless, but the listener was unable to establish the connection that would resolve the incongruity. Or possibly the listener did "get" the point, but for personal reasons did not consider it amusing. Roughly the same sequence of presentation, confusion, cognitive understanding, and emotional response that occurs when we hear a joke also takes place when we either enjoy or fail to enjoy a pun, a cartoon, or a humorous anecdote. To explore this topic further, see Attardo and Raskin (1991), Oring (1992), and Veatch (1998).

Considering the functions of humor and the role that resolving incongruity plays in recognizing humor, we can see that humor is a cognitive as well as a social skill. Statistics may not impress you any more than they did Mrs. Robert Taft, who insisted, "I always find that statistics are hard to swallow and impossible to digest. The only one I can remember is that if all the people who go to sleep in church were laid end to end, they would be a lot more comfortable" (Radin, 1997). Nevertheless, when 329 CEOs of the Fortune 500 corporations were asked about humor in business, 97 percent stated that humor is important in negotiations and that in hiring they always look for a sense of humor (Morreall, 1991). Humor smoothes social encounters, develops a tolerance for ambiguity and change, and reduces stress. It also fosters creative problem-solving, divergent thinking, and risk taking. The nonhumorous tend to be mentally rigid; the humorous, mentally flexible (Morreall, 1998).

Humor enables us to view ourselves with greater objectivity and to think about things from other people's perspectives. Humor stimulates intellectual curiosity. We discover that if we are not sure which situations are normal in a cultural environment, we cannot recognize discrepancies when we encounter them (Holt and Willard-Holt, 1995). We also learn that not all incongruity is humorous. Cultures evolve their own rules as to who can laugh, when, and at what. For instance, Asian students in my classes did not see the humor in jokes about baldness—a condition that rarely occurs in their cultures and therefore is not a worry that motivates joking.

To understand the humor of any culture, we need both an awareness of its value system and familiarity with the cultural referents that are juxtaposed to create that challenging incongruity. A study exploring the responses of international students to the humor of American cartoons (Morain, 1991) underscored not only the difficulty of comprehending the humor of a foreign culture but also the devastating emotional impact of the failure to understand. Participants spoke repeatedly of their alienation when the group laughed and they did not know why. Typical was this remark: "I feel I will never be in this group. I feel apart." Such comments provide a poignant rationale for including a dimensional exploration of humor in the curriculum.

But humor is tricky business. The controversial topic of "political correctness" is linked to the role that prejudice plays in the creation of humor (Apte, 1985; Davies, 1990; Saper, 1995). "The trouble is," said the *New York Times Magazine* (September 4, 1994), "cruelty and humor are old pals." Humor makes use of stereotypes, which are often neither flattering nor accurate. But deprived of stereotypes, where would humor be? Asimov (p. 211) explains that "the world of jokes is . . . a world of stereotypes—conventions understood by jokester and listener alike—which offer shortcuts to laughter. Because the laugh is quicker and surer, the stereotype is reluctantly abandoned, even when it is outmoded. The rolling pin remains the symbol of the angry wife waiting for the belated husband, even when few kitchens boast one." It is important for our students to know that stereotypes represent "social reality" rather than "objective reality" (Dundes, 1971) and that it is possible to enjoy a joke without believing in the stereotype (Apte, 1985). As Luke (1987) reminds us, "Those with a sense of humor do not laugh *at* a person; there is simply a feeling of delight in the ridiculous wherever it is manifest and such laughter does not condemn the other or oneself." (p. 10).

How does a teacher go about fostering this benign humor in the classroom? It seems easy to encourage humor in a folklore course, but I have taught eleven other subjects and humor self-generated in all of them. Skeptics might read the Berk and Nanda article (1998) describing how these professors used humor successfully in statistics courses at John Hopkins. Their meticulously plotted approach is not my cup of tea, but it improved attitudes, reduced anxiety, and increased student achievement. Whatever the content area, the teacher's role is to create a learning atmosphere that welcomes humor. Here are some suggestions that worked for me.

1. Forget Miss Karlson. Smile on day one and every succeeding day of the semester. It is self-indulgent to inflict your grouchy moods on the students.

2. Call your students by name and devise ways for students to learn each other's names. Humor is more likely to develop among friends than among strangers.

3. Share favorite cartoons on your office door; they offer clues to your particular sense of humor. If you meet your class routinely in the same room, display humorous clippings and images that relate to the course and will stimulate discussion. Change them frequently so they don't petrify on the walls.

4. Use words in intriguing and humorous ways: similes that surprise, proverbial sayings with a twist, puns, and hyperbole. Students appreciate the verbally unexpected. Once—on the day he received his Ph.D.—a student gave me a booklet entitled *Quotes of Professor Genelle Morain, An Unauthorized Compilation Surreptitiously Recorded During Summer Session, 1990*. I read with varying degrees of incredulity and dismay such items as "The Fourth of July was made for the trombone smear"; "I've never had a Babad in my class in 700 years of teaching"; "It might be kissing as we've never imagined with our limited lips"; "I don't know why ghosts always come to the foot of the bed; but it's better than having them crawl in."

5. Use teaching strategies that invite the creation of humor: weave anecdotes (Churchill called them "the gleaming toys of history") into the fabric of your lectures; recount examples of your own blunders; devise learning activities that involve all five senses; challenge your students with riddles; confront them with incongruities; share pithy quotations; make assignments that call for divergent thinking; involve students in role playing, skits, and small-group work. All of these provide a store of shared experiences that generate the in-group humor that makes a class memorable. Draw on it when creating exams: encountering oblique references to shared class humor diminishes test-taking tension.

6. One caveat: don't feel compelled to play the stand-up comic. Leno and Letterman pay zillions to the professionals who create their "spontaneous" monologues. Studies show that college students are turned off by a professor's self-conscious efforts to "be funny." Relax, and let humor emerge naturally from the moment-by-moment context of your class.

In my life as a teacher I followed two passions. One was to help students *question* intelligently. I wanted them to explore ideas creatively: *to think edge-wise.* My second passion was to encourage students *to value cultural differences as positives instead of negatives.* Kisly (1987) affirms that "rigidity, fear, defensiveness, and fanaticism are clearly incompatible with humor" (p. 3). I found that teaching a course where humor is welcomed created a climate in which students knew and liked each other, felt free to express diverse opinions, shared anecdotes that added important dimensions, conducted research they really cared about, asked each other questions, taught me things I didn't know, and laughed whenever they felt like it. And—sorry, Miss Karlson—I laughed too.

References

Apte, M. (1985). *Humor and Laughter: An Anthropological Approach.* Ithaca, N.Y., and London: Cornell University Press.

Asimov, I. (1971). *Treasury of Humor.* Boston: Houghton Mifflin.

Attardo, S., and V. Raskin (1991). "Script Theory Revis(it)ed: Joke Similarity and Joke Representation Model." *Humor* vol. 4, nos. 3 and 4: 293–347.

Berk, R., and J. Nanda (1998). "Effects of Jocular Instructional Methods on Attitudes, Anxiety, and Achievement in Statistics Courses." *Humor* vol. 11, no. 4: 391–405.

Crodkin, M. (1993). *Every Kid Counts: 31 Ways to Save Our Children.* San Francisco: HarperCollins. Quoted in *Teaching Tolerance* (1994), vol. 3, no. 1: 6.

Davies, C. (1990). *Ethnic Humor around the World: A Comparative Analysis*. Bloomington, Ind., and Indianapolis, Ind.: Indiana University Press.

Dundes, A. (1971). "A Study of Ethnic Slurs: The Jew and the Polack in the United States." *Journal of American Folklore* vol. 84: 186–203.

Gruner, C. (1978). *Understanding Laughter: The Workings of Wit and Humor*. Chicago: Nelson-Hall.

Holt, D., and C. Willard-Holt (1995). "Humor and Giftedness in Students." *Humor* vol. 8, no. 3: 257–71.

Kisly, L. (1987). "Focus." *Parabola* vol. 12, no. 4: 3.

Luke, H. (1987). "The Laughter at the Heart of Things." *Parabola* vol. 12, no. 4: 6–17.

Morain, G. (1991). "Humor Across Cultures: X-raying the International Funny Bone" in J. Alatis, ed. *Linguistics and Language Pedagogy: The State of the Art*. Washington, D.C.: Georgetown University Press.

Morreall, J. (1991). "Humor and Work." *Humor* vol. 4, nos. 3 and 4: 359–73.

——— (1998). "The Comic and Tragic Visions of Life." *Humor* vol. 11, no. 4: 333–55.

Oring, E. (1992). *Jokes and Their Relations*. Lexington, Ky.: University Press of Kentucky.

Radin, D. (1997). *The Conscious Universe: The Scientific Truth of Psychic Phenomena*. New York: HarperCollins.

Saper, B. (1995). "Joking in the Context of Political Correctness." *Humor* vol. 8, no. 1: 65–76.

Shea, D. (1990). *Quotes of Professor Genelle Morain, An Unauthorized Compilation Surreptitiously Recorded During Summer Session, 1990*. Unpublished manuscript.

Veatch, T. (1998). "A Theory of Humor." *Humor* vol. 11, no. 2: 161–215.

◆　　◆　　◆

Genelle G. Morain grew up in a small town in Iowa, the state whose name means "Beautiful Land." After graduating from Simpson College (where she later gave the Sesquicentennial Commencement Address), she taught English, speech, and dramatics in high school. Later, she studied folklore at Indiana University, married her college sweetheart—who was recalled to the Army on their honeymoon— and taught again in high school while he was in Korea. Her husband eventually practiced law in Council Bluffs, and they had two children.

Dr. Morain was widowed in 1960, and—while teaching French at Indianola High School—won an NDEA Fellowship for a new program at Ohio State University that would permit her to go from a BA degree in French to a Ph.D. in Foreign Language Education by carrying twenty hours per quarter for twelve consecutive quarters. Surviving, she came to UGA in 1968, clutching her diploma in one hand and dragging her children with the other. She enjoyed a joint appointment between Romance Languages and Language Education until she developed the folklore and cross-cultural understanding courses that, added to her duties as a professor of foreign language methodology and supervisor of student teachers, necessitated a full-time commitment to the College of Education. She won the Meigs Award in 1994. Dr. Morain retired after twenty-eight years of doing what she loved and is now enjoying other things she loves: baking bread, feeding birds, traveling with her son and his wife, flying to catch her actor daughter's performances, adding to her folklore library, and cherishing her friends.

TEACHER BURNOUT

Ronald L. Carlson

"I CAN'T DO this any longer," Fred Plummer announced as he came into his old friend's office.

"Can't do what?" asked Rupert Wallace, the longtime associate dean of the college.

"Any of it," Plummer responded. "The teaching. The commit-tees. The backbiting. The complaints by the students. The whole ball of wax. I have had it."

"Wait, slow down," Rupert advised his junior colleague. "How long have you been at this?" Rupert had a rough recollection of Plummer's years of service, but he wanted to hear it from Plummer.

"Almost fourteen years," said Plummer. "At first it was okay. Good, really. But the last few years I have been gritting my teeth and dreading the second half of every semester. The start of the term is fine, with the new faces. But by the end, it degenerates into a real grind."

"You have the incipient, early stages of a terminal case of academic burnout," said Rupert. "I have seen it more than once. There is a cure, but it's not easy."

"I'm not sure I'm up for a self-help program, but go ahead," Plummer sighed.

"Part of it is back to basics. The other part requires some path-breaking, and taking some risks."

Burnout Across the Board

The problem identified in the foregoing conversation is not unique to a university setting. From kindergarten through high school, teachers are turning off and dropping out. The source of the turnoff may be different, but the result is the same: frustration and dissatisfaction. Grade school instructors struggle during evening hours to balance family responsibilities with endless professional paperwork. Time during the day to prepare lesson plans and the myriad of reports expected of these instructors is slim and none.

For the middle school teacher, the chief problem may be class size. Overcrowded schools make it impossible to give one-on-one instruction, and discipline responsibilities become paramount. From K through 12, faculty members justifiably resent the amount of energy they must devote to enforcing discipline instead of instructing. As in many human enterprises, it is frequently a few bad actors whose out-of-control conduct ruins things for everybody.

There are other sources of discontent as well. One public school instructor complained about the hundreds of dollars she took out of her own pocket to fund special projects that added to the educational mission. There was no money in the school budget for anything "special."

The role of parents, particularly the positives that they can impart to the educational enterprise, declines as the student matures. Especially later in the schooling process, middle school and particularly high school, parental indifference abounds.

The result of this mix of problems is the high rate of K–12 educators quitting the profession. In places where student populations are expanding, it is increasingly difficult to hire enough qualified teachers. For those who do enter and remain in the system, burnout is epidemic.

In the university context, those outside the educational enterprise may wonder why there is any concern for "academic burnout." To the public at large, the job of university educator appears to be an idyllic existence. Invisible to the public eye are the disputes with colleagues over curriculum or with students over grades or the difficulty of balancing time between teaching schedules, drafting committee reports, meeting article deadlines, writing job recommendations, and responding to multiple inquiries from administrators, students, and alumni. The drain of daily interpersonal contact with so many constituencies is telling. In the classroom, repeating information taught many times before wears on the professor.

The expectation that faculty members will be good teachers and at the same moment good researchers sets a demanding standard. Work is never just left at the office and occupies us for hours at night. Peer pressure, student pressure, and administrative pressures are all imposed on the teaching professional.

In some universities, draconian cuts in funding have resulted in hiring and salary freezes, where larger classes and more part-time faculty have become the rule. Diminished appreciation for the valued role of the true teaching professional is keenly felt by instructors trapped in these settings.

Across the board, teachers hunger for affirmation and recognition. They look for signs that people understand what they are trying to do and the difficulty it takes to accomplish it. Sadly, when there is an absence of this commodity, disillusion abounds. Earlier in my teaching career at another school, a colleague dejectedly remarked, "My next great career goal is retirement." He was in his early forties. Barring an evolution in his attitude, I foresaw twenty grueling years ahead for him.

It is no mystery why most universities have institutionalized programs of released sabbatical time to help professors recharge batteries. And while understanding the burnout problem by the public is important, for the teaching professional it is critical. Perhaps the most important thing a professor can do about burnout is to understand it. As noted, the issues of burnout and its antidotes are presented here mainly in the context of a university setting, but it has broader application. It can affect educators of all kinds, high school teachers, junior college instructors, anyone. Only the precise source of the problem changes with the setting.

Overcoming Burnout

This essay began with a downcast college professor receiving advice from the associate dean, Rupert. Rupert laid out for Plummer a number of steps that are remarkably similar to those that have worked for me in combating malaise. It is valuable to mention a few of these.

Saying "Yes"

While seeking a golden mean in terms of one's commitments, it is inevitable that a person will err in one direction or another when he says "yes" or "no." Typically he will do one of these two things too often. The question is should the error be in the direction of over-commitment or undercommitment? I agree with the basic proposition that too little stress is worse than too much stress. Boredom is corrosive and kills the spirit. Accordingly, while endeavoring to reach moderation in all things, saying yes too many times is less of a mistake than saying no. As a first matter of importance, resolve today to be receptive to new challenges.

Engagement with Younger Colleagues

Second, to remain engaged in his or her college or department, the successful professor should seek governance opportunities. Association with younger members of one's faculty is most meaningful when all are collectively performing needed governance tasks of the department or college. The curriculum or the hiring committees provide two good examples. Many veteran professors might initially react to this advice by saying, "I have done that." Do it again. What you will find is that you may not have changed but the other members of the committee have changed as your department has evolved. Do not emulate those who are prone to tell ancient war stories: "When I was personnel chair, we did things this way or that way." Rather, get in the game, roll up your sleeves with the younger members of the department, and accomplish a needed governance task.

The same advice holds true for the K–12 teacher, although the specific applications may be slightly different. The point is, reach out for opportunities that bring one into contact with younger members of the teaching staff. The association in worthwhile projects is challenging and exhilarating. Mentoring a younger colleague is useful and may be fun.

Academic Causes

Third, contribute to worthwhile academic causes. They are presented to us constantly. Academic freedom requires diligence, activity, and watchfulness on the part of professors. Stifling speech codes or proposals to end the tenure system merit our scrutiny, and opposition. Elevating the respect for teaching on campus is another meritorious cause. Building a strong teaching academy at a university is a project worthy of participation and support.

Teacher Renewal

Fourth, recognize the value—indeed, the nobility of doing a task well on a continuing, sometimes repetitive basis. This applies emphatically to the teaching function. It is a tragedy that when professors or other teachers attain the peak of their ability to relate to the students, often that is the time when they lose their interest in teaching. Yet the greatest people in our profession are those who remained constant to their original calling. In 23 Ga. Law Review 709 I put it this way:

> [There is great value in providing] consistency of effort. This refers to the professor, who, year after year, produces quality writing and inspirational teaching. Regarding the classroom, professionals who are dedicated to the goal of effective teaching must constantly bear in mind that the messages we bring to the students are new for them each season; regardless of the number of times that we have taught the course, the fresh faces before us deserve a renewed effort, laced with the latest in case developments and creative techniques to communicate and challenge them. Consistency in performance means avoiding burnout in one's research efforts as well.

A High Calling

We need to recognize that the high calling of the professoriate provides a unique service to our communities and our nation. It has been wisely remarked that university professionals have not told their story very well. The story of American higher education merits telling. America's university professors have provided a remarkable model. We are constantly reminded of our trade deficit with foreign countries. It seems clear that American business has not always done as well as American universities in the face of foreign competition. Our universities draw people from around the world who wish to study here. It is our responsibility to keep it that way.

Personal Reflections

The prior list of suggestions for renewal and engagement contained in this essay assisted my thirty-five-year career in law teaching. One other factor requires mention. That is openness to new adventures that complement teaching or research. For me that came in the form of opportunities as a legal commentator and broadcaster. When the university communications office asked me to consider broadcasting my views and insights on the O. J. Simpson case, I said "yes." That led to a sideline that continues to this day, providing reactions to legal issues for the public, with cases ranging from Jon Benet Ramsey to footballer Ray Lewis. My views have appeared on radio and CNN, in *USA Today*, and in many other media outlets. Keeping up with high-profile cases has provided me with countless object lessons to bring back to my law students in our coursework together. It has been exciting, and this extra duty provides a perfect educational complement to my courses in litigation.

Conclusion

Burnout issues cross party, class, and gender lines. The impact of burnout can be felt in a declining passion for teaching, our jobs, and even going to work. When one doubts the importance of what he or she is doing, it is time to take stock. Have I lost my energy and drive? Am I tired of students? Do I dislike my colleagues and my boss? Is my work irrelevant? If your answers to these questions are "yes," you need to address your decline as quickly as possible. Potential avenues for renewal have been suggested in this essay, because the chief responsibility for recovery is on the individual teacher. But others can help. Overcoming burnout is sometimes a team effort. The academy can provide sabbaticals and other opportunities for renewal. Students have an important role in motivating teachers. Showing respect in class, preparation, and expressing appreciation for a favorite teacher are helpful. A recent airplane trip brought me into contact with a student from another University of Georgia college. The student and I were traveling to the same distant city. As we got acquainted, the student spoke glowingly of her educational experience studying under a valued professor. When I got back home I passed along these remarks to the professor, which brightened his day and week.

Few seek fame or fortune in the teaching profession. In the end, our enduring legacy is the positive impact we have upon our students. Recognition of this eternal truth may be one of the keys to overcoming burnout.

One final observation requires mention. The professor whose frustration began this essay and his dean have been given assumed names, for literary purposes. The names Fred Plummer and Rupert Wallace have no relation to real persons, living or dead. However, the professor in the described incident did put to work some of the suggestions from the dean whom I have called Rupert. The conversation reported in the opening paragraphs occurred in 1995. Today, the professor remains at the college and seems to have recovered his enthusiasm—and last year won the school's outstanding teaching award.

◆   ◆   ◆

Ronald L. Carlson is the Fuller E. Callaway Professor of Law at The University of Georgia. He has authored thirteen books on evidence, trial practice, and criminal procedure, in addition to professional articles in journals like the Duke, Cornell, Vanderbilt, Iowa, North-western, Georgia, and Minnesota law reviews.

Professor Carlson joined the UGA faculty in 1984. At the end of his first year on the faculty he was honored by the law students with the outstanding professor award. In 1989, he won the university-wide Josiah Meigs Award for Excellence in Teaching. In 1992, he received the Federal Bar Association's highest honor, the Earl W. Kintner Award for Distinguished Service to the Federal Bar Association.

Professor Carlson in July 2000 was presented with the Harrison Tweed Award for special merit in CLE given by ALI-ABA, recognizing his "career achievements in advancing the education of the bar." Believing that outreach to bench and bar is an important obligation of a lawyer and teacher, Carlson has provided programs for judges and lawyers all over the country. For example, Judge Myron Bright and Professor Carlson have presented their all-day program "Objections at Trial and How to Deal with the Difficult Lawyer" in over sixty cities, from Boston to Honolulu.

Prior to Georgia, Carlson was on the faculties of the University of Iowa College of Law as well as Washington University Law School in St. Louis. Summer teaching assignments have taken him to the University of Texas, St. Louis University, and Wayne State University.

Professor Carlson earned the following degrees: BA 1956, Augustana College; JD 1959, Northwestern University (Clarion DeWitt Hardy Scholar); LL.M. 1961, Georgetown University (E. Barrett Prettyman Fellow in Trial Advocacy).

INSPIRING STUDENTS TO EXCEL

Brenda H. Manning

INSPIRING STUDENTS TO excel is an important, yet elusive characteristic of an outstanding teacher. I can think of no praise more valued than to have a student say, "You inspired me to achieve more than I believed possible." With this comment, we glimpse part of the definition of "inspiring our students," i.e., believing in them, stubbornly and unrelentingly—keeping the faith that students can obtain the highest standards and ideals, even when they are skeptical, at best, and have totally given up, at worst.

Fortunately, for me, my students have continued over two decades to tell me, write me, and e-mail me that I have inspired them, sometimes after many years have gone by. Last week I heard from a young woman who graduated in 1986, and I could still remember where she sat and how she changed over the term. She was telling me about her family and her profession, and her compelling need "to inspire others as I had inspired her." I've often pondered and analyzed what it means "to inspire" as the apex of teaching.

Different Students/Different Ways to Inspire

I think about my students often. When their faces/names flash before me, I realize the ones I have reached and inspired to excel are not a homogeneous lot. Therefore, when I analyze "inspiration," I realize what inspired Sharon was not at all what inspired Vic. Although I propose some generalizations and even some steps for inspiring students to excel, I do not believe they explain "inspiration" for every student. I note emphatically that exceptions are a reality, and three examples appear next. Such exceptions (to general expectations as we enter our classrooms) are what add the spice, the excitement, and the unpredictability to the teaching profession.

Case 1—Inspiring the Student Who Already Knows Everything

The problem in Case 1 is not one of low expectations, but an unrealistic, inflated sense of self-efficacy. I have experienced some measure of success with Case 1 students by giving them the attention they seem to crave. I say things like, "Beth, you know about proleptic instruction—tell us what you know." This public acknowledgment, said without sarcasm, often lets Beth know she knows very little. I spend extra time before and after class letting the "know-it-all" experience my interest in her/him as a person. Often the "I already know this" is a front behind which a person with low self-confidence is hiding. Once this becomes apparent and okay, then Steps 1–5 in Chart 1 (see page 137) may be useful and helpful.

Case 2—Inspiring the Student Who Is Not Interested in Learning

This student may be in college because his/her parents insisted upon it or because going to school beats working. The uninterested student is one of the greatest challenges to teaching. In my teacher-preparation courses, I require each student to talk to me in individual conferences for at least thirty minutes at the beginning, middle, and end of the term. I discover extremely valuable information about my students. Then I make every attempt to incorporate something of their interest within the curriculum that might capture the attention of the uninterested student. Sometimes I encourage the student to take a break from school until he or she is more motivated to learn. Above all, I depersonalize the student's lack of interest in my subject. We aren't all interested in the same topics. From time to time students land in the wrong major. I help them find a way out, so there is a chance they'll get inspired to excel elsewhere.

Case 3—Inspiring the Student Who Is Hostile, Cynical, or Cold

One way to explain how I've approached this challenge is to share an exchange I recently had with another educator about a Case 3 student. I'm writing to a colleague about a hostile student in my class:

> She's tough, cynical, cold—my favorite type—to see if I can break in and find out what's really inside. Almost always I find hurt, and lots of it! But it takes pushing in when the recipient is pulling away and keeping on being warm until something gives. For example, I say good-bye to her as she leaves every class, tell her to have a great weekend, and call her by her name and mean my sincerity. She would grunt good-bye or ignore me at first and look at me with distrust. I just kept right on returning her cold with my genuine support and warmth, and then she began to wave good-bye over her shoulder with her back to me, without looking back at me. And yesterday, after seven weeks of this, she came up to me after every other student was gone. I was deliberately stalling my "packing up" because I noticed she was hanging back. She said, "I know you are really busy, but I want to talk to you ... could I come talk to you? I'm not happy with most of my classes. Yours is the only one I like. The others don't challenge me." She went on and on and I listened, making strong eye contact and nodding a lot, letting her know that I knew she would figure it out for herself, that she is bright, and needs to act on her gut. She made an appointment to come talk about her life as a student at UGA. And I have a strong sense that she's on her way to less hostility. I'll stay until she's ready to move on to become a strong student. I'll keep you posted.

If you don't have a colleague with whom to share "student stories," writing in a journal might also serve as a beneficial outlet.

Expressing your classroom frustrations and successes in a journal often brings about welcome insights and answers.

Truthfully, I rarely know when I'm inspiring students. I only know after the fact because they choose to tell me: "You inspired me to try harder." "I found your words so inspiring!" "You were an inspiration to me. I'm now teacher of the year in my state." I'm still trying to figure out what it means "to inspire our students to excel." However, in this essay I'll share what I've concluded so far! This is a work in progress as I don't claim to have found *the* answer.

Generally Speaking, What It Means to Inspire Students to Excel

When we inspire students in our classrooms, we witness positive changes in thinking, attitude, disposition, and behavior. Inspired students are able to accomplish beyond their own expectations as they reach higher ones. These higher expectations may begin as ones held by the teacher for the student. Nevertheless, as students consistently see themselves through the teacher's lens as more accomplished, more capable, brighter, more creative, these "inspired" students adjust their original expectations set for themselves, moving them in line or higher than the teachers' expectations. I've seen this happen over and over again with students who have "gotten by"; they weren't treated as "durable learners"—ones who have what it takes to make great strides in the college classroom. I believe they will, and they often do! This positive and challenging teacher view of students' highest abilities and most diligent efforts serves as the foundation for inspiring them to excel. Intertwined within these greater expectations is a deep caring for the student so that the challenge is one of warmth, support, and encouragement—a scaffold of respect for their highest diligent learning efforts. No laziness, sloppiness, and skimpy learning are permitted from students in this context of academic learning efforts. Fostering verbal and nonverbal classroom environments, conducive to inspired learning, are suggested in Chart 1, below.

Chart 1
Steps to Inspire Students to Excel

Step One   Teacher *naïvely believes* each student is capable of great accomplishments in the university classroom and beyond.

Step Two   Teacher *clearly communicates* verbally and nonverbally a positive and challenging view of students as accomplished, creative, and capable.

Step Three Teacher *stubbornly maintains* a genuine stance of respect, caring, and encouragement, even when particular students are returning negative affects or nothing.

Step Four   Teacher *consistently treats* students with respectful challenges and *consciously distances* himself/herself to serve as expert guide, motivator, and model of enthusiasm for the subject being taught and, hopefully, learned.

   a) **Expert Guide.** Students are not likely to be inspired by a teacher who does not know in-depth the subject he or she is teaching. The university professor who inspires first knows well what he or she is teaching. And I believe it is incumbent upon us not only to know the most current research in our areas but to be active researchers ourselves. We not only bring in the latest literature but also create knowledge in our field so students feel the excitement of having a "researcher in the field" teaching them related topics. We view our students, including undergraduates, as future researchers in our fields and treat them accordingly. We direct them toward the classics and the current studies, scaffold the analyses of our literature, and expect them to choose the topics that interest them the most. Thus, I believe a major prerequisite to inspiring students is that we enter the classroom as well-informed, well-read, and current researchers in the subject we teach. Accompanying our expertise should be the ability to excite others about what we know and how we came to know it! We can accomplish this by being a motivator and a model of enthusiasm for our subject area.

b) **Motivator.** Not only do we know our subject but also we value its importance. This passion for what we teach is what stirs our students—wakes them up to their own insights, the "ahas" of learning. If we don't believe what we are teaching is important to study, to share with others, to learn, it is highly unlikely that anyone else will either. We don't inspire students to excel unless we are motivated to know, to question, and to discover in our respective fields. One of my mentors, Dr. Paul Torrance, said that teachers should frequently strive to ask questions for which we have no answers. By so doing, we demonstrate our own curiosity and motivation to continue learning. In addition, students realize the importance of posing questions that frame worthy investigations. Thus, the way to inspire is to be inspired. As university teachers, our first link to inspiring students to excel is to sincerely reveal our motivation to know more about the subject we are teaching while simultaneously exhibiting excitement for what we already know.

c) **Model of Enthusiasm.** When my students talk to me about how I inspired them, the teaching characteristic they mention most frequently is my enthusiasm for the subject I'm teaching. Indicators of enthusiasm include starting class on time with energy and interest, maintaining a lively pace, providing vivid examples, asking challenging questions, varying techniques (lecture, discussion, small group, jigsaw, etc.), and changing technology appropriately (e.g., PowerPoint, overhead, video, filmstrips, board, charts, etc.). Monotone, half-dead teachers do not engender inspired students. Energy begets energy, enthusiasm is contagious, and inspired teachers inspire others to excel.

Step Five Teacher *tediously balances* support and extremely high expectations even in the face of resistant or reluctant learners.

Conclusion

The consistent application of Steps 1–5 often will wear down and win over even the most defeated learners with seriously low expectations. And even though they never intended to get inspired to do well in college, they often do; they excel. Indeed, they often excel far beyond their own expectations, because they are borrowing the teacher's high expectations at first until they internalize the teacher's as their own. Note that the students with the worst attitudes about learning need our positive attitudes and belief in them the most.

Thus, all students need our highest expectations because their own expectations are frequently not as high as possible. I'm not always successful at inspiring students; however, when I have been, these students make dramatic, life-changing reversals or huge advances in how they view themselves as learners. And once they have experienced well-earned success in a challenging, supportive classroom, they often transfer these improved learning dispositions to their personal lives outside our university. My files are full of letters verifying such inspired change and growth. This is the reason I teach: to reach, to change, to advance, and to inspire.

◆　　◆　　◆

Brenda H. Manning is Professor and Graduate Coordinator, Department of Elementary Education, School of Teacher Education, College of Education. She joined The University of Georgia (UGA) faculty as an assistant professor in September 1981. At UGA she has taught undergraduate (freshman to senior level) and graduate (master's, specialist, and doctoral) students in seminars of five to twenty students and lecture/discussion classes of twenty-five to a hundred students. In the 1998–99 academic year, Dr. Manning moved from teaching graduate assistants about exemplary university teaching, fall semester, to teaching freshmen in the Arts and Sciences' Seminar, spring semester. She is equally fulfilled teaching freshmen or teaching doctoral students, as well as all levels in between. Her focus is teaching prospective and practicing teachers about classroom planning models, research-based classroom strategies, procedures, guidance models, and evaluation techniques. Dr. Manning's area of research is metacognition as a component of self-regulated teaching and learning. Previously, she was a public school teacher in grades two to eight and a mathematics teacher in the fifth, sixth, seventh and eighth grades. She won the Meigs Award in 1995.

On a personal note, Dr. Manning has a wonderful husband, Stewart, who cries at weddings and designs commercial kitchens—a Georgia Tech graduate. He is currently designing the first home they've built together. They have four grown children: two are married, three live in the Atlanta area, and the baby (twenty-four years old) lives in Austin, Texas. Dr. Manning's hobbies include the study of natural remedies for excellent health and nurturing her family. They spend lots of their free time together in Highlands, North Carolina, and hope to retire there in years to come.

WHAT I THINK ABOUT WHEN DESIGNING A NEW COURSE

Alan J. Jaworski

A RECURRENT THEME in many essays in this book is that our past experiences play a large role in our approaches to teaching. Certainly this is true in my case. For that reason it is important, as an introduction to this essay, that I provide you with some idea of my background in teaching and the types of courses I have taught.

For the past twenty-eight years I have been heavily involved in teaching the large general biology courses at The University of Georgia. Much of my teaching has been in classes of more than three hundred students, most of whom were non-science majors. Usually I taught two sections each day. Until recently, the Franklin College of Arts and Sciences required all Bachelor of Arts students to take a biology sequence with labs. These students comprised approximately 80 percent of those who enrolled in my classes, with the remaining 20 percent being either science majors or students who elected to take a general biology course.

Collectively, my students taught me most of what I know about teaching. I thank them for whatever success I may have had in the classroom because I do not consider myself a natural-born teacher.

Indeed, I need student feedback to help me understand what works in a classroom. Students help me see courses through their eyes, a perspective that I consider of paramount importance in designing a course. While faculty members know best what to teach, students can greatly inform us on how to teach. The latter does not mean "give them what they like" but, rather, "try to do what works." Let me illustrate this point with the following example.

One summer in the late eighties, I was planning to teach a general biology course to about two hundred students. At that time, both science majors and non-science majors took the same introductory biology course. Because of the large class size, we took a picture of each student and pasted it on a card that had personal and academic information about the student including his or her major. Lectures that summer were expanded to seventy minutes, which meant that the pace of the course would be much faster than other quarters with fifty-minute lectures. Consequently, I decided to give students an occasional break in the middle of the class period to allow them to freshen their attention. What I did for the break was pass out cards to each of the students. They were to provide their name and answer four questions: (1) What was the most interesting thing said in lecture during the past week? (2) What was the least interesting thing said in lecture during the past week? (3) What was the most difficult subject matter covered in lecture during the past week? (4) What was the least difficult subject matter covered in lecture during the past week? Because their names were on these cards, I could go into my card file with the student pictures to sort out responses according to academic major. To ensure that the students would give serious thought to the questions, I told them that I would give them bonus points toward their course grade each time they filled in a card.

Student responses to the four questions profoundly affected the way I thought about introductory biology courses. While many answers were somewhat surprising, others were quite predictable since I had read them before in course evaluations. But one response made by many students shocked me. A large proportion of the class wrote that they enjoyed my lecture on water relations in plants. During this lecture I explained to the students with words and diagrams how water enters a plant and what mechanisms are operating to get the water to move from the roots up to the top of the plant. Like many of my fellow biology teachers, I assumed this was boring stuff, especially to non-science majors. I was wrong. Because the student response was so unexpected, I spent some time thinking about why the students liked to hear about water relations. The answer was simple. During the last five minutes of the lecture period, I told the students how they could apply the basics of water relations to some of their past experiences. For example, I explained why one cuts off the bottom of flower stems before placing them in water. To me this was not a necessary part of the lecture, but to the students, it was the most important part of the class period. It provided relevance for the subject matter and made that lecture much more interesting. In retrospect, I should have realized that, but the fact is, I didn't fully appreciate that important aspect of course design until it was made obvious by the students.

From a series of student responses generated throughout the summer session, a central theme became apparent: majors and non-majors have different needs based on their unique perspectives. Non-majors need a greater emphasis with regard to relevance of the subject matter to their everyday lives, while majors, as potential practicing scientists, need more of an emphasis on the process of science and an identification of the critical experiments that have led to the principles we teach. The question here is one of emphasis in the course because both majors and non-majors should be exposed to the process of science; also, each group will enhance its learning if students are taught the relevance of the subject matter to their everyday lives. The most important point here is that I came to a better understanding of how to approach teaching general biology by getting feedback from students in an organized way. This recognition of the difference in the perspective of non-science majors vs. science majors was the basis for the decision to begin offering separate courses to the two groups. Note that the student feedback was not generated by the traditional student evaluations normally done at the end of a course. Information was gathered on a weekly basis and allowed individual students to express themselves freely about their reactions to the subject matter of the course.

The above anecdote serves to underscore my view that consideration of the perspective of the student is paramount when designing a course. It also provides an example of a mechanism to gather specific information about that perspective. In my view, one has to be careful about the way one gathers information relative to the student perspective. The best feedback I have obtained from students happened when I asked specific questions about particular topics. I don't rely on the students to tell me what topics should be covered in a course, but I do need their input as to how to approach teaching the individual topics.

Consideration of the student perspective leads one to ask why the course is taught in the first place. Are students enrolled because they are required to take the course, or is the course an elective? Does the course serve as a prerequisite for other courses? Is it an alternative course that satisfies a particular curriculum requirement? Answers to these questions determine how one should approach the course. For instance, if the course is required, students should know why it is required, and the course content should reflect the reason the course is required in the first place.

Our introductory biology offerings treat the science majors and non-science majors differently because the two groups of students are in those courses for very different reasons. In the case of science majors, the introductory course sequence serves as a prerequisite for all upper-division courses. For that reason it is important to provide these students with a solid foundation for the upper-division courses. It doesn't hurt to tell the students that a particular concept is fundamental background for a particular course that will follow. When they are told explicitly why they need to understand a concept, students are much more likely to put in the extra effort to learn that concept. This is equally true for a non-science major taking a general biology course to satisfy a core curriculum requirement. What professor hasn't heard students ask why they should learn something or heard students claim that they should not have to learn something because they will never use it? A little bit of effort by a professor to let students know the relevance of a course will go a long way toward generating a positive attitude when learning about a particular subject. Admittedly, it is easier to point out the relevance of some courses compared to others. But that only means that the more difficult it is for students to see the relevance, the more effort one should expend to make the student appreciate that relevance.

From my own experience in teaching a general science course, the idea that the relevance of a course needed explaining did not strike me until I had taught the course many times. My original focus was on the content. As a science major, I took my general biology courses with an enthusiasm for the subject matter. I did not need to be told why I should learn particular topics, and I certainly did not need to be lectured to about the relevance of the subject matter, for I was getting ready for more advanced courses. That was my reality, so course content was all I needed. Unfortunately, most of my students have had a very different perspective.

Courses we teach today must form the foundation for students well past their graduation. When thinking about what to teach and how to teach it, I try to envision the students going about their daily lives five years after graduation. Given the large size of my classes and the diversity of the students enrolled, this may appear to be an overly complex task. In reality, it is not. What students will remember about a course in five years is precious little if you focus on the details of the subject matter. However, if you consider the fact that you provide a perspective and a basis for rational thinking about your subject, then it becomes clear what a teacher needs to try to accomplish with a course. This is particularly important in a science course such as biology where the amount of published material is so great. It has been estimated that the knowledge base for biology doubles every three years. Some estimates indicate that the knowledge base doubles every year. This makes it very tempting to teach students "the latest stuff" because so many new discoveries are very exciting. But the truth is that students who took our courses five years ago could not have heard this new information because it was not discovered yet. What about them? Aren't there a lot more past students than current students?

By paying attention to the student as a future citizen, it becomes clear that we do our best job teaching if we prepare them to be lifelong learners. That changes what we do and how we do it. For example, lab exercises are intended to provide students with hands-on experience that helps them to understand scientific principles better. A criticism of labs, though, is that they are merely cookbook exercises that teach students very little and are boring because the outcomes of each exercise are known beforehand. While I do not fully subscribe to that belief, I do think students will be more apt to continue learning about science if we make an effort to engage them in the process of science while they are taking our introductory courses.

One way this can be accomplished is to expose students to discovery-based labs. The basic idea here is to get students to pose a question and then design experiments to answer that question. This is much more difficult than it sounds, but it can be successful if the professor puts in the effort. Students exposed to this type of lab are much more engaged in their own learning and as a consequence are better prepared to continue learning well into the future. The fundamental point here is that we will develop ways to prepare students to be lifelong learners if we design courses that give strong consideration to what the student will be doing after graduation.

As an added bonus, if we try to generate lifelong learners, then there is less pressure on us to "teach it all" during the short period students are in our classes. That premise has allowed me to focus on the essential concepts and to try to teach them well while I look at my students as professional learners. The more I focus on the latter, the more respectful I am of the students, which hopefully leads to a positive attitude on the part of the student.

This article was written with the hope that it might be of some benefit to those who want some tips on what works in the classroom. As stated above, my ideas about teaching have come primarily from my students. They have taught me much with regard to how to design a course. It is my hope that your students will do the same for you.

◆   ◆   ◆

The late Alan J. Jaworski was a much loved and respected teacher, researcher, and friend. At the time of his death, he was Professor and Head of the Department of Botany at The University of Georgia. When he joined the Botany faculty in 1971 as an assistant professor, his very first teaching experience came as an instructor in the large introductory biology courses. Prior to that, he had not taught even a lab section because he was on a research assistantship while in graduate school.

Until recently, most of Professor Jaworski's teaching was in these large introductory biology classes where he taught an average of over a thousand students per year. Dr. Jaworski remarked that he always found it very exciting when he walked into the classroom the first day of class to meet a new group of three hundred students. The responsibility he felt was awesome. For these large classes, Professor Jaworski preferred to give a lecture that was accompanied by preprinted notes that outlined the main points of the lecture. During the lecture, he liked to ask questions that helped students focus on the subject and think about why they should learn the material. In contrast to the large lecture sections, Dr. Jaworski also taught honors biology classes to groups of fifteen or more students. Primarily, these classes were discussion sessions on articles that were read before class. He also taught upper-division courses in developmental biology and graduate courses in plant or fungal physiology. Most of the latter courses were seminar courses taught to groups of ten self-selected and highly motivated students. These smaller classes were much more personal and allowed him to get to know each student in the class. Dr. Jaworski won the Meigs Award in 1993.

When not working, Dr. Jaworski liked to cook, work in the yard, fish, watch college football, play golf, and travel with his family. His most relaxing vacations were those where he spent a week at the beach with books. He liked both fiction and nonfiction.

WHAT MY MENTORS TAUGHT ME ABOUT TEACHING

States M. McCarter

IN 1998, I had the chance to read Tom Clancy's book *Into the Storm*, a nonfiction account of the ground war in Desert Storm. Near the middle of the book, I turned a page and was startled to see a name that I immediately recognized but for the life of me could not remember from when or from where. In the middle of the night, my mind returned to 1959 to a high school in South Carolina, where I was doing student teaching as part of a teacher-training program at Clemson University. Clancy's "hero" was a student in one of my high school classes. How are these events related to my subject? I will get to that.

The high school teacher (hereafter Mr. J.) who served as my supervisor and mentor at the host school was recognized widely as one of the best agriculture teachers in South Carolina. During his long teaching career, Mr. J. had received many honors and accolades related to teaching. Also, he had served as president of his state professional association and was active nationally in vocational education circles. Thus, when Billy (a friend and Clemson classmate) and I were asked to choose a supervisor for our student teaching, selection of Mr. J. was a "no-brainer" on our part. How could we go wrong in this selection?

At our arrival at our host school, however, Billy and I were almost immediately disappointed with Mr. J., our new supervisor and first professional mentor. He was not at all impressive in the classroom. His lectures were not exciting. His lesson plans (our Clemson education professors had repeatedly stressed the importance of complete lesson plans and required us to take a bundle of perfect ones to use at our host school) were sketchy or nonexistent. He was slack in his record-keeping and other paperwork. He even had other weaknesses I will not mention. Mr. J. simply did not fit my image (as developed in the Clemson education department) of an outstanding teacher. Initially, Billy and I often sat up late at night debating why Mr. J. had such a celebrated reputation as a teacher. It took me years to completely understand that.

Now back to Clancy's "hero." Early in our training program, Mr. J. called Billy and me aside, and quietly he "sized up" almost every student in his freshman through senior classes. He specifically pointed out two senior students who, he believed, were destined to accomplish important things in life and asked us to work closely with them. Clancy's "hero" was one of the two. As Billy and I worked with and watched this student, we were only a little more impressed with him than we had been at first with Mr. J. Certainly the student was academically talented, but he seemed to lack focus and was often mischievous. How could this student have as much potential as Mr. J. seemed to think? After all, he was not a serious student like Billy and me. But the student did become a great success!

What we failed to recognize at the time was that Mr. J. had the uncanny ability to recognize potential in his students. It took me some years to develop that ability. However, this ability alone was not the reason that Mr. J. was so successful as a teacher. Our respect for Mr. J. grew significantly as Billy and I observed his willingness to spend the time required to develop whatever potential his students had. Classroom contact was only the beginning of his teaching effort. During breaks and after school, his classroom was often filled with students seeking assistance with, and advice about, various matters. In those days, high school guidance counselors were rare. The days (and often nights) spent at that school were long for Billy and me, but we learned about the time commitment required to be an effective teacher. We learned that Mr. J. was successful as a teacher because so many of his students became successful in a variety of endeavors. Clancy's "hero" was just one of many. To Mr. J., teaching was a mission—not just a profession.

In retrospect, I do not know why I was so slow in recognizing Mr. J.'s strengths as a teacher. After all, the path that I had taken after high school was the direct result of one of my own high-school teachers (hereafter Mr. M.) who recognized potential in me, a potential that I never imagined I had. Mr. M. believed I could, and should, also become a high school teacher. But of course becoming a high school teacher required a college degree, and in the 1950s in the somewhat rural area of South Carolina where I grew up, attending college was not a routine or expected event as it is today. Only the academically talented, academically prepared, financially able, and sometimes culturally privileged were considered to be "college material" in my high school. There were few scholarships and no loan programs available, and there were no regional colleges or universities. Few in my high school even considered attending college as an option. Most male graduates became farmers, factory workers, and the like. Yes, attending college would be a great leap for me both for cultural and financial reasons.

These considerations were in no way deterrents to Mr. M. He set about getting me prepared mentally for college, encouraged me in every way possible, and helped me apply for and obtain significant scholarship help that made college a reality for a farm boy who otherwise had little hope of attending college. Mr. M. did for me what I saw Mr. J. do for Clancy's "hero" and many other students several years later. Like Mr. J., Mr. M. spent the time necessary to develop potential in his students. I eventually became a college graduate because of his commitment. Mr. M. was an effective teacher because many of his students were successful.

In college, I observed in certain professors the same commitment that I had observed first in Mr. M. and later in Mr. J. One of these professors had a significant impact on my career plans. My intention of becoming a high school agriculture teacher was interrupted in my senior year when my path crossed with that of a certain plant pathology professor (hereafter Dr. E.). Dr. E. had spent most of his career in plant pathological research at an off-campus location and only recently had acquired the reputation as an effective classroom teacher of plant pathology courses on campus. Although he had been on campus for a relatively short time, his interest in students and his willingness to work with students outside the classroom environment were known.

I first met Dr. E. when he served in one of these outside roles as faculty adviser to Alpha Zeta, a service and honorary fraternity to which I belonged. During his period of service with the fraternity, Dr. E. was always subtle in his comments about his profession, but it was obvious that he took pride in being a plant pathologist and sometimes shared his enthusiasm with others. As my admiration for Dr. E. grew, so, too, did my interest in plant pathology, a field, up to that time, in which I had never taken a course. Dr. E. never "recruited" me or anyone else for plant pathology, but he often encouraged students with excellent academic records to consider graduate training. To me, a graduate program in plant pathology seemed to be the obvious choice when the time came. Once my decision was made, Dr. E. arranged for me to receive a National Defense Education Act (NDEA) fellowship, the very best financial aid possible. Another mentor had set my path for life.

As I have looked back over the years in preparing this essay, I have been overwhelmed with thoughts of the devotion and time dedication of a few teachers and mentors, including the three who were singled out. But on a negative note, I am even more amazed (and perhaps discouraged) about how few of these there were. My gratitude for the few and my concern as to why there were so few became perhaps the motivating forces that led me to write this essay. Why was only Mr. J.'s room full of inquiring students? What were the other teachers doing with their spare time? Although I ranked number one academically in my senior class, why did only two teachers (Mr. M. and one other) of some twenty that I had in high school suggest to me that I should consider college upon graduation? Did they not want to spend the time necessary to help me overcome my financial obstacles? Was it because no member of my family had ever attended college (I was number ten in a family of ten)? Did they not really care about me as a student or person? In college, why was Dr. E. the only professor who encouraged me to continue in graduate school and arranged for the financial support to make it happen? Why were so few professors willing to serve students outside the classroom?

In my zeal to stress the importance of teacher involvement with students outside the classroom, I have not intended to belittle in any way the importance of excellent classroom instruction. Having good lesson plans, presenting stimulating lectures, and the like are known indicators of effective teaching. But these were not the things that made me remember certain mentors for forty years or more.

I am thankful that during my some twenty-eight years of teaching at the university, I was fortunate enough to teach mostly small classes that allowed one-on-one interaction with students. Even with relatively large classes, I always attempted to create small group activities, i.e., small laboratory sections that facilitated my getting to know students. My mentors taught me the importance of this. Working with students and student groups outside the classroom was always high on my list of priorities. Although I fully understand that pressures and time constraints at modern universities discourage the kinds of activities that I have described, I hope that more than a few faculty members will espouse the philosophy of my mentors, which I now share. Technology will offer new tools for instructional purposes, but it will not replace the person who shows a genuine interest in a student.

◆　　◆　　◆

States M. McCarter is Emeritus Professor, Department of Plant Pathology, College of Agricultural and Environmental Sciences at The University of Georgia. A native South Carolinian, he holds the BS degree in Vocational Agricultural Education and the MS and Ph.D. degrees in Plant Pathology from Clemson University. From 1968 to 1996, he taught undergraduate, mixed undergraduate/graduate, and graduate courses including Elementary Plant Pathology, Etiology of Plant Diseases, Bacterial Plant Pathogens, and Disease Diagnosis and Control. These courses were small to medium in size and were taught in a lecture/laboratory format that allowed considerable interaction with students, particularly in the laboratory. He also led graduate seminars and served as the department's undergraduate adviser. He won the Meigs Award in 1993.

Prior to coming to UGA, Dr. McCarter held research positions at the U.S. Army Biological Laboratories, Fort Detrick, Maryland, and at the Coastal Plain Experiment Station at Tifton. He also held an extension position at Auburn University. His hobbies include gardening and reading, and the McCarters operate a Christmas tree farm in South Carolina. Dr. McCarter and his wife, Jane, have two children, Beth and Steve, both UGA graduates, and two grandchildren. All of the McCarter family currently reside in Georgia.

Teaching "Outside the Box"

Dan T. Coenen

When we think about teaching, we tend to focus on our work with students in pursuing academic subjects in academic settings. We think about classroom teaching. We think about making assignments, giving feedback, and coming up with grades. We may think about communicating with students via computer or in question and answer sessions in our offices or after class. All of these components of teaching are vitally important. Through our subject-centered work with students, we deepen their knowledge, hone their analytical and communication skills, and perhaps even stir in them a lasting love of learning. Most teachers understand the value of these goals. But many of us—precisely because we think of teaching in terms of academic subjects and academic settings—may not see that there is another and a more subtle dimension to our work.

This element of teaching involves making positive connections with students as individual human beings. It calls on us to reach out as whole persons to students as whole persons, finding ways to attend to their needs, hopes, and fears. This aspect of teaching entails dealing with students' vulnerabilities by becoming more vulnerable ourselves. It envisions efforts to create an environment in which students can flourish because teachers help to give them a sense of belonging and worth.

Much good work along these lines takes place in the context of teaching courses. But there is an enhanced opportunity—often missed, I suspect, by even the most well-intentioned teachers—to foster meaningful connections with students in informal settings and unstructured ways. This work involves teaching "outside the box" in the sense that it requires a rethinking of what teaching means. It also involves teaching "outside the box" because it moves our work beyond the physical spaces we normally think of as venues of instruction onto ground that we, as teachers, do not dominate or control. We may not think of this sort of teaching as being teaching at all. Yet if some of our most meaningful interaction with students can and does occur outside classrooms and offices, does not some of our most meaningful work as teachers necessarily occur there too?

Student-sponsored events offer one important setting away from institutional spaces in which to build strong personal bridges to students. Year after year, I find that students deeply value the attendance of faculty members at functions like student-organized speeches or colloquia, end-of-the-year banquets of student organizations, intramural sports games, and on-campus social activities. Students notice who attends these functions, and they appreciate the signal that they are valued enough that their teachers will drop by. These events also offer opportunities to make small, but meaningful, connections: to chat with a student about a recent job-search setback, to share thoughts with a small group about course selection or summer work, or to serve as a sounding board for student frustrations and complaints. In these encounters, I often look to share a tale or two about some of my most memorably *bad* classroom teaching, the latest litany of complaints my children have lodged against me, or the story of some lapse or challenge during my own time in school. When we reach out to students in these ways, we convey our humanity and touch their humanity too. Students welcome these encounters and often find in them—as do I—sources of learning and encouragement.

Working with student organizations provides another way to forge special student-teacher bonds. In the law school, we have a nationally prominent moot court program that engages the efforts of twenty to thirty upper-class students each year. The success of this program is attributable in large measure to connections made between faculty and students that are unrelated to in-class work. Students consult informally with faculty members about their cases. Teachers meet with students, often in the evening, to make critiques of their practice arguments. And teachers follow the results of competitions, ready to offer words of support for winners and losers alike. Through collaborations of this kind, there is created a community that is built around a spirit of shared effort and common mission. And because this community is essentially a student community—with faculty participation in it a purely voluntary choice—students seem to greet the counsel that teachers offer with an added measure of receptiveness and appreciation.

Last year, I experimented with a new way to meet students on neutral ground, holding periodic brown bag lunch sessions for my seventy-member first-year Contracts class in a meeting room set apart from the law school's teaching areas. These sessions were informal and optional. Attendance varied greatly: sometimes fewer than a half-dozen students would show, sometimes more than fifty. The key idea was that this time belonged to students. It was their questions that would be discussed, their comments that would be welcomed, their gripes that would be aired. Sometimes we discussed schoolwork. More often the conversation turned to law practice, job searching, stress management, and the like. I hope my students picked up some useful tips along the way. But the real objective was to give them a chance to blow off steam, to provide an ear for listening, and to help induce reflection about how law study fit into the broader purposes of their lives.

The home provides another venue for spanning the distance that separates teacher and student. Several times each year, I invite groups of students to my house, and every time I am reminded of what great company they are. My goal in hosting these get-togethers is to provide a welcoming and relaxed setting in which simple human connections can be made. Students meet my family, they pet my dogs, they shoot baskets in my driveway. Sometimes at these gatherings we talk about school-related matters—about admissions or placement or casebooks or about what to change in my classroom teaching. Sometimes, these occasions allow me to look into how individual students are coping with the stresses of school. Sometimes we just relax, chat, and laugh. Whatever the direction of the conversation, however, these sessions seem to reduce, if only in a small way, the sense of alienation that can surface in the academic environment and the sense of antagonism students sometimes attach to the student-teacher relationship. I find in particular that, following these gatherings, students become more willing to ask questions after class or to stop by my office. By heightening my approachability "outside the box," I seem to create a greater possibility for dialogue and learning "inside the box" as well.

Another site for teaching in this broader sense is in the hallways and common areas of the school. In these locations we make dozens of potentially positive connections with students every day. Merely greeting a student by name sends a message of shared purpose and personal affirmation. Chance encounters create valuable opportunities to note a student's recent accomplishment or to provide a word of encouragement or praise. It is easy to underestimate the importance of these moments, but that temptation should be resisted. Seven or eight years ago, for example, I sensed in a passing student a feeling of discouragement. I stopped the student and took her aside. I told her that I had been impressed by her recent recitation in class, that I thought she had a real aptitude for law, and that I believed that someday she would make an outstanding lawyer. She was obviously appreciative, but the real lesson came years later when she wrote me a long letter. The letter explained how that moment had made a significant difference in her life, how it had kept her going in the face of much self-doubt, and how she would always remember my words of support.

It will, of course, be a rare encounter that produces a reaction of this magnitude. But small measures of encouragement, especially in the aggregate, matter greatly too. As we push students to meet their full potential, we must be attentive to making them feel good about that process and good about themselves. A few well-timed words can make all the difference in enkindling or renewing a student's delight in learning.

Teaching "outside the box" does not mean "partying" with students. It certainly does not mean gossiping with them or listening to personal attacks directed at other students or at faculty colleagues.

(Such conversations, for me, are strictly off-limits.) Teaching "outside the box" does not mean becoming "one of the gang" or "letting it all hang out" or abandoning a proper sense of formality and reserve. In reading the letters written by former students in support of my Meigs Award nomination, I was struck by the emphasis on this point. These students appreciated personal interest, but they also valued professional distance. They viewed it as a sign of respect and a necessary pre-condition for having a productive teacher-student relationship. Maintaining a professional distance also involves teaching by example—a form of teaching that is distinctively powerful and that (whether we like it or not) we engage in continuously both inside and "outside the box."

As I plead the case of more neutral-ground encounters with students, I confess that, far too often, I do not practice what I preach. (In particular, it seems harder as I get older to link up with students in this way. Is it because of the ever-increasing competing job demands that come with more senior status? Is it because an expanding age gap breaks down natural affinities? Is it because my weakening knees have finally left me unable to keep up with my students on the basketball court?) A serious commitment to "outside-the-box" teaching also raises inevitable questions of judgment and discretion. I have, for example, occasionally taught seminars in my home. Would it be worthwhile to teach in a student's home? Would it be fitting? One of my colleagues says that some of his most successful teaching experiences have come in pubs and cafés. Would it be productive to hold serious class sessions with a small number of students in these or other off-campus settings?

Of course, teaching "outside the box" is not a one-size-fits-all matter. This aspect of teaching, like more traditional aspects of teaching, must, to be genuine, reflect the practitioner's own personality and style. The critical point, however, is that, whatever that style, there is a special opportunity for genuineness—precisely because we share more of our whole selves—when we interact with students outside institutional spaces. If I am right on this point, then teaching in such ways and places holds the potential for greatly enriching our students' learning. There can be no doubt, after all, that the chance to reach, to teach, and to inspire our students is in large measure a function of the intangible connections we forge with them. I also suspect that, especially in the longer run, sharing more of ourselves with our students is vitally important to us. If a basic goal of our work is to find meaning in it, how can building deeper and stronger human connections not be a source of fulfillment and renewal? And if we aspire to stronger human connections, is it not self-evident that we should reach out to those with whom we seek to connect in ways and in places marked by openness, informality, and warmth?

◆   ◆   ◆

Dan T. Coenen has taught in the law school at The University of Georgia for thirteen years in the areas of constitutional law and contracts. Coenen's style of teaching is built around use of the so-called "Socratic method," which involves posing a sequence of questions to students who are called on at random. Questioning of this kind requires the student who is called on—and all students as they participate vicariously—to prepare carefully, to construct the sorts of arguments lawyers routinely make, to engage independently in problem-solving, and to explore thoughtfully the proper limits of governing legal principles.

Professor Coenen grew up in Appleton, Wisconsin, and received his bachelor's degree from the University of Wisconsin. He attended law school at Cornell University, where he was editor-in-chief of the *Cornell Law Review*. After clerking for Judge Clement F. Haynsworth of the United States Court of Appeals, in Greenville, South Carolina, and Justice Harry A. Blackmun of the United States Supreme Court, Coenen practiced law for six years in Charlotte, North Carolina. He won the Meigs Award in 1998.

At the center of Professor Coenen's life is his family. He and his wife, Sally, have three children: Michael, seventeen, Amy, fifteen, and Claire, twelve. Coenen reports that an ever-increasing amount of his time is spent attending cross-country meets, plays, soccer games, and music recitals. Coenen coaches his children's basketball teams every winter and has become involved in a number of civic and community activities. According to Coenen: "I sometimes jog, occasionally go backpacking, and play a variety of sports quite badly. Mostly, I try hard just to spend more time with my family and the many dear friends we have made since moving to Athens."

Teachers as Role Models

Judith C. Reiff

Teaching is learning and learning is teaching.
Teaching is making connections to self.
Teaching is making connections to our students.
Teaching is making connections to future generations.

As MY MOTHER frequently told family and friends, "From the time Judy was two years old, she was playing school and teaching anyone who would 'listen' to her." In fact, my career goal never wavered throughout elementary, secondary, or college schooling. And, over the last twenty-five years, I have been fortunate to have been able to pursue my career dreams as a preschool teacher, elementary classroom teacher, reading specialist, and college teacher.

Many individuals and life experiences have contributed to my own philosophy, beliefs, and actions: a father who modeled discipline and unconditional love; a mother who models patience, graciousness, and diplomacy; teachers who modeled enthusiasm for knowledge and an excitement about their students; teachers who modeled apathy and sarcasm; a husband who shows a passion for living, travel, and lifelong learning and who demonstrates through example the importance of valuing all cultures and peoples; colleagues who model encouragement, professionalism, and friendship; and three children for whom I was a model and from whom I also learned.

I am likewise fortunate to have had many mentors at The University of Georgia. One of my first mentors emphasized to me that students are the primary reason we are in this profession and never should we lose sight of their importance and our purpose for teaching. He modeled the qualities of being a dedicated teacher and compassionate person through his actions within the classroom and beyond. Other mentors have shown me that we need to stimulate and motivate students to go beyond the surface of instruction and to become lifelong learners. These UGA mentors expect their students to succeed and do their best while encouraging self-evaluation; they expect a level of student discomfort to occur but in a nonthreatening environment. They also allow creative expression and opportunities to learn through multiple paths.

I am thankful that I work in an atmosphere of scholarly teacher-researchers who model an excitement and commitment to excellence in both research and teaching. Respect for colleagues and respect for students in the classroom are conducive to a positive work and learning atmosphere. Being selected a UGA Senior Teaching Fellow provided me with the opportunity to interact with faculty across campus who are scholarly teachers. The conversations and interactions with these colleagues stimulated me to reflect on the reasons I initially chose education as a profession and afforded me the opportunity for renewal.

A professional organization is another source for rejuvenation and rededication by being associated with colleagues who model enthusiasm and personal commitment to teaching. While I was a graduate assistant, my adviser involved me in the Association for Childhood Education International, an organization that emphasizes the importance of teaching and serving the needs of diverse children. For the past twenty years I have actively participated in annual conferences and have also served as national vice president. When I return from a conference, my renewal to teaching is evident as colleagues have told me they can tell a difference in my attitude and interactions.

What I have learned from students is that they want to be challenged, but they also want their teachers to be fair, supportive, and accessible. Students appreciate teachers who model the importance of reflecting on one's own life and how to implement the changes that this reflection inevitably brings. In other words, students want their teachers to exhibit a human personal quality along with being the expert in the field. They also like their teachers to be interested in them after graduation and are grateful when previous instructors continue to help them as alumni.

One goal I have had is to encourage my students to envision a better society and how to accomplish that dream. Consequently, I believe teachers need to model the importance of college students becoming politically literate individuals. We want learners who are capable of critically analyzing social issues while envisioning a better society and becoming advocates for positive change. We want to empower our students with the confidence, knowledge, and enthusiasm to be lifelong learners and involved citizens.

I strongly advocate a multicultural perspective in planning classroom activities, managing instruction, and assessing teaching. Teachers of children and adults must accommodate the diversity of individuals and relate instruction and assessment to students' needs and differences. By varying my teaching approaches and by giving students choices for certain assignments, I attempt to accommodate different styles of learning and provide an environment for more equitable learning. As social theorists maintain, students and teachers learn from one another when they are engaged in discussion, problem-solving, case studies, or other meaningful activities. I believe college teachers should model being flexible, organized, enthusiastic, and knowledgeable for effective learning to occur. Even when we are teaching college students, culturally responsible instruction and assessment will promote learner sensitivity by recognizing student style differences. With effort and creativity, the college classroom can be a model not only for what to teach but also for how to teach diverse students.

One important outcome for me from the Senior Teaching Fellows experience was the receiving of information and motivation from faculty in business and law about using case-based instruction. Since then I have taught entire education courses based on cases that require students to discuss issues and make decisions. Case-based instruction promotes flexibility, cooperation, and the analysis of situations and problems through various perspectives. By recognizing that each group of students represents a variety of learning styles, personalities, cultural backgrounds, interests, and abilities, we can make the content more applicable and personal. Case-based instruction bridges theory and application in a diverse classroom. Students are teachers, and teachers are learners. Students learn a great deal from one another, and instructors learn from their students. Students respond to their being involved in the learning process and by being valued.

The integration of research and teaching with application is fundamental to my philosophy and practices. An understanding of brain development and research has implications for any classroom. An understanding of the complexity of the brain and its relationship to our individuality provides a framework for my approach to teaching, and specifically, in the course I developed on teaching and learning styles. Brain theory is the umbrella for the multiple perspectives of how we learn and teach, and the explosion in brain research challenges all educators to consider the complexity and potential of every individual. Unfortunately, much of the discussion and application related to brain theory is frequently overgeneralized, trivialized, and misunderstood.

For instance, a student turned in a project entitled "Enlightening of an Educator: A Challenge to Change," which described her initial reluctance to consider brain theory and individual learning differences. However, she wrote in her conclusion about her renewed excitement for teaching. She believed that with the knowledge and ideas gained from brain theory she would better facilitate learning and accommodate the needs of her children. I believe the following terms[15] capture what I intend to accomplish and model through my instruction.

Orchestrated immersion is to take the information off the printed page and blackboard and bring it to life in the minds of the students (Caine & Caine, 1994). The students are totally involved in learning the content through a variety of experiences to accommodate diverse learners. Too often, teachers superficially cover content rather than teaching for deep or meaningful understanding of the material. More meaningful learning occurs when teachers plan or "orchestrate" different ways for students to become involved or "immersed" in the content. For instance, when I teach brain theory, in addition to teaching via the lecture/discussion format, I also have students create a visual representation of how they construct meaning. They also describe or illustrate what brain-based education means to a classroom teacher. Each description or illustration is displayed and discussed throughout the term in relation to the concepts and key definitions. I plan and "orchestrate" activities for students to be "immersed" in the curriculum.

Active processing is to learn and internalize information in a personally meaningful and organized way (Caine and Caine, 1994). It involves the emotions and is meaningful or deep learning rather than surface learning. By having choices for their assignments, students are experiencing active processing because they can relate or connect their assignments with their own worlds. The brain is continually searching for common patterns and can make better connections when meaningful learning is occurring. Individuals need time to reflect and to make new connections in learning. The use of metaphors and analogies is an excellent strategy for personalizing and creating meaning.

Relaxed alertness is feeling comfortable and safe in an environment to maximize learning (Caine and Caine, 1994). The use of humor and personal stories promotes this type of atmosphere. When students have choices, opportunities to interact with one another, and freedom to disagree, then relaxed alertness is promoted. Quick-writes (two-minute reactions) over material read or after a lecture are nonthreatening and stimulate thinking. Think-pair-share is another strategy to encourage relaxed alertness. First the student has time to think about an issue or question; then the student shares thoughts with a peer before discussing them with the entire class. Brain theory emphasizes that for meaningful learning to occur, students need to avoid downshifting or blocking out the situation.

The best compliment teacher educators can receive from students is that we model not only what to teach but how to teach. We need to be able to practice what we preach and live the ideals we purport. A teacher committed to excellence will model high standards and expectations for self and for others but will also exhibit flexibility while valuing learning differences.

A poignant comment by a student summarizes this essay the best: "The ability to model is a critical attribute of an excellent teacher."

◆　◆　◆

Judith C. Reiff is an early childhood education professor and department head in the Department of Elementary Education, School of Teacher Education, College of Education at The University of Georgia. She has worked with a number of doctoral students and taught undergraduate and graduate courses in early childhood education curriculum, trends and issues, problems and challenges, organization, and management. Learning and Teaching Styles in the Elementary Classroom and Research in Multicultural Teacher Education are graduate courses that she developed and taught. For twenty years, Dr. Reiff supervised practicum students and student teachers in surrounding schools. Consistent with her beliefs about teaching and learning, she uses a variety of instructional strategies to meet the needs of diverse learners. She primarily teaches classes of fifteen to thirty students. Dr. Reiff won the Meigs Award in 1998.

Her husband, Richard, is Executive Director of International Education at The University of Georgia. They enjoy traveling, reading, cooking, and watching old movies. Their son, Cam, graduated from The University of Georgia in telecommunications. One of their twin daughters, Becky, graduated from Earlham College in Richmond, Indiana, with a Biology degree. She is currently a teaching assistant in Science Education at Indiana University in Bloomington. Her sister, Kayla D'Anne, lives in Roanoke, Virginia, and is pursuing a teaching degree in English.

GREAT MYTHS OF SUCCESSFUL TEACHING

Carmen Chaves Tesser

There is an inevitable divergence,
attributable to the imperfections of
the human mind, between the world
as it is and the world as men perceive it.

James William Fulbright, 1964

IN THE ACADEMIC culture of a research university, myths that explain the professoriate portray the successful teacher as a hero, as an autocrat, as a half-wit who does not know the rules of the culture, or as a genetically marked individual who is prewired for the profession. These are a few of the stories that we have created and helped nurture as we go about our business of "teaching, serving, and inquiring into the nature of things," as our university motto tells us. These stories provide for us a comfortable existence in that dubious space "between the world as it is and the world as men perceive it." My purpose here is to review and analyze six specific myths that have been constructed to identify successful teaching: (1) "Teaching is easy." (2) "Great teachers are born, not trained." (3) "Successful teachers are always thoroughly prepared for class." (4) "Great teachers are able to reach every student." (5) "Successful teachers are confident and self-assured." (6) "Teaching and research are not compatible: faculty cannot do both equally well and have to decide which track to pursue."

Every year, we hear variations of these stories being repeated among our graduate students, young colleagues in the beginning of their careers, and senior faculty. As these stories are handed down from generation to generation, they gain credibility and strength through the many examples that accompany them. Faculty aren't the only ones with strong opinions on teaching. Professors have been stung by criticism from outside commissions in reports and books that challenge us to readdress teaching priorities. The following, which relates directly to my own field of research and teaching, is just one example.

About twenty years ago, a federal commission was formed to study the issue of foreign language teaching and international studies in higher education in the United States. The "Perkins Commission" or "the President's Commission," as those of us in this field have come to know it, finished its task with some fascinating and frightening conclusions. Among them, the one most often paraphrased among us—professors of languages and literatures other than English—is that Americans' knowledge of foreign languages and cultures is abominable. We must take immediate and strong steps to rectify this situation by teaching our youth . . .

Although this particular conclusion and its recommendation was the one that got national attention—and even landed a spot on the evening news with Walter Cronkite emphasizing the word *abominable*—the recommendation that caught my attention was buried among the pages of the report. This was that every teacher should have a course in drama, specifically in the techniques of performance. The proponents of this recommendation explained that teaching was akin to a well-rehearsed and well-coached performance. The main difference between "acting" onstage and "acting" in front of a class, according to the report, is that the successful teacher must be a student of his or her field.

As I studied the commission's recommendations back in 1979, I became aware of the fact that most of us in the academy chose this profession because of our love for "inquiring into the nature of things."

We love the discovery process that is usually associated with being a student. In many respects, what came "easily" to us was in fact our research task in the professoriate, not teaching. Ironically, research is the part of our graduate education and professional lives that has received much attention and mentoring by our professors and our senior colleagues. In contrast, the teaching part of our task—the delivery of what we find in our research—did not come easily to many of us and until very recently was not considered to be part of our professional development. If the other authors in this book are like I am, they received virtually no formal teacher training to prepare them for classroom instruction. In my particular case, I was given—on the first day of classes—a copy of the textbook from which I was to teach.

Most of us who "profess" for a living came into the academy because we were the nerds in our schools. In my field, we were the ones who preferred reading and thinking—both solitary endeavors—to the social interactions associated with youth. Yet, as we began our work as graduate students or as young faculty, we were faced with that which we shunned most of our lives—performing in front of a group; persuading a group of less enthusiastic people that what we *know* to be exciting is worth their time.

Having presented this bit of historical trivia as well as my own existential crisis at the beginning of my career, let me return to the six great myths of the successful teaching previously listed.

1. *Teaching is easy.* I am sure that we have all heard the cynical adage: "Those who can, do; those who can't, teach," implying that if we were *able* to do anything else we would not be in the classroom. After more than thirty years in academe, I find teaching, especially successful teaching, to be one of the most difficult tasks around. I also find teaching to be one of the most enjoyable tasks during my working day—particularly after a successful class experience.

In the early 1980s, I was involved in a national project designed to foster the development of good foreign language teaching from kindergarten through graduate school. The project director, Claire Gaudiani (now president of Connecticut College), described teaching as "spontaneity carefully planned." The phrase describes how teaching may appear easy when, in fact, it is a daunting task.

As a shy and introverted person, at the beginning of my career I had to learn how to "act," and in so doing I began to discover ways of delivering my subject matter to my students. Today, when I counsel graduate students and young colleagues, I tell them that teaching builds from the knowledge base of our subject matter and to be able to teach successfully takes time, practice, and patience.

2. *Great teachers are born, not trained.* I believe this is partially true. Teachers seem to have been born with a hunger for understanding the world around them, with a passion for seeking answers, and with a desire to explain new concepts to others. I'm not convinced that we can teach students to want to learn—whether they are undergraduates or future colleagues—but we can show the committed student how to deliver his or her message in a way that will be convincing. Yet, outstanding teachers tend to be strong communicators, a learned skill, and they excel at motivating and inspiring others. Much of this comes from a teacher's personal commitment and effort to improve his/her teaching tools, skills that are acquired through practice and experience. So I would say that great teachers are born, but they also can and do learn to teach.

3. *Successful teachers are always thoroughly prepared for class.* This is the myth that most of us, and I include myself here, would probably accept. If we think about our most successful experiences in teaching, I am sure that we will remember the preparation for those classes. But sometimes our best teaching moments happen spontaneously, without preparation, such as when a student makes an insightful comment or asks a question that opens a window for important learning. Great teachers recognize these moments and seize them. And who among us hasn't found themselves periodically less prepared than desired, trapped by a shortage of time for the appropriate class preparation? We aren't perfect and we all occasionally experience "failures"—a class that did not "click" or students who did not learn the material. In my own career, when my teaching has been a disappointment, I have tried to learn from these failures. And as tempted as I have been to blame the failures on "student apathy," "a ball-game weekend," or "the weather," upon further reflection, I can usually point to my own insufficient

planning. To rephrase Claire Gaudiani's statement, spontaneity hardly works without careful planning. As we mentor our students and young colleagues toward successful teaching, we must admit our own failures—even if they are failures at preparing for class. In so doing, we accept that they, too, will also experience some failures that can be used as lessons for the future.

4. *Great teachers are able to reach every student.* This is a statement that appears in many teaching portfolios of successful teachers. However, most of us know that we cannot reach every student. Indeed, we reach fewer students than we wish to admit. Some rewards come from seeing "the lightbulb go on" when a student suddenly understands what we are explaining. Other rewards may not come for several years until one of our students from the past contacts us with a success story. But reaching everyone is not likely to happen regardless of one's teaching ability. Perhaps a truer conclusion is that great teachers "get through" to a higher percentage of their students than do teachers in general; moreover, great teachers tend to change lives in positive ways.

In 1906, Santiago Ramón y Cajal, a Spanish physician, won the Nobel Prize for his description of the human nervous system. Always a dedicated teacher, Ramón y Cajal in accepting the prize described the joy of teaching as that of a flower gardener who plants the seeds, cultivates the garden, and waits patiently until the spring to see the results of months of hard work. I would add that not every seed produces an orchid even when given loving attention.

Successful teachers accept these realities and move on; they do not dwell excessively on their failures. I also believe that in the academy students gravitate toward those professors to whom they are able to relate. Similarly, my impression is that one way effective teachers improve their success rates is to recognize, find, and recruit successful students.

5. *Successful teachers are confident and self-assured.* This is a story often told by old-timers, maybe even by some of the authors in this book. I accept that experience, time, and patience have led professors to appear self-assured, but most of the successful teachers I know still have doubts about their teaching effectiveness. Whenever

teachers gather to discuss issues of success and failure in the class-room, invariably the horror stories and nightmares of self-doubts are aired.

For most of my career, I have had several versions of a basic dream. In one version, I'm standing in front of a class completely engrossed in my own teaching and I don't realize that the room is empty. In another version, I am dreaming about "this dream" and try to determine whether I have any students before starting the class. As I look at the room full of eager eyes, I discover that I forgot to get dressed that morning and find myself standing in front of the class wearing nothing but very clean white socks. On other occasions, I dream that I finish what I consider to be a fine lecture only to find that I'm in the wrong classroom—these are not my students. In yet another version of this nightmare, my students stare at me expressionlessly. Upon a close inspection, I notice that they are wax figures who respond only to high temperatures, but who certainly do not respond to my attempts at teaching. Finally, in another variation of the dream I find myself looking at blank sheets of paper rather than the meticulously typed class notes that *I knew I had prepared.*

All versions of my dream have in common a classroom; they also point to obvious feelings of insecurity and inadequacy. Although I am understandably relieved when I awake from such a dream, I am also quite aware of the insecurities that I feel despite the successes that I have experienced. "Goose bumps" are normal, common, and healthy. They make us teachers work harder and get better prepared. Still, part of the performance that we must perfect is the part that gives forth the appearance of confidence and self-assuredness. It is hard to lead and teach students who see our self-doubts.

6. *Teaching and research are not compatible: faculty cannot do both equally well and have to decide which track to pursue.* Here is another myth that has been the bane of the professoriate for years. Great commissions of important and successful people have studied this particular story over the generations. From time to time, we read a new report about the relationship between these two sides of our professional lives, one of which is the newest Boyer report

on undergraduate teaching in research universities. In my own experience and view, I cannot separate these two sides of the profession.
We are not engaged in a zero-sum game. Faculty can and must do
both simultaneously. Research enhances teaching and teaching stimulates research. I almost wish that we could coin a new term—"tre-
search" or maybe "reaching"—to describe what we do.

As I described in the beginning of this essay, many of us came
into the academy because of our love for research—for discovering
new knowledge or for linking former ideas to create new ones. We
chose the academy because it is the one job in the marketplace that
allows us to continue to be students; it is the one culture that allows
our eccentricities and often rewards us for them. But a key benefit
that research provides is passion, a passion for our fields, at times
seen as outlandish by those outside of academe, which gives us
energy, makes our classes come alive, and helps us pass on the excitement of learning to our students. But the benefits are two-direc-
tional. Faculty members likewise benefit. On more than one
occasion, a simple question by an undergraduate has led me to investigate a new topic, framed a new research idea, piqued my intellectual curiosity, and let me experience being a student myself.

I believe that we need to model this kind of cross-pollination for
graduate students and young faculty colleagues. It is very fashionable
in my field to talk about the "seamless curriculum" that integrates
language skills, literature, and culture in the teaching and learning of
languages other than English. We should make it part of the conversation to speak of the "seamless academic," the one who combines
teaching, research, and service in carrying out daily activities.

Conclusion

In conclusion, what can we learn from this assessment of some of the
great teaching myths? The importance seems to lie not in the battle
over truth versus fiction but rather in what these myths can teach us
to help us become better teachers. Reflective thinking on teaching
myths can help us interpret the unexplainable and understand the

uncomfortable. Myths are stories that can guide us in daily tasks, facilitate our ability to control situations that may well be out of our jurisdiction, and help us satisfy our desire to determine our destiny. They can also give us a better understanding of our professions' traditions and customs. Ultimately, our goals should be to improve our teaching and help our students fully develop their capacities to learn. A most important responsibility for a university professor is the mentoring of the next generation of teachers. To this end, what we believe, what we state, how much enthusiasm we say it with, and what we practice as professional teachers and researchers will likely have a major influence on their academic priorities. Therefore, it behooves each of us to clarify our objectives. Soul searching by examining teaching myths is a positive step toward these worthy goals.

◆   ◆   ◆

Carmen Chaves Tesser is Professor of Romance Languages in the Department of Romance Languages, Franklin College of Arts and Sciences. She has taught Portuguese and Spanish language/literature/culture courses from the most elementary to doctoral-level seminars. During the last four years she has been a member of the national task force that wrote *Standards for Learning Spanish and Portuguese (K–16+) in the 21st Century*. True to the project's objectives, she believes in active participation by her students in the learning/teaching process whether she is in a small-seminar setting or in an Introduction to Spanish Literature class of seventy-five undergraduates who are still having trouble with Spanish language skills. Before joining the faculty at UGA, she taught Spanish and Portuguese at Mississippi State University and at the University of Pittsburgh. She won the Meigs Award in 1992. She is married to Abraham Tesser. She has two daughters, a stepdaughter, a stepson, and four grandchildren.

FREE SPEECH IN THE CLASSROOM

Calvin M. Logue

IN THE UNITED STATES, as we begin the twenty-first century, too often street and school rage has replaced civil discourse. In the political arena, podium frenzy routinely substitutes for reasonable explanations of stands on vital issues. On religious circuits, ethical tenets can deteriorate to self-indulgence. When demagogic acts monopolize participation and decisions, the body politic and individual well-being suffer.

In contrast, enlightened communicative initiatives by citizens of diverse voices can contribute substantially to the uplifting of the human condition. While poised ignorance and corrupt promises are protected by the Constitution, a free exchange of judicious experience and instructive judgment can expose those rhetorical excesses. Requisite to an informed dialogue beneficial to people and institutions is the understanding, appreciation, and mastering of the liberal art of public speaking. In a nation and world still experimenting with democratic procedures, I can think of no higher calling than to teach free, disciplined, and effective public speaking—the practical art—as I have strived to do for more than three decades.

I have instructed undergraduates how to isolate and define a socially significant issue, research that problem systematically in a variety of authoritative sources, meld their own good judgment with reliable findings published by credible authors, draw inferences of their own, organize and style a coherent and original message, and present a defensible argument for their cause competently to a live audience, including students, instructor, and outside guests. After speakers have taken a turn at the podium, they then are asked to sit, listen, and question overtly the oral cases communicated by classmates. These are rhetorical understandings, skills, choices, and practices requisite to personal success and to democratic decision-making that are difficult to master. In short, applying Emerson's vision of the American Scholar as "Man Thinking," I have sought to help students become Thinking and Responsible Citizens Speaking.

With permission of students, authentic typed manuscripts of well over three hundred of their final original persuasive speeches on socially significant issues, given in class, have been deposited in the special manuscripts collection of The University of Georgia Library. Seventy-seven of those texts, ranging from Carolyn Tippett's "Help a Friend Who is Dependent on Drugs" to Brett BenDavid Berns's "Anti-Semitism: The Hatred Continues," were published in *Student Speeches in Georgia: Last Score of the Twentieth Century*, sponsored by the Honors Alumni Association of The University of Georgia.

While teaching and improving public speaking are worthy endeavors, I know of no more challenging tasks—a peculiar blend of pain and pleasure indigenous to all instruction. In evaluating my teaching of the fundamentals of public speaking at the end of one term, an undergraduate wrote anonymously: "I wondered if Logue realized I was scared sh——less!" Indeed, some students change their majors rather than take a required public speaking course. A number postpone the class until their last term in college. Others register for public speaking and drop it before the first oral assignment. A few remain but miss those days when assigned to speak. For those who stay the course, and I who teach it, there is no place to hide.

In instructing undergraduates in the appreciation, understanding, and practice of public speaking required for involvement and survival in a highly competitive free-market economy and in a rough-and-tumble democratic state, I have tried to be sensitive to their fears. Because a few are so frightened, they are allowed to give their first speech from their desks, rather than risk the podium. Others initially sit at a table in front of the class. One recorded his speech on audiotape in private for me to evaluate later. Eventually, most of those students choose to present their final speech in the course at the podium.

Although they are at times bothersome to me personally, I have also been tolerant of diverse views expressed by students concerning numerous controversial issues. How indulgent an instructor and society should be has come under increasing scrutiny with the dawning of the age of political correctness and speech police. This issue is of concern to all teachers of all subjects. On campus, in the classroom, and among regents, alumni, legislators, and parents, many ask, "What topics will be allowed? By whom? With what results?" One professor decreed that no speeches on religion could be given by students in his public speaking course. This pedagogical edict denied religion a voice on such significant issues as cloning, drug addiction, redwood groves, crime, self-righteous politics, atomic bombs, rock music, family, personal values, and the decline in membership of mainline churches. Is society better off when one segment of thought is forbidden? Is the classroom?

My own policy, however, is about as extreme as the professor's decision that disallowed speeches on religion. In teaching public speaking annually from 1962 until 1999 (and continuing), I authorize students to choose their own topics and goals. During this long period of instruction, I have not censored a single student's choice of subject. I do have a few guidelines. For example, to protect students captive in the classroom from serious accidents, I no longer allow real guns as visual aids. But I welcome speeches for and against gun control.

In an era often linked to incivility in public discourse, can one still justify freedom of expression in the classroom? What if a student walks to the podium and maligns African-Americans, women, or the elderly? Does a pedagogical axiom of free expression allow such abusive attacks? First, if one is searching for a comfortable profession, look beyond the classroom. A university is no longer a sheltered retreat. What we do there is under constant scrutiny. People residing there are busy and expectant about the known and unknown, often uncertain about their investigations and findings. Teaching is not for the timid. I recommend that, along with extra chalk and light-bulb for the overhead projector, one carry to class a bottle of Pepto-Bismol. Over the years, listening to more than twenty thousand speeches, and censoring none, I have thrown up on occasions afterward, both to my left and right. For example, for an assignment in which I required each student to persuade the class "to do something," one member, employing the basic canons of research, language, delivery, organization, and argumentation that I taught, sought to actuate fellow undergraduates to become arsonists—to burn their old cars, clothes, and furniture for insured profit. So much for my efforts throughout the term to indirectly instill values of civic responsibility.

My challenge, then, has been to find a way of holding fast to my own standards of responsible citizenship—the ideal that Quintilian envisioned in his course in rhetoric, as the "good person speaking well"—while allowing students the constitutional range to defend their convictions in class. This pedagogical dilemma has been quite challenging, as I have come increasingly to believe, through my own teaching and research on communication by black and white Southerners during slavery, Civil War, Reconstruction, and the twentieth century, that extremism in any direction can be detrimental to communal health. In teaching, then, my personal preference would be to stoke the moderate and calm the extremist. While this bias probably leaks into my syllabus and classroom instruction, it hardly tempered the student who advocated burning possessions for profit. Because I have permitted students to defend their own judgments, I have evaluated speeches delivered on every imaginable theme from every possible direction, by conservatives and liberals—by Ralph Reed, former head of the Christian Coalition, and Robbie Owen, active in blocking capital punishment in Texas for a time—both formerly enrolled in my public speaking course. As faculty adviser for the Demosthenian Literary Society for seven years of Thursday evening debates, I was also fortunate to hear and critique the persuasion of Ralph, Robbie, and their contemporaries beyond the traditional classroom setting.

Some would contend that it is morally and educationally inde-
fensible to allow persons, under the protection of a course assignment or a free speech postulate, the option of abusing women,
African-Americans, the elderly, and others. With every fiber of fairness that is within me, I, too, oppose such rhetorical vile. In the final
analysis, in part, maybe I have been fortunate. Because, in teaching
some four thousand undergraduates public speaking, I recall no one
defaming an individual or group directly. Certainly I have heard
many talks where the language, assumptions, and inferences were
embarrassing or ignorant. In one speech, for example, a student
based her solution to overpopulation on the premise that men over
forty were incapable of having sexual intercourse. Even then I
resisted the temptation to interrupt and terminate her folly in its
tracks. I have also heard arguments seemingly based on racist or
sexist perspectives. In my judgment, however, these unenlightened
and abusive premises can be confronted and unpacked by the
instructor and other students during commentary after speeches are
given. Indeed, this is a proper function of a liberal arts education,
to seek values that uplift the human condition.

But what would (should) the teacher do if, under the guise of an
assignment in a course syllabus or under the First Amendment, an
undergraduate walked to the podium and began portraying African-
Americans in the derogatory idiom deployed by Gene Talmadge and
J. B. Stoner in gubernatorial campaigns in Georgia in the twentieth
century? Should each student be required to submit a proposed public speaking topic and purpose in writing for approval by the teacher
prior to each speech? I can vividly recall sitting through the entire
speech in which the student in my class advocated arson as a means
of gainful employment. Although his goal was illegal, I did not interrupt and stop that talk—although I squirmed a lot. During that speech,
and a number of others heard over the years, I envisioned a headline
in the *Atlanta Constitution* reading: "Professor Supports Arson for
Students for Profit." And some claim that tenure is unimportant! After
listening to that speech promoting arson, as is customary, insofar as
time allowed, I led the class in a critique of the speaker's research,
content, organization, language, strategies, delivery, adaptation to

audience, and the *appropriateness* of his topic—one of the oldest canons of oral rhetoric.

As a teacher, finally responsible for what takes place in "my" classroom, what would I do if a student began a blatantly destructive diatribe against African-Americans, women, the elderly, or others? Having not faced this situation, I am not certain. Would (should) I interrupt and terminate the speech? If I do, what then? Or would (should) I hang on, as I did with the promoter of arson, until the speaker finished and then "lecture" and discuss the importance of informed and responsible civic discourse? I admit that I would be strongly moved to interrupt such a speech, a painful prospect pedagogically for me. Under this interrupt-and-end approach, my instructional policy would change from one of free expression to: "You are free to speak on any topic of your choosing as long as you do not insult another human being." If one adopts this means of moral censorship, where does the limit on student speakers in classrooms end? For example, many in my classes are highly repulsed when exposed to persuasive speeches on one side of the abortion issue or the other. Under this interrupt-and-end policy, one could even rationalize not allowing speeches in class on religion.

Certainly, in one sense, I have been fortunate. Will an instructor teaching public speaking or other courses the first three decades of the twenty-first century risk giving students freedom to select topics and purposes? Will the First Amendment apply to the classroom? Or, if trends of rhetorical incivility continue, will flagrant racist and sexist discourse be too rampant not to regulate pedagogically? I like to think, however, that my experience of not having heard direct, abusive persuasion by students in class has not all been due to luck—that my disposition in teaching public speaking has discouraged students from abusing others. I agree with Richard Weaver that language is "sermonic." What speakers say and how we say it do have consequences and can help or harm others. Routinely, in lectures, discussions, and critiques of speeches, when explaining principles of research, content, argumentation, organization, language, appeals, audience adaptation, delivery, and appropriateness of subject, I have tried to promote a better understanding and appreciation of diverse ideas, cultures, and constructive dialogue in democracy, both for advocates and consumers. I have attempted to assist individuals, whether they be ideologically moderate, liberal, or conservative, in becoming not only better but also more responsible communicators.

But how can the teacher orchestrate tolerance in the classroom, not necessarily for a particular point of view, but for the right to express and hear diverse opinions? Equally important, how can one encourage initiatives by individuals that contribute to the well-being of others rather than denigrate them? Teachers should attempt to re-create the classroom as a sanctuary of inquiry. We should foster the art of enlightened exploration. This laboratory for imaginative inquiry should fit individuals with an assortment of new lenses through which to observe social issues. Every term I hear myself saying to students: "I don't give a damn if you are a Bleeding Liberal or a Bloodless Conservative, but I do care greatly that you be an informed advocate." Students must acquire reliable means of observing ideas, events, and people. Too often persons approach social problems like the physician who glances at the rash on a patient's arm and calls surgery to schedule the removal of a left arm! Students must be taught that one's understanding of the causes of a problem often determines what one recommends should be done to solve that problem. Learners are taught to exhume information skillfully, examine those materials judiciously, measure them systematically, and collate them inquisitively with previously found remnants. First, then, we have a moral and pedagogical responsibility to require students to study what knowledgeable and reliable authorities have uncovered about socially significant issues; otherwise, we merely pool our ignorance. Students must be taught, for example, how to distinguish between reliable and unreliable information located in faceless sources on the computer Internet.

With these insights and practical experiences investigating social issues, students find that even experts disagree, for example, on whether genetic engineering is best for individuals and society or whether criminals should be locked away from society or rehabilitated. By becoming familiar with the most dependable information and views available on a particular subject, individuals in the class are licensed to join the continuing debate and to assert their own informed and responsible judgments. In a classroom environment where individuals are actively searching, purposeful inquiry becomes contagious. Mastering known laws, theories, hypotheses, hunches, and interpretations, students step toward the unknown. As pedagogical referee, the instructor can lead the class in a discussion of the consequences and implications of rhetorical choices, for example, of advocating that audiences burn their property for profit.

With this investigative attitude and practice established, the instructor can then explain and apply the principles and practices indigenous to one's field, in my case, the ethics of communication; reliable means of research and note-taking; use of language that is clear, accurate, vivid, and appropriate; organization that is coherent and purposeful; reasoning that is valid; audience adaptation that is responsible; and delivery that is clear, interesting, effective, and accountable.

Through a continuing process of shared inquiry, evaluation, and encouragement, instructor and student strive to grow in knowledge, discernment, and appreciation of the worth of the individual, cultures, ideas, values, and opportunities for personal and societal advancement. As with any art form, in seeking these bold ends, results are inevitably mixed. More times than not, however, I have been gratified to watch as students confront challenging issues in class responsibly and leave the university to participate productively in small and large communities as consultants, lawyers, politicians, doctors, civil servants, clerics, business representatives, executives, sellers, parents, advocates, and teachers. Any part that I might have played in preparing them to contribute publicly and constructively in society has been worth the periodic episodes of stomach unrest. This is the rocky path I have chosen and one on which I shall continue.

◆   ◆   ◆

In 1967, Calvin M. Logue came to The University of Georgia as an assistant professor of Speech Communication. As a professor in that department in the Franklin College of Arts and Sciences, he taught public speaking, rhetorical criticism, and communication strategies in social movements to undergraduates and rhetorical criticism and the history and criticism of American public address to master's and Ph.D. students until he retired on June 1, 2000. Enrollment in Dr. Logue's undergraduate classes ranged from twelve to fifteen in a freshman seminar to forty-five in courses for persons majoring in communication. While he preferred the give-and-take of relatively small classes, Dr. Logue also taught a large section in which he oriented first-year undergraduates to rhetorical and interpersonal communication studies. Before coming to The University of Georgia, he served three years in the United States Marine Corps as a private and sergeant in artillery and taught at Birmingham-Southern College, Louisiana State University (as a graduate assistant), and the University of Arkansas. More personally, he enjoys wood carving, vegetable gardening, family, and teaching Sunday School. He won the Meigs Award in 1995.

Understanding Our Role as Teachers: One Professor's Journey

Peter J. Shedd

In a song that Rod Stewart made popular during 1998, he sang, "I wish that I knew what I know now—when I was younger!" That phrase captures well my feelings as I begin this essay on my journey as a teacher at The University of Georgia. Actually, the beginning occurs even earlier, when I was a student at this university during fall quarter, 1971. I distinctly remember the combination of excitement, anticipation, and intimidation that I felt just walking the campus and wondering what wise scholar occupied a particular office or laboratory. Little did I know then that I would be given the special opportunity of joining the faculty in 1978 and be blessed with the journey that has been the past twenty-three years!

My first opportunity to enter a classroom as an instructor actually came during my third year of law school. In 1976, I was selected as a teaching assistant in the Legal Studies Program in the Terry College of Business and was assigned a discussion section of an introductory Legal Environment of Business course. I clearly remember my first class. I was so nervous that I could not pass out the syllabi. My hands were shaking to such an extent that I had to place the stack on the podium and pick up one syllabus at a time. Fortunately, in subsequent classes, it has never taken me so long to pass out the syllabi. Once I started to speak about the subject matter covered in this introductory course, I felt much more comfortable. Within minutes, I was quite relaxed and even recall thinking that I was a natural at this sophisticated level of communication known as teaching. I thought that I was gifted regarding this task. After I explained that this course would cover topics such as constitutional law, governmental regulations, contracts, property, and *torts* (which is the area of law involving the noncriminal, noncontractual breach of a duty), a student on the front row raised her hand. While I hesitated to interrupt my eloquence, I did call on this student. Her question—"Mr. Shedd, what is a *tart?*"

That question so popped the dream bubble that I was a great communicator that the feeling of excellence and self-confidence I momentarily had that first class has never returned (despite the many courses I have taught). From that early moment, I realized that as a lecturer, I could not be certain that my students were understanding (or even caring about) what I was saying. The communication was so one-tracked—from professor to students—that the feedback—from students to professor—was lacking.

Despite the lesson I learned from this very first class, my initial focus as a teacher was on not embarrassing myself in front of my students. Like other new assistant professors, I spent hours preparing those initial lectures. And the real reason for my efforts was to make sure that I had enough material to fill the allotted class time. One point that my senior colleagues impressed upon me was that letting students out early is viewed as a sign of insufficient rigor. So, my primary mission in getting ready for each class was to make certain that I had more points to cover than I could possibly get to during a given class. The fallback position that I occasionally relied upon then (but never recently) was to go over the end-of-chapter review questions.

Sometime during my third or fourth year of teaching, I began to change as a teacher. I gained a sense that perhaps I had something worth sharing with my students. That is, I began to feel that my perspectives on life were sufficiently refined to be worthy of class time. Although I developed some interesting examples from my life's experiences to share with my students, I now realize that my focus was on me and not on their learning.

Around my seventh or eighth year of teaching, it occurred to me that students had experiences and perspectives that were worth sharing with one another. My teaching shifted to a third phase during which I concentrated on encouraging in-class discussion. I always had asked questions and expected a student (hopefully the one I called upon) to respond correctly. But now I was recognizing that students could and should contribute to the situations that needed to be analyzed for the application of legal principles.

With my focus on students as active learners, my transformation as a teacher was on its way. Can you recall a time and situation that had a profound impact on your life? It is interesting to ponder why some times and situations produce this influence while others do not. I suspect that the key to a life-influencing experience is less in the deliverer of the message than it is in the receiver of the message being open to what is being said or to what is happening. Such an experience occurred in my life during 1992. I had the privilege during that year to chair our university's Instructional Advisory Committee. This committee, which is made up of some of the finest people any campus could hope to have as faculty, had just completed its monthly meeting.

Although I'm quite sure that we had a good meeting involving some important issues of instruction, I cannot now access any memory of this specific meeting. However, immediately after the committee members departed, I was speaking with Dr. Ron Simpson, the director of the Office of Instructional Development. During the course of this conversation, Ron told me, "The decade of the nineties would see the professor moving from the 'Sage on the stage' to the 'Guide on the side!'" I confess that as Ron spoke these words, I did not comprehend what he meant. While the words immediately became emblazoned on my mind, it would be quite some time before I understood how wise they were. I have talked to Ron about this conversation, and he admits that he doesn't specifically remember it. While the quoted phrases above may not have been original with Ron, it was his expression of them that I have never forgotten. From this I have concluded that as faculty we need to be ever mindful of what we say because the listener might be profoundly impacted even if we don't intend to cause this impact at that moment. Equally important, from this conversation, I began a journey of reinventing (or reengineering) what I do as a teacher.

The year I chaired the Instructional Advisory Committee, my fifteenth year on the faculty, was a period when I spent a good deal of time pondering if I could keep doing what I had been doing for another fifteen years—assuming a thirty-year career. Much of what I thought about did not please me, for my enthusiasm for teaching the same topics again and again (even given the variations produced by updating material) was dwindling. This personal struggle might explain why I was open to being struck by Ron's statement about the changing role of the teacher.

Fortunately for me (and I hope the university), the Terry College of Business supported my desire to retool. I focused much of my study and energy on teaching Negotiation and Conflict Resolution. As I began to teach these subjects during the spring of 1995, I started to understand how my role as a lecturer (provider of knowledge) changed to a facilitator of learning. In the typical negotiation class that I teach, students are interactive with one another through actual negotiation scenarios. As they return to class, there is an energy and desire to share experiences that I have never seen in my other courses. During a debriefing discussion of a negotiation, I realize that I do not have the answer: the correct response is within each student's individual experience. The self-reflective nature of these courses causes me to reevaluate and better comprehend that my value to the students is to make the classroom experience as thought-provoking as possible. In essence, my role is to create a good question, not simply to provide answers.

During the same period that I was developing and teaching this new series of courses on Negotiation and Conflict Resolution, I had the very good fortune to be a university representative in a four-year (1994–97) national project focusing on teaching. Our university was one of twelve asked to select six faculty to participate in the American Association of Higher Education's Peer Review of Teaching Effectiveness. Relatively quickly, all those involved began to realize that we really were studying ways to have faculty colleagues actively engaged in a collaborative effort to improve our personal efforts in teaching. While my designated peer, Jere Morehead, and I experimented with numerous ways to understand each other's teaching, the most valuable tool was interviewing each other's students. The experience of visiting with a group of students (during an hour-long conversation) and discovering what they believe is good teaching and how to improve the learning environment was extremely stimulating. Through these interviews, I came to appreciate that students can and should play a significant role in creating and evaluating the learning aspects of any course. Students are not just the receptacles of knowledge delivered by the faculty member; students and faculty are coparticipants in the learning experience.

A final occurrence that has most recently refined my thinking about my role as a teacher was an assignment I was given to teach a master's-level course via the Internet. I did not ask for, and did not welcome, this responsibility. I have come to believe (and this has been confirmed through many student interviews) that an essential element in the creation of a productive learning environment is a personal connection between the faculty member and the students. To teach a course via the Internet seemed to deny the opportunity to create this connection. Fortunately, this "distance" course does involve some face-to-face class time during which these connections can be established. What I learned from this course is that my primary function as a teacher is to create *learning opportunities* for students to work together in teams to discover and learn. Through this experience, I have established a more complete comprehension of the phrase "Guide on the side." I am now experimenting with incorporating these learning opportunities in traditional courses.

One example might help to illustrate my point. In the past, during class time on the litigation process, I shared (mostly through lectures) my experiences that document the complexity of litigation. To emphasize this point, I now ask my students to work in pairs as they "strike a jury" based on materials that I have created for a fictional case and jury panel. The feedback I receive from this and similar exercises indicates that learning is occurring that has an impact on the students. They have more to remember than my words from a lecture. (Let me quickly add here that learning opportunities are not limited to one type of exercise. An effective learning opportunity certainly can involve some lecture. Truthfully, learning opportunities are limited only by the lack of creativity of the teacher and students working together.)

To this point in my journey as a teacher, I realize that my job should not simply be to fill the class time with some knowledge-delivery function that focuses on my telling my students what I know. Rather, I should focus on encouraging my students' active participation in the creation of a learning environment that involves learning opportunities for both my students and me.

To paraphrase Rod Stewart's quote at the beginning of this essay, "I wish that I knew now what I will know when I am older." Then again, maybe not! The anticipation of another opportunity to learn is what makes our individual and collective journey of life so fulfilling. All of us, as students (whether young or old), should keep this focus close to our hearts and minds.

◆   ◆   ◆

Peter J. Shedd is Professor of Legal Studies in the Terry College of Business and Associate Vice President for Instruction at The University of Georgia. His home department goes by the lengthy name of Insurance, Legal Studies, and Real Estate. During his twenty-three years at The University of Georgia, Peter has taught a variety of undergraduate and master's-level courses. These courses typically range from 40 to 120 students per section. The style of teaching, as discussed in the essay above, has varied over the years and over the different class sizes and course levels. In addition to his teaching, Peter has served The University of Georgia in several administrative capacities, including Associate Dean of the College of Business, Executive Assistant to the University President, and currently as Associate Vice President for Instruction. Peter is the author of numerous scholarly articles as well as the coauthor of a leading *Legal and Regulatory Environment of Business* textbook. Peter and his wife, Margie, have three children, all of whom hopefully are developing a love for the spirit of lifelong learning. He received the Meigs Award in 1993.

STATEMENT ON TEACHING

Hubert H. McAlexander

DESPITE THE ELECTRONIC revolution and the resulting media explosion, I feel that there is still room for the sort of experience that good teaching offers the student. Despite the appeal of multimedia encounters and the lure of the information highway, many students still respond to (and, in fact, long for) the experience of direct contact with a text and with another mind.

When material of value is presented by a mind thoroughly engaged with that material, students rise to the lure. Teaching offers such a constant challenge because we have to remain responsive to what we teach. That is probably more difficult with remedial work than anything else. In that case, I have tried to teach grammar as a sort of mathematical construct, emphasizing the value of learning the body of information and applying it to writing. This is the most difficult of tasks. One has somehow to impart excitement to something that, most feel, lacks it intrinsically.

The teaching of writing, of course, goes on at every level. It begins with our aspiring for precision in the discourse of the classroom, and our encouraging that aspiration in our students. Ideally, then, our verbal struggles in class have an effect upon the written attempts outside. As we begin to teach more advanced students, increasingly we should function as editors, catching errors and confusions, and suggesting improvements—and grading according to quality.

The everyday life of the classroom, however, consumes most of our time. And it is in that intellectual give and take that most teaching takes place. The intrinsic intellectual value of the material covered should be our first concern and, after that, the level of our own engagement with that material. For our excitement must breed their excitement, and we can maintain the intensity only if we find compelling the process by which they learn. If we can remain interested in that process, then we can learn from them, for as they discover a work or a writer, the widening of vision often reveals things we have never seen. Thus the process of learning and teaching becomes truly symbiotic, and teaching has its reward in the process itself.

◆ ◆ ◆

Hubert H. McAlexander, winner of the Meigs Award in 1997, is a professor in the English Department who came to The University of Georgia in 1974. Four times named Outstanding Honors Professor, he has twice held a General Sandy Beaver Teaching Professorship (1983–85 and 1991–94). He is the author of *The Prodigal Daughter: A Biography of Sherwood Bonner* (1981) and editor of *Conversations with Peter Taylor* (1987) and *Critical Essays on Peter Taylor* (1993).

On Becoming a Contructivist Mathematics Teacher

Larry L. Hatfield

My journey as a mathematics teacher has spanned the past four decades. It began when I was an undergraduate teaching assistant in astronomy labs at the University of Minnesota. It has included several years as a high school mathematics teacher. In more than thirty years as a mathematics teacher educator at UGA, it has included teaching mathematics in grades K–16 with students ages six to sixty!

Through my teaching, I've experienced many of my most significant professional moments. In this brief essay, I'll try to share the details of certain particular events related to my teaching and address some of the meanings of those experiences. In doing so, I'm trying to portray the transformations in my teaching and in my personal theories upon which I base my teaching.

Moments of Love and Lust

While an undergraduate at the University of Minnesota, I chose to be a school mathematics teacher, because of my love for mathematics. In my early years as a teacher, I was totally dedicated to showing my school mathematics students the power and magic of mathematics. I wanted all of them to understand and appreciate what I had found in mathematics. For example, when I taught geometry, I exerted great energy and enthusiasm for the beautiful proofs and constructions of classical Euclidean geometry. I even experimented with inductive approaches—using a "lab" or measurement approach to discovering all of the theorems about circles, angles, arcs, and chords. I knew that I was effective at explaining and modeling, and, despite my lust, most of my students appeared to be successful. Lust? Indeed, for I focused my efforts on getting my students to know and appreciate the mathematics—but just as I knew its beauty, excitement, fulfillment. I treated mathematics as a finished display, like a classic Greek marble sculpture, rather than contexts for challenging experiences to be creative, generative, involved. I wanted their understanding to be like my understanding.

Early in my career, I encountered two significant events that would affect deeply my perspectives as a mathematics teacher. In my first year of teaching, I participated in a special evening course for seventy-five Twin Cities–area mathematics teachers at Control Data Corporation. We learned to construct FORTRAN programs for simple mathematical procedures—a laborious, error-prone process. Yet, as a novice I caught a glimmer of the potential of the context for promoting something very powerful in mathematics—"teaching the computer to perform a procedure that was *your* design!" When I joined the mathematics faculty at University High School the next year, our mathematics teachers learned of a brand-new computer language called BASIC, and we began using it to stimulate our students to build, test, "debug," and refine or extend their own computer algorithms for most topics of the curriculum. This became a major theme of my research and development activities, which has continued here in my role as a mathematics teacher educator. The infusion of computing tools into school mathematics teaching and learning is now a major goal and pedagogical emphasis in all of our courses—and it continues to be a major problem area of our field.

In that same early period, I participated in the curriculum reform efforts known as "the new math." While this reform is often criticized today, it was a shift toward teaching mathematics for understanding, and it emphasized deep conceptual analyses of fundamental mathematical constructs. Clarity of meaning was to result from being precise in our concepts and language (e.g., the distinction between "number" and "numeral," or the use of unifying ideas such as sets or structural properties). These notions had an impact on my own conceptual understandings of mathematics, and as I taught with these emphases, I experienced the joy of being able to illuminate with greater clarity and precision the details of my subject while also revealing the overarching theory. Further, I was impacted by much greater attention to student activity in the learning process, more "hands on," guided discovery. These were fundamental shifts in the way I was thinking of the psychology of learning and teaching, and these impacts still serve as a major emphasis in my work as a teacher-educator. In helping teachers to become more effective in their teaching, I strive that they will reflect deeply upon the meanings of basic mathematical concepts and then ponder what kinds of problematic situations can be posed to students to stimulate and support their development of such meanings and understandings.

Moments of Inspiration and Excitement

In 1968, I joined the newly created Department of Mathematics Education at The University of Georgia. It was truly an exciting period of growth in our embryonic field, when serious research and scholarship to address fundamental questions of mathematics learning and teaching were established.

The role of the computer, and then the handheld calculator, in school mathematics became even more important questions. First, distributed processing via time-sharing terminals and then the introduction of the microcomputer for classroom-based work fueled the potentials, and my teaching was impacted and changed with each technological hardware and software innovation. While the emphasis upon teaching structure in the "new math" was replaced by curricular designs based on neo-behaviorist hierarchies of performance objectives, in my teaching I continued with a central interest in mathematical problem-solving, discovery, and reasoning processes.

In my teaching of teachers, I enacted these ideas by treating my explorations of computing in terms of the design of mathematical procedures as problematic situations—computer programs were operational embodiments of the student's reasoning about an algorithmic problem. With such programs, students and teachers could then go on to explore and investigate with speed and accuracy well beyond what could happen normally. I found that students and teachers found great excitement in "teaching the computer," and in many cases it inspired the kinds of mathematical questions and inquiries that were not easily provoked with traditional "chalk and talk" teaching.

The results were exciting—such as the time a group of seventh graders came running down the hall, trailing their computer printouts and excitedly announcing that they "had found it." With my help, they had designed a simple program to test any number for primeness, and this had led to getting the computer to help them find "Where do the primes live?" A program was developed to print arrays (sieves) showing asterisks for primes, blanks for composites (and 1). What they had discovered was that, except for 2 and 3, every prime number can be found "in front of, or behind" a multiple of 6. Despite my graduate study of number theory, I did not know this! We went on to find a simple proof of this theorem and eventually to generalize the ideas to sieves of other orders.

When guiding my students to construct a computer program, I found a new context for questioning their thinking and for focusing upon mental processes. With teachers, this became a way of challenging them to be more directly involved with their own students' mathematical thinking. However, I was not fully aware of the more fundamental shifts occurring within my epistemology, and of the impacts upon my pedagogical views.

Moments of Epistemological Shift

Through a collaborative National Science Foundation (NSF)–supported research project in the late seventies, I became involved in investigating the early mathematical development of children. In a

Soviet-style teaching experiment conducted across two years at Whitehead Road Elementary School, I worked with second graders wherein the basic question was explored: Can children invent their own methods for computation? Arising from my views that older students could, indeed, construct their own algorithms (within the computer programming context), I was certain that if we teachers encouraged and supported beginners, they too would generate methods that were based upon their own meanings. Traditionally, elementary teachers model the textbook (adult) procedure for each whole number operation, and typically children struggle to make sense of the "mysteries" of, for example, borrowing to subtract or the complex maneuvers of long division. We know of widespread failures to achieve acceptable learning of arithmetic. My premise was that children would find ways that embodied what made sense to them.

My struggle was to redefine my role as a teacher. How in the world could I provoke and support such invention? Without reporting the rich details of my experiences, I found that these young children *did* invent their own methods, and that there are clear pedagogical approaches that teachers can take to encourage such thinking. Essentially, one needs to help establish fundamental conceptual meanings (e.g., meaning of the operation of division) and action schemes for modeling the task (e.g., using counting strategies on representations with the task). More important, as a teacher one needs to de-center—get out of the way, step aside, and allow the learner the opportunity to engage the challenge, per se. Wait, watch, listen—intervene to help focus, or to clarify, or to provoke analysis, or to reflect.

In this project work, my colleagues included Ernst von Glasersfeld and Les Steffe, and I encountered their early development of radical constructivism. What I came to realize is that by artistic intuition, I had been striving to become a more constructive mathematics teacher. I shifted in my conception of mathematics as a wonderful body of knowledge "out there," finished, real, to a view of mathematics as a human construction that must be made by each individual person. I realized that by exhibiting and modeling "finished" mathematics, I was essentially "robbing" my students of opportunities to make mathematics.

Moments of Dilemma and Frustration

Adoption of a constructivist epistemology brings with it new dilemmas in teaching. If each student's knowledge is idiosyncratic, then how can there be a science to teaching? Are there any generalizations about teaching that can guide what I do? How can I ever plan for a teaching episode if the fundamental need is for me to attend to the personal construction of each student? Indeed, how can I even begin to manage a classroom where everyone is building his or her own knowledge uniquely? How can I, on the one hand, be responsible and accountable for learning but also accept that I can never be so? How can I cover the required content, when a more constructive approach will surely be slower and take longer? Given their prior experiences in learning mathematics, how can I get my students to accept and shift to the personal responsibility implied by constructivism?

What about explaining, or telling—is there no place for this? If the goal is to activate the mental schemes of the child, how can I be sure what I'm doing even "fits"? If Vygotsky's "zone of proximal development" applies, how do I determine this and then teach in ways that reflect lots of different zones among my students? Is there no social dynamic for building up mathematics, or must it be an isolated independent matter? What, then, is the fundamental nature of the teaching-learning relationship? The premises of constructivism can appear to be an impossibility within classroom teaching of mathematics.

Moments of Pedagogical Growth

As a teacher educator, I work with both pre-service and in-service teachers of school mathematics. Teachers in grades K–12 bring their own backgrounds of experience in mathematics and its teaching. Predictably, these experiences seem to be largely traditional—almost never have they had any challenge or opportunity to approach a mathematical situation as their own construction, per se. When I seek to have them experience such constructive approaches, they sometimes resist or rebel. "Why are you expecting us to do this? Just tell us clearly what we have to know for the test, and I'll show you I can do it! Beside, kids can never do mathematics on their own—the teacher must show and tell so they can learn to imitate correctly." Expectations—of oneself and of one's students—can be a major determinant for shaping how one chooses to learn or chooses to teach others. Confronting one's expectations is a major challenge if we are to transform the nature of school mathematical experience.

At the root of this confrontation for me are fundamental questions: Why do we teach school mathematics? (It is the only subject that now spans all grades, preK–12.) What should be the nature of students' experiences? For most of the teachers who study with me, their answers often involve goals of preparing their students for post–highschool education or work. To them, students need to learn basic arithmetic, algebra, and geometry, with perhaps a bit of statistics, probability, and trigonometry in order that they can do well on the SAT or can do basic mathematics on job entry tests. Some teachers express ideas about "getting them to think" or learning to solve applied problems. Almost never do they see mathematical experiences as intrinsic to the formative development of intellective thinking, per se. The notions of Piaget, the eminent theorist of developmental psychology who characterized the development of thought in terms of mathematical structures and processes, don't appear for most classroom teachers as a basis for the goals of mathematical education.

Finding Balances in Mathematics Teaching

Mathematics is among the most dreaded (and sometimes hated) school subjects. Many adults respond with notable negative energy, expressing their fear and dislike for their memories of their own school mathematics experiences. By contrast, mathematics has a widespread reputation as an important subject that can have great value in determining educational and career opportunities and choices. The emotional dimensions of mathematical experiences appear to be significant factors in how people feel about mathematics, and as such, may well be overwhelming determinants of how mathematics students approach their learning of the subject.

In my journey as a mathematics teacher, I've seen myself explore, question, and alter how, why, and even what I teach. Today, I'm deeply convinced that the quality of the experiences of our mathematics students is the fundamental issue and dilemma. Social, economic, and political forces increasingly pressure mathematics teachers to cover more and achieve higher standardized test scores. Despite evidence arising from international comparisons of mathematics achievement and practice, we seem unwilling to acknowledge that "less is more." In Japan and many other countries, mathematics teachers often take much longer to help students develop new ideas; U.S. curricula cover many more topics in less time with more focus on extensive practice at the expense of conceptual understanding—a curriculum that has been said to be "a mile wide, an inch thick." For most mathematics teachers (and myself as a teacher-educator), the struggle to change is a matter of finding balances among conflicting perspectives and demands while the nature of doing mathematics is undergoing radical changes due to the ubiquity of powerful computer tools. In the twenty-first century we will surely see major transformations of school mathematics, its goals, contents, and teaching. I'm eager for my personal journey to continue!

◆　　◆　　◆

Larry L. Hatfield (1990 Meigs Award) is Professor and Head, Department of Mathematics Education, College of Education, The University of Georgia. He was raised in the 1940s and 1950s on a Minnesota family farm, and jokingly says that he is "from Lake Wobegon"! He attended a one-room rural schoolhouse through grade seven and strongly believes that his conceptions of teaching were greatly influenced by the one teacher who effectively taught all (typically fewer than a dozen) of the children in grades one through seven. He has taught mathematics and mathematics education at all levels and in many places, including the University of Minnesota, the International Schools of The Hague, Teachers College-Columbia University, Western Australian Institute of Technology, and East Tennessee State University. While serving for two years as Program Director and Deputy Division Director, National Science Foundation, he says that his major challenge was to teach government bureaucrats about quality mathematical education.

As revealed in his essay, Dr. Hatfield's philosophy and epistemology are those of a transforming constructivist. In his role as a teacher-educator, he seeks to help teachers confront their own beliefs about the nature of mathematics, how they see themselves as mathematicians and mathematics teachers, and their preconceptions of their students' thinking. He promotes a problematic approach using powerful computer tools—emphasizing that within the processes of investigating and searching for solutions to nonroutine problems, students will have profound opportunities to understand concepts, discover generalizations, and reflectively appreciate themselves as thinking humans. His theory of mathematics teaching is that artistry as a teacher must be constructed by the individual, and that every great teacher is reflectively searching and re-searching his/her own practices. A primary goal of great teaching is to connect, deeply, with the thinking of the students—and this is also the primary dilemma of teaching.

WHAT I WISH SOMEONE HAD TOLD ME: ADVICE TO NEW TEACHERS

Sharon J. Price

BECOMING A TEACHER was my childhood dream, and memories associated with my walking into "my" first classroom in a public high school in northern Illinois are still vivid. There were feelings of excitement, anxiety, and fright, as well as recognition of the awesome responsibilities associated with being a *teacher*.

As an undergraduate, I took courses lauded to be the ones that prepared you to teach. For example, in Methodologies of Teaching the emphasis was on how to cut stencils (this was before copying machines), work a movie projector, design bulletin boards, and prepare a "teaching plan." These experiences may have provided some marginal preparation for teaching but did not ensure an in-depth understanding of being a teacher.

So there I was: a high school teacher facing a classroom of bouncy adolescents, a graduate teaching assistant and instructor confronting vast numbers of undergraduates, and later a faculty member responsible for numerous undergraduate and graduate classes. Upon reflection, I fervently wish someone had provided advice and counsel to me before these experiences. Therefore, in this contribution,

I will attempt to provide ten points that I believe are important. I base this advice on four decades of teaching but also realize this list is not exhaustive. Hopefully, it will foster your thoughts as you move ahead in your career.

Excellent Teaching Is Hard Work

Good teaching is about content, substance, and students as consumers. It takes endless hours of reading, reflection, and rumination about the far edges, and everything in between, in your field of scholarly endeavor. Good teaching involves devoting endless hours to grading papers, designing and redesigning courses, preparing materials related to the objectives of each course, and, of course, talking with students. It requires one to move beyond the cubicle called your office and the borders of your campus in order to seek out knowledge in your field. Good teaching reflects a lifelong commitment to learning.

I estimate that the first time I teach a course I spend approximately eight hours outside the classroom for every hour in the classroom. Of course, as one gains experience and builds on the body of knowledge, this time may be modified. Still, any reduction is minimal; the knowledge base is expanding much too fast.

Listen to Your Students

Learning is a transactional process: students learn from faculty, and faculty learn from students. It is not pontificating from on high to empty vessels. Many students have knowledge and experience that contribute to the focus in the classroom. One needs to be able to maximize the use of this rich diversity of knowledge and experience since it will provide value and added dimensions to the learning environment.

Good teaching involves listening, questioning, and responding to students. It is the capacity to engage reticent students in discussions and foster an atmosphere of trust and respect where students feel free to ask questions and state opinions. It is using techniques and presentation styles that provoke discussion and dialogue. To paraphrase an adage, "Listen unto others as you expect them to listen to you."

Be Flexible

Don't be concerned if you get off the schedule you have established for a course or a class. Syllabi and class plans are nothing more than guides. They are not Linus-type security blankets, even though some teachers carry them around as if they are. The world is not going to end, nor will you fail in the eyes of your colleagues, if you don't cover all that you had planned.

There are many ways for students to be exposed to class material. The best classes often are those when the students and teacher lose all track of time and the original outline of the syllabus. In many ways, these are periods when learning is at its optimum. Nurture your ability to experiment, don't be so anxiety-ridden that spontaneity is minimized, and develop response patterns that are adaptive to ever-changing circumstances. An intellectual free-for-all is invigorating for participants, and you will know this when, at the end of a class, you feel good, even though you have deviated far from your intended plan.

Keep Your Sense of Humor and Self-Perspective

Faculty often are able to accept the fact that students are human; accepting themselves as such is, unfortunately, more difficult. Humor is an endearing quality of being human, even to the extent of finding it in our own behavior. We all need to have the capacity to laugh at ourselves and with others. We also need to see the humor in our subjects of study. The subjects for review in classrooms are, of course, serious intellectual excursions; however, these journeys need not be monastic. Having humor as an integral part of each class you teach will contribute to a more relaxed and enjoyable learning atmosphere. Successful teachers, however, are not stand-up comics or clowns. Rather, they are committed professionals with a deep, abiding, and engaging sense of humor.

The Atmosphere for Learning Is the Teacher's Responsibility

Good teachers assume responsibility for ensuring the physical integrity of their respective classrooms and recognize these aspects make a difference. Often the discussion is not putting students to sleep—it's the temperature! It is not that students are visually impaired—it is the lighting! It is not that the discussion is interfering with learning—it's the ringing of cellular phones and the beeping of pagers!

Good teachers ensure that the learning atmosphere is optimized by effective classroom management that minimizes unnecessary disruptions, establishes comfortable levels of lighting and heat, and provides good seating. Take time to make sure that needed equipment is in the classroom and working (including bulbs in projectors). Check the temperature of the room. Define the policy for receiving and making calls on cellular phones and the use of pagers. The dividends are worth it!

Evaluating Students Is Difficult and Sometimes Boring

I believe evaluating students is very difficult. This may stem from my doubts regarding the various methodologies used for this process, or it may come from my nagging sense of a lack of confidence to consistently do this in a fair and equitable way. These doubts are especially present late at night and/or under the pressure to have grades submitted by the designated deadline.

I believe the majority of the faculty (and all good teachers) recognize that grades definitely impact the lives of students and want students to succeed. Giving a poor grade is not fun, and most good teachers have questions about their own competencies when a student performs at a low level. The perennial question is: What could I have done to help this student perform better?

Reading the same responses over and over is not exciting and will sometimes put you to sleep. But it is necessary and very important. In contrast, we are all invigorated when we read new and novel responses that put innovative slants on our knowledge base. The reality is, however, that evaluation of performance is an integral part of our responsibilities, even though papers may fall into the category of "life is not always fair."

It Is Okay to Be Nervous When You Enter a Classroom

I have been teaching for four decades, and I am still nervous the first time I walk into a new class. I believe this is a common characteristic of persons who are conscientious about the quality of their teaching, as many of my colleagues who are recognized as excellent teachers express the same or similar sentiment. In my opinion, these initial bouts of anxiety are a reflection that no two classes are alike and that every class has its own personality. The dynamics of each class are different because of the variance among the interactions of the students, teacher and students, and the nature of the course. This aspect is part of the surprise of teaching. You can expect to be nervous; it is only detrimental when it impedes, rather than facilitates, your teaching.

Good Teaching Is Entertaining

There are those who confuse entertaining with being popular, and teaching is not simply a matter of being entertaining for the purpose of increasing popularity. Teaching is not a popularity contest. Neither is entertaining a substitute for substance.

To be entertaining is to engage students in the learning process. It is a process of "working" the classroom from corner to corner and doing this with enthusiasm for the topic, the learning process, and for what each student can contribute. While not falling into the category of "Let Me Entertain You," there is effective behavior that contributes to students becoming involved in the intellectual fray.

Don't Expect Yourself to Know Everything

No one commands full and complete knowledge of everything! Don't expect yourself to be able to answer any and all questions that students, or colleagues for that matter, raise in discussions. Don't be afraid to say, "I don't know," and engage yourself, along with the students, in the process of seeking the information that will provide the answer.

If you expect to be all-knowing, your behavior will reflect this self-imposed omnipotence. Furthermore, you are likely to teach well above the competencies of the students in an effort to avoid being asked a question you cannot answer. In every respect, this is a defensive system that will be a debilitating factor to your teaching and your students' learning.

If You Don't Like to Teach, Evaluate Your Choice of Profession

If you find you have no enthusiasm about your field and/or about teaching, perhaps you have chosen the wrong profession. Reality, however, is that on some days nothing goes right—even for enthusiastic and excellent teachers. Your brain feels like mashed potatoes, your thoughts remind you of tossed salad, your lecture notes look as if they were written by a stranger, the instructional equipment has no intention of providing working support, and the ever-present recalcitrant student continues to ask endless and mindless questions. You are having a bad day, and it happens to all of us. But these days should be the exception, and when you reflect back over your expe riences in the classroom, you should feel that you had fun and experienced the pleasure of knowing that students learned. Take pride in the role you might have played in a student's decision to pursue graduate school, helping a student find the right niche in a discipline, or easing a student through a difficult transition in life. Yes, if the bad days are the rule rather than the exception, get out of teaching. You may not be a bad teacher, but you certainly will not become a good one. Good teachers experience and expect good days—and settle for nothing less!

Finally

In summary, teaching is a wonderful, rewarding, and in many ways, unique profession. Be glad and rejoice in the experience! True, it has its "ups" and "downs," but overall you will have numerous positive experiences. I am glad you are part of the teaching profession!

◆　　◆　　◆

Dr. Sharon J. Price is Professor Emerita and formerly Department Head and Graduate Coordinator in the Department of Child and Family Development at The University of Georgia. She holds a BS from MacMurray College for Women, Jacksonville, Illinois, and an MS and Ph.D. in Sociology from Iowa State University. She was on the faculty at The University of Georgia from 1973 to 2000; prior to that time she was on the faculties at Tulsa University and Iowa State University and was a high school teacher. She taught numerous undergraduate and graduate courses in family studies but primarily in theory, research methodology, family problems, and various seminars. During her career she taught classes that ranged in size from fewer than ten to over five hundred students.

Dr. Price has published widely in professional journals and is the author or editor of four books, *Divorce: A Major Life Transition,*

Families and Change: Challenges Related to Family Transitions, Remarriage: A Program and Handbook, and *Families Over Time: A Lifecourse Perspective.* Her current research focuses on widows who live on family farms.

In addition to being a Meigs Award winner in 1990, Dr. Price received other awards for teaching, including the Osborne Award, presented by the National Council on Family Relations, for distinguished teaching in Family Studies. She has been active in several professional organizations, including having served as president of the National Council on Family Relations, and was also instrumental in developing a national program for the Certification of Family Life Educators in the same organization.

While students are extremely important to Dr. Price, the most significant people in her life include her husband, Dr. David Coker, Associate Provost-International Studies at The University of Georgia (retired); her mother, Sylva Price, who still lives on the family farm in Illinois and was the major inspiration in Dr. Price's decision to become a teacher; her stepson, Steven David, and her daughter-in-law, Linda Groce, who live in Southlake, Texas; and her nieces, Christine Price (on the faculty at the Ohio State University) and Wendy Price (on the faculty at Mary Washington College). Time hindered the development of many hobbies, but she presently enjoys gardening, reading, and needlework and is pursuing golf.

Reflections on a Life in Music

Egbert Ennulat

My father died in 1935, leaving my mother with a struggling business, a very grown-up son, Hans-Georg, twenty-four, and two little boys, ages six and eight. To keep us off the streets, Mother arranged piano lessons for my brother and me. Frau Kern was a very kind teacher but somewhat limited and set in her ways. Her approach did not foster much accommodation for the more enthusiastic and talented students. Nevertheless, music became my world, and one day I decided to become a professional musician. At first Mother was not concerned about it, thinking it just a phase that would blow over soon. When I persisted, she really began to worry.

"There is no way, Egbert," she told me, "that you ever will be able to make a living in music." Knowing how well children listen to their elders, she confided her concern to a neighbor.

"Frau Ennulat," said Frau Mueller, "I do not see this as a problem at all." She went on to tell my mother about something she had just heard about, the *Musische Gymnasium*, a preparatory school for musical boys selected by nationwide audition. This unique state-funded institution was situated right there in Frankfurt. "Why don't you have him tested at the next audition?" Frau Mueller suggested. "Probably he will not pass it, and that should take care of your problem."

"Indeed," my mother responded gratefully, "this is a great idea." She followed her friend's advice.

At the audition, we waited our turn along with about thirty sets of nervous but proud parents with their *Wunderkinder*. Mother was as cool as a cucumber because, for her, the purpose of all this was quite different from that of the other very anxious people. After my audition, the director of the school told my mother that she should have brought me in much earlier. That day I was the only boy to be admitted. I looked forward to my new life.

The school had been envisioned by Leo Kestenberg (1882–1962), a Jewish professional musician, philosopher, and music educator who served as chairman and councilor of the music division in the Prussian Ministry from 1919 on. The Nazis, always quick to recognize good ideas and declare them their own, were generous with their support. Thus came into being our school, a combination of high school (then and now much tougher than most U.S. schools) with daily music instruction, instrumental practice, and rehearsals.

I was truly overwhelmed by this curriculum. The only time for homework was study hall from seven to nine at night. Often, free opera tickets became available, and I never could resist. I saw a lot of glorious operas, and while my grades suffered, the exposure to good, live opera early in life increased my desire to devote my life to music.

When World War II ended, our school was abruptly dissolved, leaving the students on their own to find their way home to their families. Back home in Frankfurt am Main, life turned out to be a struggle for pure survival. At first there was no infrastructure, transportation, mail or telephone service, and there was general starvation. But we were very happy to be alive. Eventually things got better, and some cultural life resumed.

One of my earliest experiences of an organ recital took place at the Church of the Redeemer in Bad Homburg, and it was packed. I even remember what was on the program: it was the *Great Organ Mass* by Johann Sebastian Bach, one of his greatest achievements. The impact of this music was so profound that I began to turn to Baroque music, and in particular to the works of this composer. This was also the time when I realized that "Man does not live by bread alone." Unfortunately, with increasing prosperity, the attendance at such events declined in opposite proportion.

From my education in Germany I remember that, for the most part, higher education in music took place in music conservatories where applied music reigned supreme. Other subjects, such as music history and theory, were only tolerated as adjuncts. Methods courses for music education majors were nonexistent, and the subjects music teachers later were expected to teach in addition to music had to be taken at the university, an institution not connected with the conservatory. With this education I became a very good, but not very knowledgeable, performer.

In 1961, I arrived in the United States, a very frightened immigrant, for studies at Yale University toward an MM with a major in harpsichord under Ralph Kirkpatrick. The micromanaging of graduate students petrified me. Having been accustomed only to strict lecture courses in Germany in which professors did not even know the names of individual students by the end of a semester, it was new for me to be questioned out of the blue during classes, to be held responsible for homework assignments and assigned readings, and to be subjected to tests and final examinations. This really got me going, but it took a Herculean effort to succeed, both because of language problems and the different educational approach. I found the study of style and theoretical and historic concepts very exciting, and from then on the performance of music became unthinkable for me without understanding everything about it.

At this time, I also became interested in teaching and have since shared with great enthusiasm what I had come to understand with my students. In hindsight, I came to the conclusion that the teaching approach in the States is more effective because the faculty/student relationship is much closer and also because the development of students is closely monitored. To this day I have remained convinced that a good instructor in music must be a concert-level performer and a well-versed music historian and theorist.

In my teaching I make it a priority to reach the *entire* spectrum of students. Early on, I realized that when only a fraction of the students came up with the expected test results, it was I who had to change. And change I did. I came to understand that the most important elements of good teaching are to have complete command of the material, to be well organized, to make the right choices concerning what to include or exclude, and foremost, to keep the class actively engaged. Although no easy task, I always found a good dose of humor very invigorating. In turn, I myself became very enthusiastic about sharing what I love. For instance, I enhance my lectures with references to social and political developments that influenced the arts throughout history. My background allows me to broaden our discussions further with the personal experiences I had in Germany. I am a firm believer that if you know your past, you will understand yourself.

Enlightened musical performances, the equivalent of scholarly research, are educational for the entire community. In college settings, live concerts reinforce true understanding of the information studied in the lecture courses. In turn, it is inconceivable that uninformed musicians can be truly outstanding performers; good musical interpretations must be governed by understanding. Music is but one facet of the arts, but my life has been enriched by the great privilege of being involved in the education of the young and the dissemination of the arts.

◆   ◆   ◆

Egbert Ennulat, Professor Emeritus of Music at The University of Georgia, was born in Germany in 1929 and attended the *Musische Gymnasium* as a boy. From 1945 on, he studied at the *Staatliche Hochschule fuer Musik* in Frankfurt am Main, graduating in 1951 with the equivalent of a master's degree in music. During these years, Dr. Ennulat served as a graduate assistant to his major professor, Helmut Walcha, an internationally famous organist and harpsichord performer. In 1950, Professor Ennulat won a Bach Award in a nationwide organ competition. During the next ten years, he established his reputation as a specialist in Baroque keyboard music, performing and recording internationally until his emigration to the U.S.A. in 1961.

In 1964, Dr. Ennulat earned an MM from Yale University under Ralph Kirkpatrick, and, in 1971, a Ph.D. in historical musicology at Case Western Reserve University. He has taught at Oberlin College

(Ohio), the College of Wooster (Ohio), and, since 1965, The University of Georgia, where his teaching activities have been recognized with several awards, including the Josiah Meigs Award for Excellence in Teaching in 1992. His history and theory courses on both graduate and undergraduate levels have always emphasized the link between performance and scholarly research.

Professor Ennulat has remained active as a performer and scholar, accepting guest professorships in Germany, South Korea, and Brazil and presenting concerts and research papers at international conferences in Brazil, Uruguay, and Argentina, as well as concerts in Venezuela, South Korea, and Japan. In June 1999, he traveled to Germany and recorded Baroque organ music on an Arp Schnitger organ built in 1680. The CD was released in early 2000.

Dr. Ennulat's publications include an edition of *The Collected Works* by Johann de Fossa (A-R Editions, 1978), a book entitled *Arnold Schoenberg Correspondence* (Scarecrow Press, 1991), and several contributions to professional journals.

Since 1989, Professor Ennulat has been fascinated with oriental watercolors, and it will be this endeavor that occupies him for the remainder of his life.

Coming Full Circle: Teaching for Beyond the Classroom

Michelle Henry Barton

PERHAPS ONE OF biggest advantages of being an educator of professional students is the fact that both you and your students know the chosen career for which they are preparing. As an educator of veterinarians, I can count on approximately 95 percent of our graduates entering private practice. For any educator, a key to engaging and challenging students and holding their interest in your subject is to give them a purpose for what it is that you are trying to teach. In other words, give them a purpose for their education. I remind our students that they are not just learning the material to get through the class or to pass the final exam. Rather, I am teaching for experiences that reach far beyond the classroom. Students are learning for life.

As an educator, I so often recall the incessant words of my parents: "Someday when you grow up, you'll understand this." It's so true. Until you personally experience something, it's difficult to take the leap of faith that what someone is trying to teach you is true, real, accurate, or will have any importance in your life. Take the example of the toddler wanting to help cook something. You warn her about the fact that the stove or oven is hot and if she touches it, it will burn and hurt. But what is "hot"? "How much will it hurt?" Until she personally experiences what "hot" is, it is a virtual concept that is very difficult for her to understand. Once "hot" is experienced, the education comes full circle. The toddler now believes that hot is hot. More important, she truly understands what hot means. Now I am not suggesting that everyone needs to "get burned" to become educated! But as an educator, if you can help your students take the (perhaps) mundane facts and channel them into a real-life experience, they are more likely to remain engaged and to store the information until they experience it in life.

Because the majority of veterinary students enter private practice after graduation, perhaps our obvious educational goal is to prepare them for that endeavor. In the classroom setting, the didactic facts must be discussed at some point, but if the facts can be channeled into real-life case scenarios, it gives purpose to the facts. Instead of teaching minutiae, we teach problem-solving skills with broad application. What should be stressed and taught is the thought process and methodology for how to take the facts and apply them to a real case scenario. Given any particular clinical case, a competent veterinarian should be able to recognize and correctly arrive at a diagnosis. More important, the ultimate goal should be to understand how to correctly gather the clues, interpret diagnostic tests, and sort through the findings to be able to arrive at the correct diagnosis. By first presenting the didactic facts and then giving those facts application by telling stories or discussing actual clinical cases, we accomplish two key objectives. Students remain interested because they can relate the facts to real-life situations that they will encounter, while at the same time problem-solving skills are taught in lieu of memorization. They are being prepared for life beyond the classroom.

So how does a teacher provide useful or practical guidelines for preparing students for beyond the classroom? You must be able to "practice what you teach" and for that matter, "practice what you preach." As a clinician (an educator in clinical practice), I have that very advantage with fourth-year veterinary students. In the last year of their professional curriculum, the students rotate through the different sections of the hospital and receive and work on actual (animal) cases as they are presented to the Veterinary Teaching Hospital. In my particular area, Large Animal Internal Medicine, the students spend one-month rotations with me in the Large Animal Hospital. We have a tremendous amount of contact time together (an average of sixty hours per week) and really get to know each other well, warts and all! In the clinic setting, students are thrust into the real-life situation of being responsible for all aspects of patient management. They have to take their education beyond the classroom and apply it. The intriguing part for me is to observe them during this transition period from classroom learning to life. They have to act as detectives, assembling facts, clues, findings, and test results to arrive at a diagnostic plan or a diagnosis. Then this information must be transferred into appropriate treatments and translated to the patient's owner. If I previously was successful in making the connection between the classroom and beyond the classroom, the transition into the clinic is less intimidating for students. They have been prepared for the application of their basic science knowledge base and have learned lifelong problem solving skills. Their education has come full circle.

If students struggle through the transition into the clinic, they still have the opportunity to fine-tune their problem-solving skills through "apprenticeship" with the attending clinical educator. This can be a very critical point in their education. Students need a role model whom they can observe in the same situation that they are in, as well as appreciate that the educator can and does "practice what he/she teaches." Students need to be nurtured through their attempt to handle solving a clinical case puzzle with poise and a sense of accomplishment. The educator must provide a fine balance between letting students see their own mistakes in problem-solving while not letting them become discouraged by making a mistake. It's the best example of why clinical medicine is referred to as "practice." Even after they graduate, learning is for life. Each individual case is unique. Not all cases "read the textbook" or follow the class notes on what clues or signs should be present and what tests should be positive or negative. Each case is in essence a "mini-experiment" for the veterinarian. The information that veterinary students process from each case and the experience they will gain from it add to their knowledge base. Instead of looking at a projector screen in a classroom or reading a description of a disease or seeing a picture in a textbook, students experience the power of observation firsthand. So we are back to the toddler trying to understand the concept of "hot." Once experienced firsthand, the education process has come full circle. I so often wish that I had the experience and wisdom of my mentors and elders, without having to get gray hair to obtain it.

The concept of educators serving as role models for their students is crucial. A bond can form between a student and an educator that extends beyond the student's formal education. If the student can relate to the educator, accepting and trusting the teacher's ability to patiently lead him/her beyond the classroom, he/she can also learn to respect that even an educator can be "wrong" or struggle through problem-solving. It brings a sense of reality and humility to life's experiences. It teaches the student that it's okay to be wrong, as long as you can ultimately recognize when you are in error, why you were incorrect, and how to correct the mistake. Honesty, recognition of one's own mistakes, a good work ethic, and a sense of humor are teacher characteristics that will help prepare students for life's punches.

◆ ◆ ◆

Michelle Henry Barton, DVM, Ph.D., is a professor at The University of Georgia's College of Veterinary Medicine. She teaches principles of large-animal internal medicine to second- and third-year students in large classroom settings, as well as instructs small groups of first- and third-year students in laboratory settings. The majority of her time as an educator is spent in the Veterinary Teaching Hospital with fourth-year veterinary students, interns, and residents, receiving patients referred from former alumni and practicing veterinarians in Georgia and surrounding states. She is married to Dr. John Barton, an Interventional Radiologist at Athens Regional Medical Center. They live with their four daughters on a twenty-five-acre horse farm in Madison County. Dr. Barton's hobbies include horsemanship, gardening, landscaping, and being "Mom."

MY BEST COURSE

Charles M. Hudson

I HAVE ALWAYS felt out of place and foolish in discussions of how to teach. As the first in my family to complete college and the first in my county in northern Kentucky to earn a Ph.D., I do not come from anything that even vaguely resembles an academic culture. I bumbled into college teaching without knowing what I was getting into, and I have never felt adequately prepared to do anything I have done in my career in academia.

Like all college teachers, I suspect, I was fortunate enough to encounter a few exemplars along the way. When I was an undergraduate anthropology major at the University of Kentucky, it was Frank Essene, an iconoclastic teller of vivid stories with a sly sense of humor. As a graduate student at the University of North Carolina, it was John Honigmann, a dedicated scholar of the old school who was famous for his wide-ranging interests and prodigious organization and work habits. Far from thumping for a theoretical party line, he delighted in fostering the creativity of his students. Both Essene and Honigmann loved anthropology.

Whether because of my own naïveté or because I began teaching at The University of Georgia in 1964, just before its ambition to become a first-rate research university was ratcheted up, I had the luxury of assuming that the most important and most characteristic part of my role in the university was to teach. My first responsibility, as I saw it, was to learn to be a good teacher. Subsequently I learned to be a researcher, but even then my research has always been closely connected to what I taught in the classroom.

In retrospect, I believe that my career as a teacher-researcher has benefited from two values I have held. First, I have always loved English prose in the plain style of such writers as Jonathan Swift, Daniel Defoe, Henry David Thoreau, Mark Twain, and John McPhee. I have read their works not only for what they wrote but also for how they wrote it. Early on, I adopted the practice of writing out my lectures rather fully, and in class I endeavored to speak as I had written.

A second value that has served me well is a hedge against burnout. That is, I promised myself that my research would always be animated by a subject matter I loved. No matter what theoretical winds were blowing, no matter where the research money was glowing, I determined that I would pursue only those questions that vitally interested me.

In the 1960s, the sine qua non of research in social anthropology was firsthand field research in an exotic culture. In 1965 and 1966, I dutifully put in two stints of fieldwork with Eskimos in Canada. But I did not take to Eskimo research, and I have never been able to explain why. I can only say that I did not resonate with the far north.

The field of anthropology was very weakly developed in Southern universities in the 1960s, and I soon realized that no anthropologist since John Swanton had inquired deeply into the history and culture of the Indians of the Southeastern United States. I, in fact, had learned very little about them in my undergraduate and graduate studies. As I read Swanton's voluminous works, I saw that while he was a diligent collector of facts, his work was unreadable to any but a specialist scholar, and even for them Swanton's prose can induce deep sleep.

I decided to teach a course on the native peoples of the South, and I meant to write a book out of it. This effort became incarnated in ANT 441/641, Indians of the Southeastern United States. I taught it first in 1970, and I taught it once or twice a year almost every year thereafter. My intent was to construct a basic introduction to the Southeastern Indian way of life. I wanted to grasp the essentials of all their basic cultural and social institutions and to set this forth plainly, in accessible prose. Each time I taught the course, I edited and improved the text, and I endeavored always to add new material. I showed a veritable storm of 35 mm slides as I lectured. I played recordings of Southeastern Indian music and recordings of birds that were symbolically important. I brought artifacts into the classroom and took my students on field trips to archaeological sites.

As I taught my course, time and time again, I could see in the faces of my students which parts of my lectures worked and which did not, and I constantly pruned and added to the manuscript. Without question, ANT 441/641 was the most satisfying teaching experience of my entire career. It was a peak experience that I have since tried to duplicate, but I have never quite succeeded in doing so.

In 1976, *The Southeastern Indians* was published by the University of Tennessee Press, and it has been continuously in print ever since. Several of my former students have told me that when they read this book, they can hear me lecturing. Bumbler that I am, once the book was in print, I encountered a problem I did not anticipate. That is, with my entire course of lectures in print, I felt foolish continuing to present these same lectures in class. Temporarily off balance, I began developing the material further, amplifying it and injecting a much needed chronological structure into it. I divided the course into two parts: ANT 447, The Rise and Fall of Southeastern Chiefdoms, and ANT 448, The Indians of the Old South, both of which I have since taught many times.

Indirectly, *The Southeastern Indians* led to the most important research of my career. That is, I realized that the book contained a huge unanswered question. Neither I nor anyone else had shown what connections lay between the large, complex mound-building native societies of the Southeast in the 1500s and the less spectacular and less numerous Indian societies of the early 1700s. It seemed obvious to me that a major social transformation had taken place between the sixteenth and eighteenth centuries, but no one could describe precisely how it had happened. My students would ask questions like "Were the Etowah mounds built by Creeks or Cherokees?" I could not answer this or any similar question.

Around 1979, it occurred to me that if the route of the Hernando de Soto expedition of 1539–43 could be laid on a map with some accuracy, this string of events could be combined with archaeological information on the late prehistoric era, and in so doing we could reconstruct at least the outlines of the Southeast in the 1500s. And if this could be done, we could then proceed both backward and forward in time from that point of reference. If the social and cultural landscape de Soto traversed could be fleshed out, it could open up two missing centuries of Southern history.

In 1980, I taught a graduate seminar on the de Soto expedition. As my students and I began working out segments of the route of de Soto's expedition, along with the related expeditions of Tristán de Luna (1559–60) and Juan Pardo (1566–68), other historians and anthropologists became interested in what we were finding. Our results were significantly different from the research that John Swanton had done on the de Soto route, and his is the research that had inspired the installation of numerous place names and historical markers from the Atlantic Coast to East Texas.

The people who lived near these place names and historical markers were irritated by our claims, and they said so most volubly. I was obligated to respond to this controversy, and the four years I planned to spend on de Soto stretched out to sixteen years. And quite by chance, the Columbian Quincentennial fell during this period of time. My research became relevant to several state, regional, and national de Soto and Columbus commissions. In addition to many articles and chapters, I edited and authored four books from the project, including *Knights of Spain, Warriors of the Sun*, probably the most important book that I will write.

All of this, I would argue, had its seed in my best course, ANT 441/641, Indians of the Southeastern United States. People ask me whether I will revise *The Southeastern Indians*. I tell them that I cannot. What is needed is a new book covering the subject matter in a new way. Perhaps for the first time in my life, I feel that I know how to do this next necessary step. But now that I am retired, I am concerned that I will have enough time and energy to complete it. Even more, I am concerned about whether I will be able to write it in retirement, without benefit of the motivational and intellectual context of teaching.

◆   ◆   ◆

Charles M. Hudson is Franklin Professor of Anthropology. He joined the faculty of The University of Georgia in 1964, immediately after graduate school, and with only momentary exceptions, he has hardly budged from there since then. He has taught introductory anthropology throughout his career, as well as upper division undergraduate courses on comparative belief systems, ethnohistory, and most particularly the history and culture of the native peoples of the Southeastern United States. He has taught undergraduate sections of 300+, small graduate seminars, and one-on-one with graduate students and honors students. He is a mediocre but eternally optimistic gardener. His wife, Joyce, has published several novels, a travel book, and a book on Jungian dream interpretation in a Christian context. He won the Meigs Award in 1994.

IN PRAISE OF HOLISTIC TEACHING

Katharina M. Wilson

The true purpose of education is to cherish and unfold the seed of immortality already sown within us: to develop, to their fullest extent, the capacities of every kind with which the God who made us has endowed us.

Mrs. Jameson, *Winter Studies and Summer Rambles*

Learning without thought is labor lost; thought without learning is perilous.

Confucius, *Analects*

MRS. JAMESON AND Confucius, worlds and millennia apart, both advocate what I believe the essence of holistic education to be: the nourishing and cultivating, rather than the supplanting, of the learner's innate talents, her and his intellectual and emotional strengths; the fruitful interaction of reflection and knowledge, of thought and learning. It is a mode of teaching analogous to the ecological rather than commercial method of landscaping: not the systematic destruction of biodiversity in favor of convenient uniform planting, not the intermittent destruction of the native (or preexisting) flora and its supplantation by fast-growing drought- and pest-resistant hybrids, but the careful preservation, full utilization, shaping, improving, and cultivation of the existing plants in their indigenous setting.

The cultivation of a young mind is no different and no less difficult or less rewarding than the cultivation of a seed that may have to be transplanted to a sunnier or shadier spot or rescued from weeds in order to reach full flowering; analogously, the presupposition of existing thought and awareness or even the seed of genius in neophyte scholars makes the necessity to challenge and examine their assumptions and belief systems incumbent on the teacher if the goal is to encourage them to develop their full potential and strengthen their sense of value. If we can teach young people skills such as creative, reflective, and analytical thinking and values such as empathy and the worth of diversity; if we can give them confidence and passion to continue learning and not to fear the new, then we will have accomplished a feat far more important than the imparting of facts.

There are, therefore, numerous concerns facing any teacher attempting a holistic approach to education: first, how to be student-centered without compromising standards; second, how to avoid compartmentalizing knowledge while inspiring a passionate commitment to the discipline; and third, how, by extension, to make learning an active rather than passive experience, fostering thereby the application of insights and understanding gained in one context to other fields in academe and to other walks in life. This corollary concern is particularly relevant to educators today when only a precious few can expect to hold lifelong jobs, when intellectual and career flexibility seem to be key to professional success (because people will have to be retrained periodically to accommodate the rapidly changing needs of a technology-driven society), and when all of us are bombarded with increasingly subtle messages by advertisers, politicians, and other manipulative narrators in search of our votes, dollars, or loyalties. With the information explosion, the globalization of just about every aspect of human endeavor, and the radical changes in the way "work" has come to be defined, few of us can fathom what the jobs, challenges, and opportunities of the twenty-first century will be or how to prepare our students for them. Or, in other words, we can't aspire to give them answers or even permanent job skills, only a desire and passion for learning and the general skills of reflective, analytical thinking.

It is my conviction that the greatest gift a teacher can bestow upon a student is her/his eagerness to foster and reward the student's willingness to think critically, nimbly, and creatively; to apply that ability to novel concepts and diverse fields; to energetically and effectively transmute knowledge and experience from one situation to another; to become comfortable with the analogical mode of reasoning; to gain, in other words, as much intellectual flexibility as possible. The metaphor that comes to mind is that of a drop of water creating numberless concentric circles in a body of water propelled by the initial force of the energy but perpetually modifying and transmuting that energy into a myriad of interacting ripples. No different, I think, is the effect of an ideal class or learning situation. From one insight, many are bound to follow almost automatically; from one successful venture beyond the boundaries of the obvious and the traditional, a sustained desire to explore ever farther in all fields and realms of human endeavor results; and it is that gloriously epiphanic combination of desire and process that in turn facilitates the success of the holistic model of learning, because by internalizing and then activating what we learn, we stand a chance of reaching that realm where moral and intellectual developments interface. The desire to understand and explore, to reason analogically, therefore, is bound to shape the whole person and to affect personal as well as abstract processes, relationships, and patterns.

We grasp not by axioms but through analogies. The world is (and has always been) explained and is, in turn, understood in figurative language, in images. Aesop's fables, the Homeric similes, Socrates' dialogues, Christ's parables, Archimedes's discoveries, as well as contemporary commentaries on the giddiness of the stock market or the introduction of new medical technologies and astrophysical discoveries, use the criterion of the familiar to explain the unfamiliar. The process is ancient, its pedagogical application is time-honored, and in its best manifestations, it always contains moral and intellectual, as well as political dimensions. As such, it is often suspect, and is rarely comfortable. Christ and Socrates, prime practitioners of the method of analogical reasoning, challenged people to abandon self-complacency and the comforts of traditional thinking. Both taught with passion and inspired passion. Both left lasting legacies. Both were murdered.

In my nineteen years of teaching early literature and cultural history, I have tried to adhere to a holistic model of teaching and to formulate a philosophy of teaching both true to the model and sustainable in generalized survey classes at a large research university. Throughout the years I have changed and even abandoned some components of this approach to suit the needs of the students and the realities of their intellectual preparation as well as my own limitations. I would like to share that formulation here with you.

My philosophy of education rests on three pillars of convictions: first, that learning is and always has been an active, participatory activity requiring as much effort from the student as it does from the teacher; second, that participating in the learning process is a cooperative as well as competitive endeavor; and third, that the often holistic, intercultural, cross-racial, and cross-generic communication that the best of world literature embodies can and should have a pressing relevance to students' personal lives in specific and to the contemporary ethos in general.

I begin every class by emphasizing that passivity is the greatest enemy of learning and growth and that students, individually and collectively, are every bit as responsible for their education as are their parents and teachers. Learning is a process (not a product) that requires active, even enthusiastic, participation from all involved. I, therefore, insist on full participation by all students, attempting to enlist their strengths and interests into shaping the class. I firmly believe that each class, as each individual, is different and that, therefore, I have to teach each class differently. By empowering students to participate in designing the course (my syllabi are guidelines only, and I allow a 30 percent redrafting of the syllabus according to the expressed and justified desires of the class), I can, in turn, demand enthusiastic cooperation and full participation in the discussion.

To guide students through texts, I have compiled copious study notes intended to alert them to important details, questions to be raised, inferences to be drawn, and problems posed by the texts. With access to the literal level facilitated by the study notes and accomplished largely out of class, the lion's portion of class time is spent in discussion, whereby problem-solving (literary, initially, but almost invariably broadening into ethical, political, aesthetic dimensions) is approached as a systematic procedure applicable to all such endeavors, personal or professional. The activity is cooperative, we work by consensus, and I labor to underscore the fact that there are no "false" answers but different aspects of truths, different realities and degrees of appropriateness. I urge them to find personal and contemporary analogies to the discoveries they make about ancient texts and, vice versa, to bring their own experiences and insights to bear upon the texts.

By my insisting on the importance of the process of understanding rather than the product of knowing, students, often intimidated by literary tasks and tending to compartmentalize knowledge, are forced to abandon convenient pigeonholes ("I am a scientist." "I never do well in lit classes.") and excuses. They/we thus demystify the supposedly daunting esoteric nature of literary analysis by underscoring the importance of processes, methodologies, and creative, analytical tools of problem solving that they have not brought to bear on literary/cultural studies before. As part of this demythification process, I insist that students bring their own expertise and experience to bear upon the text and provide personalized entries into the work. In the literature survey class, for instance, short presentations have ranged from a premed student's discussion of battle wounds in the *Iliad* to a former carpenter's blueprint of Odysseus's raft; from an art major's evaluation of Achilles' shield to a nurse's critique of the Homeric nobleman's diet; and from a recent divorcée's lament over Dido's abandonment to a former wrestler's demonstration of Grendel's martial technique in *Beowulf*.

Students thus realize that reflective, creative, and analytical thinking should never be limited to one's field of expertise but rather should be a mode of reasoning applicable to all fields of inquiry and that empathy (to people, causes, texts) is not an inborn talent but a conscious effort in awareness.

Parallel to this lateral process of demythification (i.e., abandoning the perception of great works of art as isolated and personally irrelevant manifestations of individual genius), I also stress a vertical application, that is to say, the observation that what troubled and delighted men and women millennia ago and the way they set out to pursue their goals and attempted to grasp the great mysteries of existence are not that substantially different from our own fears, aspirations, and desires or the ways by which we deal with them. To this effect, I ask students to share newspaper clippings, observations, and experiences with the class that manifest aspects of themes or problems raised by the text we are discussing. We also experiment with applying, by analogy, the insight and wisdom gained from the source text to the contemporary situation at hand. This particular "problem-solving" exercise seems to be especially effective in bringing great works of the past alive for many students.

The great benefit of this approach, for me at least, has been that every semester, in every class, I learn at least as much as my students do. And this never-ending process of learning and thus of personal growth, in turn, has been invigorating and has never allowed my enthusiasm for the profession or for my field of study to dampen. Indeed, as one of my students recently observed, I will probably be asking "why questions" on my deathbed and waiting for a multitude of answers before I die.

◆　　◆　　◆

Katharina M. Wilson received her BA and MA in Comparative Literature from The University of Georgia and her Ph.D., also in Comparative Literature, from the University of Illinois. She has been teaching at The University of Georgia in the Comparative Literature Department since 1981. She won the Meigs Award in 1997. She is married to Christopher Wilson, who is also a teacher, and they have two children, Caroline and Tess, who, by the last count at least, also wanted to become teachers. Both Chris's and Katharina's parents taught either full time (Chris's father was Professor of Botany at UGA after the Second World War) or for portions of their professional careers, so the domestic assumptions are that there must be teaching genes running in both branches of the family. When they are not teaching or discussing pedagogical strategies, the Wilsons enjoy gardening, building, music, theater, cooking, entertaining, and, most of all, watching and fostering their children's intellectual and spiritual development.

PERSONAL TEACHING AND STORYTELLING IN THE LARGE CLASS

O. *Lee Reed*

FOR THE PAST decade, I have specialized in teaching a required sophomore-level legal studies course in the Terry College of Business. During this time, I have come to appreciate the challenge of teaching large core classes, a challenge that properly met requires the most developed skills of senior faculty. In my experience, nineteen-to twenty-year-old students often lack the motivation, focus, and seriousness of purpose necessary for productive education and, later, a successful career. Unlike graduate and professional students, sophomores often do not appreciate the value of their courses, a feeling magnified when students are buried in large core classes. I believe that these large classes must provide students not only with adequate course content but also with an enthusiasm for education in general and the course content in specific. This essay emphasizes two of these large-class skills: personal teaching and storytelling.

First, faculty who teach large undergraduate classes should emphasize what I call "personal teaching." Young adult students in particular need to see teachers as role models, not as remote authority figures, models who resemble their students, only are older and more knowledgeable. In short, they need inspiration and a model for emulation. Students get this from teachers they like, but they have difficulty liking teachers unless they feel they know them as persons, unless their teachers practice personal teaching.

For me, personal teaching means my letting the students know about who I am. In the course of a semester, they find out that I like reading, sports, movies, and friends; that I grew up in the small town of Sylacauga, Alabama, where I played baseball, roamed the woods with my buddies, and made a friend for life one evening by telling the high school librarian that she walked "in beauty like the night" (Byron); that in college I majored in history, a wonderful discipline whose structure has influenced every cranny of my thinking even though I've largely forgotten the body of facts I stayed up so many nights to memorize; and that I teach instead of practice law because I always wanted to be paid for reading, for what I would do for free. Surprisingly, it takes little time away from course content to be "personal" with the students in class, yet I believe many of them get more from the course because of my style.

Faculty who are quietly personal in small-class settings may have trouble presenting themselves in a legal studies, chemistry, or history class of over a hundred students, but I think that personal teaching is more imperative in the large, than in the small, class, if for no other reason than undergraduates usually start university education in large classes. Unless these students bring a genuine love of learning to their crowded classrooms, and I observe that many do not, then the large class is a recipe for educational disaster. Clear and organized explication of subject facts is necessary but hardly sufficient to avoid having students minimize learning and focus disproportionately on socialization, sports, and other potential impediments to higher education. Faculty who teach large classes must be carefully selected for their ability to show enthusiasm for the life of the mind through revealing themselves as persons.

Intertwined with the act of personal teaching is the second step for generating enthusiasm for learning in the large class: storytelling. By storytelling I do not intend that teachers ought to relate a series of anecdotes to students in large classes. Rather, teachers must appreciate that the lecture or modified-lecture style required in large classes by necessity is a type of story. It has a beginning and an end. It is a narration with rising and falling dramatic emphasis that may be humorous, serious, interesting, boring, or whatever.

Appreciation that large-class teaching style requires storytelling leads also to the recognition that good teaching in large classes demands attention to the elements of good storytelling, which go beyond the strict verbal element of the story (course content). Intonation, gesture, eye contact, humor, pathos, pacing, attention grabbing—all play a vital role in good storytelling. All play a vital role in the rhetoric of teaching, especially in the large classroom.

For many faculty, good classroom storytelling, including effective presentation, is difficult. They may be good storytellers around the dinner table with family, or in front of the fire with friends, but in the large classroom they become dry reciters of factual content. In major part, they cannot be themselves in front of their students, and this gets back to the importance of personal teaching. In the large classroom, good storytelling requires that teachers reveal themselves, their humor, their love for learning, the sharing of human commonalities and human interests *in the process* of effectively delivering course content. Undergraduate students are not inspired by a chalkboard or overhead projector full of course content without first seeing a living, breathing person in front of them, a teacher whose love of learning is worthy of emulation and who holds up a mirror in which students see potential for themselves.

So, how does one become a personally expressive, storytelling teacher in a large classroom? Practice, practice, practice. There is no other secret except, perhaps, that teachers need to exaggerate everything in the large classroom. As stage actors know, effective communication with an audience that is thirty to sixty feet away requires expressive exaggeration of content delivery. My family occasionally clasps hands over ears at the dinner table, but my students all hear me well.

In 1997, I gave the Honors Day address out on the quadrangle between the main library and Old College. The honors graduates, various award winners, several hundred parents, numerous faculty colleagues, and virtually every administrative potentate of the university were there. In the middle of my speech, I became aware that

I could not move one arm. My improperly fastened cowl had slipped from the shoulders of my academic gown and was pinioning my arm to my side. I wriggled, contorted, got it in place, made some joke, and went on. People actually seemed more interested. The point: be willing to let it all hang out, literally, before a large audience.

Because the Honors Day address illustrates an attempt at what I consider "personal teaching," I am concluding this essay by quoting that written speech, which I tried not to read but to deliver in natural rhythms. The speech represents my belief that not only effective teaching but human existence itself represents a type of story.

A Good Story

I love a good story.

I have always loved stories.

My father told me stories.

My mother read me stories.

Before I entered grade school, I knew the stories of the Bible,

of Greek, Roman, and Norse mythology, the Brothers
    Grimm,

Hans Christian Andersen, and Uncle Remus.

The stories of Paul Bunyan, Pecos Bill, John Henry, Mickey
    Mouse, Tugboat Annie,

the Green Lantern, Superman, and Wonder Woman.

I love a good story.

When I began to read, I couldn't get enough stories.

During the long cicada-summers of my youth, I played
    baseball, explored hilltops and creek beds,

learned with my friends how to get into trouble,

and read, read, read—often five or six books a day,

books carefully selected from the public library to avoid any taint of redeeming social value.

As I grew older, I continued to enjoy stories.

My interests broadened to include nonfiction.

I began to haunt library periodical rooms.

Every January, the high school librarian, Mrs. Hamil,

gave me a year's back issues of *National Geographic* and *Popular Science*.

I love a good story.

I read for pleasure.

When students ask me why I chose a career in higher education,

I tell them that I always wanted to be paid for reading,

for doing what I would have done anyway.

I often read a book until I'm tired of it, then, for relief,

read something else.

During one final exam week in law school,

in addition to studying twelve or more hours a day,

I reread the *Count of Monte Cristo*—all eleven hundred pages of it.

I love a good story.

As an adult I have come to think about the role that stories play in shaping our lives.

Although I suspect that our species designation,

homo sapiens—the wise animal—is both self-serving and
more than a bit misleading,

I have no doubt that we are *homo loquens*, the speaking
animal, the storytelling animal.

Our lives are ceaselessly intertwined with narrative.

Literally, every time we open our mouths and speak, we are
telling a type of story,

for words are never exactly what we are speaking about,

words are not the thing in itself, the *ding an sich*.

Words are merely the vehicle of narrative, of storytelling.

Importantly, narrative is not merely the story we tell others.

Even more, it is the story we tell ourselves.

The story is in here [gesturing] as well as out there.

What we tell ourselves shapes what we think,

how we feel, who we are.

In the most real fashion imaginable,

we tell ourselves the story of our lives.

No, we are not the wise animal.

We are the speaking animal whose life is a story.

Others have thought about life as a story.

Dante wrote about it as a divine comedy.

Shakespeare's *Macbeth* says that "life's but a walking
shadow,

a poor player who struts and frets his hour upon the stage,
and then is heard no more.

It is a tale told by an idiot,

full of sound and fury, signifying nothing."

When I think of what truly frightens me,

I don't think of Stephen King's monsters,

which can always be heroically and meaningfully opposed, or
at least run away from.

No, when I think of what truly frightens me,

I think of Macbeth's utter existential horror,

of life "signifying nothing."

But whether tragedy or comedy,

horror or *A Midsummer Night's Dream,*

for us humans, life is first a story.

I love a good story.

And it is a serious mistake to think that stories do not pervade

the highest realms of human thought.

For instance, science tells us many stories:

the story of the Big Bang, the story of evolution,

the story of quarks and quasars, of DNA and $E=MC^2$, of
fractals and chaos.

But wait, these scientific stories aren't *just* stories.

They mirror reality itself, don't they? Of course, and yet . . .

Lest you believe the equivalence of scientific models and reality
too dogmatically,

consider Thomas Kuhn's *The Structure of Scientific
Revolutions.*

Kuhn says that scientific models tell us certain kinds of stories
about the world

that scientists accept until better stories come along.

As long as science is based on human thought—and its support system: language—

no final view of reality can be totally encapsulated and frozen within a scientific model.

In the last analysis, science provides only a type of narrative, a story,

a way of peering through the glass darkly.

Kuhn's theory is itself a story.

A story about the nature of stories.

I love a good story.

That's why I've chosen a career studying law.

Law has an inherent drama to it.

The themes of law resonate through society.

They resound through prime-time television and fill the best-seller lists.

But at a deeper level, law's revelation through language

suggests its basic connection to the storytelling animal's will

to temper desire and order social functioning.

Euripides said, "Law is the lamp that lights civilization."

It illuminates the story of our human coming together,

of conflict and resolution,

of our attempts to make a living order and to reject social entropy.

It undergirds our political system at every turn, and our economic system as well.

Without law the adequate functioning of large-scale private markets is highly problematic,

a fact that Russia and Eastern Europe have had recently to confront.

Law also represents the best hope for our noblest social aspirations,

of opportunity, equality, and justice.

Law furnishes an institutional framework of sustaining narrative

for our life's journey in community.

I love a good story.

Perhaps it is why I pursue teaching.

Teaching involves the sharing of stories, the transmission of narrative down through the generations.

Certainly, all members of the community share their stories of what it means to be human.

Everywhere we meet and talk and weave the rich fabric of social narrative.

But to teach at a university, in the academy, is something special.

It represents what is the highest and best about our storytelling.

So I tell you recognized teachers today: be honored that students turn to you for this storytelling

and play your part in the plot well. Render your character with emotion.

William Arthur Ward wrote, "The mediocre teacher tells. The good teacher explains.

The superior teacher demonstrates. The great teacher inspires."

Inspire your students, so that whatever career path they take,

they will fully appreciate the importance of your subject to the human story.

Walter Bagehot said, "A schoolmaster should have an atmosphere of awe,

and walk wonderingly, as if he was amazed at being himself."

It is pretty amazing to play the human role.

As a teacher, know this and walk wonderingly, and your students will attend your stories

and follow you closely.

I love a good story.

And I say to you recognized students today: You are why we tell our stories.

We, your teachers, and we, your parents, say, "You are the reason."

You are the best of our next generation, and if you will but join the human story

with a sense of wonder and commitment, your future will be bright indeed.

Certainly, there are challenges for the future. Yes, there may be dragons along the way.

The story twists and turns.

But I have every confidence in the words of H. G. Wells,

spoken during a lecture to the Royal Institution in 1902:

All this world is heavy with the promise of greater things, and a day will come, one day in the unending succession of days, when beings, beings who are now latent in our thoughts and hidden in our loins, shall stand upon the earth . . . and shall laugh and reach out their hands amidst the stars.

What a plot! Ultimately, ultimately, we are all part of a great
narrative,

a grand drama that spins the very galaxies like a child's
pinwheel.

I do so love a good story.

◆ ◆ ◆

O. Lee Reed is Professor of Legal Studies in the Terry College of
Business. Except for a visiting hiatus at the University of Pennsylvania's Wharton School, he has taught at The University of Georgia
for the last twenty-seven years, teaching large and small legal studies classes at both the undergraduate and MBA levels. For the past
decade, he has specialized in teaching LEGL 2700, the large undergraduate core legal studies course in business. Professor Reed's preference to teach the core course reflects his training at the University
of Chicago, where introductory classes were usually taught by senior
faculty, including Nobel laureates. Although he principally lectures
to his 120-student classes, he also insists on interaction with the students. He won the Meigs Award in 1996. Professor Reed met his
wife when she was an English graduate student at the university,
and they have two wonderful sons, ages seventeen and twenty-one.
One of his pleasures is to have access to the UGA libraries, and he
has catholic reading interests. Out-of-doors, he is passionate about
the art of landscape photography and has one of the country's
largest collections of signed landscape photography books.

MY CAREER

Joseph R. Berrigan

FOR MORE THAN fifty years, I have been a student of Latin and Greek and so of rhetoric, although for a long time I was not aware of that. It began at Jesuit High in New Orleans in 1947 and continued at three universities, Loyola of the South, St. Louis, and Tulane. I am deeply grateful to all the teachers in those institutions, men who first showed me the path to learning and virtue. The most powerful impact came, in high school, from Edward Romagosa, a young Jesuit scholastic who taught me during my sophomore year. He perfected our Latin, introduced us to Homer, and gave us a sampling of philosophy in a reading group he organized on Cicero's *On Old Age*. (Why didn't he introduce us to his *On Friendship*?) That group of young Orleanians was the most gifted set of people I would know until I came to the History Department at Georgia. My most memorable teacher was our fourth-year instructor in Latin, English, and Religion, F. X. Entz, who had come to America from Alsace in the aftermath of the Franco-Prussian War. I remember visiting him a few years after I had graduated from high school. Entz told me that he was reading the Latin comic writers Plautus and Terence. "You'll have to do that when you retire," he said. I have been doing that now for two years, along with the philosophical dialogues of Cicero.

Before narrating my college years, I would like to mention that for at least fifty years I have primarily considered myself essentially a student, someone who is eager to learn something new. This desire explains my interest in languages, not only English, Latin, and Greek but also Italian, Spanish, French, and German. This sheds light on my curiosity about other cultures, other times, and other forms of humanity. How else could one make sense of my friendships with classicists, medievalists, Americanists, Chinese, and even British historians? As an eternal student, I admire and revere others who pursue the same goals, no matter how diverse their fields may be. In the best of all possible worlds, we would always be learning something new. Now, I am eager to learn new languages, especially Chinese, Hebrew, and Gaelic.

In the Korea-accelerated undergraduate program at Loyola, I majored in Classics with the prospect of entering law school. The acceleration was due to the felt need to produce second lieutenants through ROTC, and I was in that program all three years. During that time I benefited from a French Jesuit, Paul Callens, a native of Lille, who tried to interest me in Byzantine history. No chance. What should have been my fourth year of college turned into an AM program at St. Louis University, where I had marvelous teachers, especially Paul Korfmacher and Chauncey Finch. The latter directed my thesis on a fifteenth-century Latin translation of Mark Antony's funeral oration for Caesar, the version given by Dio Cassius. (My year there saw the beginning of what was to become the Pius XII Memorial Library, a rich microfilm collection of Vatican manuscripts.) Until his death, Professor Finch remained a friend and an inspiration. Every year I would visit him in the Film Library during the *Manuscripta* Conference. He was always cheerful, energetic, and eager to help, even after losing a leg to the effects of diabetes.

It was at St. Louis that I decided that I wanted to be a historian. I had come across several nineteenth-century texts by Southern classicists in my courses on Pindar and Sophocles, and I realized that I had to change my direction to make sense of men like Basil Gildersleeve and M. W. Humphreys. This decision predated my being drafted. My service consisted of two years in the Counterintelligence Corps, mostly in Japan. I felt that this was a typical military posting since I possessed an MOS as a Spanish interpreter, and where could I use Spanish in Kyoto?

When I came out of the army, I entered Tulane but as a medievalist. Enter Charles Davis, who had just come there from Oxford. He wanted a graduate student with Latin and paleography. I was the one. Gone were my dreams of Southern classicists but not for good: I have been able to work on them across my career. Charles Davis was a great Dante scholar, and I had for many years yearned to know the *Commedia*. He introduced me to that great work, to late medieval Italy, especially the early Trecento, and the Renaissance. He insisted that I do my dissertation on an obscure Lombard encyclopedist named Benzo of Alessandria. Also, he arranged for me to have a Fulbright scholarship to Italy where I could work on my thesis topic. By that time (1961), I had already begun teaching, gotten married, and had a child.

In 1958, I began my career as a teacher of history at Loyola, where I taught Western civilization, American history, and a variety of modern European history courses. I was completing my doctoral course work at Tulane at the same time. Teaching was a passion for me from the start. I loved the interaction, the repartee, and the generous friendship of the students. After all, I was still in my twenties. While I experimented with different teaching styles, I finally settled on a modified lecture format in which students never knew when I would stop lecturing and start asking questions. After a couple of years, I stopped using notes. It was my practice to offer generous office hours and engage in constant association with students. I returned their friendship and found the whole enterprise of teaching one of boundless joy. It is no accident that the greatest thing that ever happened to me was my marriage to one of my students in 1960. Can you imagine that happening these days, enveloped as we are in the clouds of political correctness?

Those eight years at Loyola really shaped me and established me as both an accomplished teacher and a published scholar. But I felt I had to leave there because of my profound disagreement with internal politics over which I had no control. I remember sitting at my desk and writing letters to the universities of Mississippi and Alabama, where I presumed I might get a position. With my last five-cent stamp,

I wrote a letter to The University of Georgia. Soon, though, I heard from Athens and got an interview on Holy Thursday, 1966. I knew nothing about Athens, The University of Georgia, or the History Department, but I quickly learned a lot about them all.

The whole enterprise was an antebellum plantation (Ed Best of Classics taught me that metaphor when we served on the In Depth Committee). Our Head was a wonderful old gentleman named Joe Parks. A historian of the Old South, he was an antebellum autocrat, charged with expanding the department and bringing it somewhere close to the twentieth century. He had already brought in several scholars by the time I arrived but would outdo himself when he brought in thirteen in 1967 alone. Joe did not use committees; he relied on his own intuition. I discovered that he liked to recruit men who were already chairmen, as Parks had been at Birmingham Southern and as I had been at Loyola.

It was exciting to be in LeConte Hall. Everything seemed possible, with so much life and intelligence abounding around us. I felt that it could not last, just as the good times at Loyola had not lasted, and unfortunately, I was right. The senior faculty in history, most of whom preceded Dr. Parks, resented the new faculty and him. They wanted changes in direction and a reallocation of departmental resources and succeeded. We still had our teaching and our research, those of us at least who did not leave for Ohio, Massachusetts, Arkansas, Arizona, and Alabama. And we taught up a storm, even after the departure of such gifted teachers as Willard Gatewood and Bob Griffith. Among those who stayed were Lester Stephens, Will Holmes, Tom Ganschow, Emory Thomas, Bud Bartley, Jean Friedman, and Kirk Willis. We were alive with teachers.

Surrounded as I was during this time by enthusiastic teachers, I came into my own as a teacher and scholar. Building on the foundation of Loyola, I worked at my teaching and took two positions as unassailable: one must know his material before he begins teaching and one must love one's students. During these years, two topics were close to my heart and evident in my teaching: Renaissance humanism and the philosophy of history. Finally, I had come to appreciate the school of Vittorino da Feltre in Mantua through the lens of his student Gregorio Correr, a Venetian aristocrat and humanist. I edited his fables, satires, and tragedy along with translations of the first and the last of these. Presenting papers on these topics and on other works of Quattrocento humanists, I developed a real interest and expertise in Renaissance fables and tragedies.

All of this work involved my Latin and Greek and awakened the echoes of my classical education. After all, the young man who had done that translation of Dio Cassius was the son of the other great Renaissance educator, Guarino da Verona. The role of rhetoric in the schoolrooms of the Renaissance provided the link with my interest in the philosophy of history, with Giambattista Vico, R. G. Collingwood, and Isaiah Berlin. How do we know the past? What do we make of the past? How do we present the past for today's students? These are the questions that confronted me in every class I taught, from introductory Western civilization to advanced graduate seminars. The bridge had to be a series of texts, no matter the subject, and there I felt Vittorino and Gregorio at my side, along with Chauncey Finch and Charles Davis. Making sense of texts—that is the goal of education, as I understand it and as I have practiced it for almost forty years.

This has been a long and absorbing conversation. It still continues in my retirement, and I feel that I am a member of a select group of teachers and students who came here to Athens over the past two centuries, men like Moses Waddel, Willis Bocock, W. D. Hooper, Joe Parks, Alf Heggoy, James W. Alexander—all men of the text.

◆   ◆   ◆

Joseph R. Berrigan was born in New Orleans on July 20, 1933. He took his AB at Loyola (1954), his AM at St. Louis University (1956), and his Ph.D. at Tulane (1963). As an undergraduate, he majored in the Classics. For the master's degree, his major field was Greek; for the doctorate, he emphasized medieval and Renaissance intellectual history. He spent the 1961–62 academic year at the Universita del Sacro in Milan, where he worked under Giuseppe Billanovich. At Loyola he taught American history, Western civilization, and courses in ancient, medieval, and modern European history. At Georgia, he taught the first in the sequence of Western civilization courses along with advanced courses in medieval and Renaissance intellectual history as well as the philosophy of history.

Dr. Berrigan's preferred teaching style was lecture-discussion. He was the major professor of five Ph.D.s and twenty-five MAs. He and his wife raised five children, two of whom are lawyers and two are engineers; the fifth is a stonemason who designs and constructs patios. The Berrigans now proudly point to seven grandchildren. They have a mountain retreat on a lake in northern South Carolina where he can walk, bird-watch, and commune with Homer, Virgil, and Dante.

Dr. Berrigan taught at Loyola (1958–66) and at Georgia (1966–97). In 1963–64, he was a visiting professor of classics at Newcomb College, where he taught a course in classical culture. In 1967 and again in 1988, he taught summer school at Tulane University; in 1988 he also taught summer school at the University of New Orleans. During 1966, he was part of the Globis program in Verona. His last course was at Jesus College, Oxford, in the UGA Oxford Program in 1997. Dr. Berrigan received the Meigs Award in 1986 and again in 1991.

My Teaching Philosophy and the Teachers Who Shaped It

Frederick J. Stephenson

ONE OF THE most valuable exercises I have ever undertaken as a teacher is the preparation of a statement of my teaching philosophy. This assignment, which I didn't attempt until late in my career, proved so beneficial to me that I urge every teacher to complete one. It made me focus on why I do what I do and what I hope to accomplish in this honorable profession. At the start, what I knew was that for twenty-nine years I had been daily going to work with a strong desire to make a difference. To be honest, though, there never was a "big picture" plan. I was engaged in a journey, and I might add an enjoyable one, but to an unknown destination. Why? Because it just made sense to me. I simply thought that teaching was the right path to follow.

The most direct benefit of this philosophy-development process was that it helped me redirect my career. Of equal importance, it confirmed that the path I had chosen was a good route and that I should keep following it. I also found new energy, which is important because teaching demands a high level of emotion and passion. But the biggest surprise was a benefit that just materialized from nowhere, a so-called "rest of the story" that was very meaningful to me and that I want to share with you. First, though, let me define my teaching philosophy.

Statement of Teaching Philosophy

Since joining the UGA faculty in 1978, I have taught more than nine thousand students. Teaching has presented me with both a huge responsibility and a tremendous opportunity, so I take my work seriously and am committed to doing my best for my students. But it is important that I remember that learning, not teaching, is the ultimate objective. Teaching, though, is so central to learning that I must do it well.

People regularly ask me what I teach. My answer is not marketing, transportation, or business but people—individuals—for teaching, regardless of class size, is still very much a one-on-one interpersonal profession. My objective is to treat each student as my son or daughter. Why? Because it keeps me focused on doing a good job. As a parent, I expect the teachers of my sons and daughter to give them their best. I don't want excuses for teacher failures or inadequacies. Every parent deserves this commitment from teachers, and if he/she got it, teaching effectiveness would improve dramatically.

I let students know they are important to me, assume that in every class there is a student who will achieve tremendous accomplishments in life, and believe that each person has the potential to learn and contribute to society. My job is to be a professional, to be reasonable and fair, to motivate students to give me their best, and to strive for excellence in everything they or I do. I believe that competency, achievement, merit, and honor are the path toward acceptance and respect.

Nothing is more important to the attainment of these goals than my own attitude. How can I expect students to have passion if I lack it? From day one, I tell students that I am excited to be their teacher and that I think they will learn a lot in the class and enjoy it. I want them to know that I trust them and believe in them, that I will treat them as adults, and that they will learn much more if they join me as coteachers in an interactive, discussion-oriented environment. I mean every word. Education is not a spectator sport. It requires effort and much practice. We can't give students an education. It has to be earned. What we can and must give students are opportunities to be challenged and to prove themselves. As long as I teach, the bar will stay high, and I sincerely believe most students are up to the challenge. But they won't have to clear it on their own. I'll help them get over it.

I want to make a difference in as many students' lives as I can. My goal is not to develop them in my image but help them realize their own extraordinary talents and capabilities. Another goal is to help them acquire a lifetime love of learning. I am constantly thinking about what will happen after they leave my classroom and whether I have prepared them for the future.

I want students to be excited about learning. My job is to create a stimulating classroom environment that inspires effort and achievement. I must help students strengthen their critical thinking, communication, analytical, and people skills as well as expand their subject-matter knowledge. It is crucial that they try to understand different perspectives and beliefs, are considerate and respectful of others, practice and not just discuss ethics, and become problem-solvers. I must be a full-time practitioner of all these traits because classrooms don't need teachers who are hypocrites. By definition, teachers are role models. It comes with the job. Therefore, I work hard every day to be a good example and a trusted mentor.

Students are this world's future. If we help them to realize their dreams and potential, to find happiness and courage, to lead successful and satisfied lives, and to share their talents with others, society will make progress. Very few professions have more opportunity to facilitate this process than teaching has, and this motivates me. My work is very meaningful.

The teachers who have shaped my life didn't do it with textbook facts. They inspired me, guided me to make better decisions, helped me to recognize my worth, built my self-respect and confidence, and demonstrated both patience and an unwavering faith in me. They gave me hope. I will try to do the same for my students. Nothing would make me happier than to see my students exceed my own accomplishments. To all of these challenges I commit my energies, talents, and skills.

The Rest of the Story

As I developed my teaching philosophy, I grew increasingly curious about the statement's origin. Where does a person's philosophy come from? Who or what shaped mine? The more I thought about it, the more I became convinced that there was a meaningful "behind the scenes" story, something that had the potential to motivate improved teaching in others. My philosophy, I began to understand, was primarily learned and acquired over time. Every day of my life, unknowingly for the most part, I had been watching and taking mental notes, long before it ever crossed my mind that I would become a teacher. I was studying people. Piece by piece I was building my teaching philosophy by very selectively borrowing ideas and values from classmates, colleagues, and especially from classroom teachers, either mine or from others I came in contact with.

I learned many things during this reflective search for answers. One of my most important conclusions was that I needed to think about teaching in a much broader context. For the first time I saw that not just professional educators but *every person is a teacher.* Clergymen, former choir directors, past coaches, people I worked for, men and women I had served with in the Navy, business colleagues and customers—from my three-year-old granddaughter to my ninety-four-year-old father, each one contributed to the development not just of my teaching beliefs but more important of me as a person. I am so grateful to these individuals for sharing their time, advice, and lives with me. If I had the luxury of unlimited time and space, I would tell you about each of them and thank them publicly. Since I don't, permit me to focus on several classroom teachers who significantly influenced my thinking about teaching.

As an introduction, I determined one day that in the process of taking classes from kindergarten through the completion of my Ph.D. degree, I was taught by 114 instructors. In that span, I honestly believe I learned something about teaching from every single teacher regardless of whether I remember them as outstanding, good, fair, or bad instructors. One of my high school science teachers, for example, asked this question on his final exam (a question worth 20 percent of the grade, I might add): "On what page of the text does the following formula appear?" I knew the formula, knew how to compute the answer, and understood what the results meant, but it had not crossed my mind to memorize the page locations. He was unsympathetic to my reasoning. From this man I learned the importance of using common sense, that students expect teachers to be reasonable, that teachers can lose the respect of their students in an instant, and that being brilliant and thoroughly knowledgeable of one's subject (he was) do not constitute outstanding teaching, at least not by themselves. Fortunately, I was blessed with more good teachers than bad, and they taught me even more about the profession.

Elementary School Teachers

The first teacher to influence my philosophy in a most positive way was Marjorie Jaswell, my third-grade teacher in the Smithfield, Rhode Island, public schools. I felt welcomed and loved in her classroom. Mrs. Jaswell made my classmates and me feel special, and her kindness affected my attitude toward education and school. She cared, I knew it, and I was motivated to learn. Mrs. Jaswell taught me that it is a teacher's responsibility to create a classroom environment conducive to learning and that sincere caring about the individuals in your class is a crucial first step.

In the fifth grade, Edith Knuschke shared her love of reading with us and proved to me that effective teaching does not require that every minute of each class be occupied with rigorous academic pursuits. Reading kindled a curiosity within me that I hope I never lose. I can still hear Mrs. Knuschke's mellow contralto voice reading *The Secret Garden* to us every Friday. It was so real that I felt I was there, inside those walls. I have been an adventurer ever since.

One of the valuable lessons I learned from Harry Westcott, my sixth- and seventh-grade teacher, was the importance of showing your human side to students. Students do not expect teachers to know all the answers; moreover, they like to learn who we are and that we have a life beyond the classroom, just as they have. Mr. Westcott would share his adventures as a volunteer fireman and talk about his family. While doing so, he infected us with his contagious energy and enthusiasm. Clearly, he loved his job and his life, and his attitude got me thinking that I, too, might like teaching. I additionally learned that classrooms can be fun without losing any of their instructional effectiveness, provided teachers have Mr. Westcott's leadership abilities to keep students focused.

High School Teachers

Two teachers made lasting impressions on me at Classical High School in Providence, Rhode Island. John McGlinchy was a superb math teacher who always had a twinkle in his eye, a subtle sense of humor, and a motivating and positively reinforcing attitude. He was the consummate professional teacher, always impressively attired, punctual, and prepared. Mr. McGlinchy held us to rigid standards and gave us four tests a week, yet I never felt pressured or ill at ease. I sensed that he had a deep understanding of students and kept life's priorities in perspective.

Elizabeth McCabe was one of the most demanding, exacting teachers I have ever had. She was very serious, rarely smiled, and kept me totally on edge. Only years later did I realize how well Ms. McCabe had prepared me in English. She was a severe but honest critic, fair to her students, and dedicated. Each week she graded an average of 150 essays and 450 tests with absolute precision and without complaint. When Ms. McCabe returned our graded essays, above each error was a number that corresponded to a section in the *Harbrace Handbook*, an English writing book that she had memorized. We had to look up each number and correct the error. I still can't believe she had the book memorized, but more important, her methods were very effective. Like John McGlinchy, Elizabeth McCabe took teaching and high standards very seriously. They believed that students would rise to the occasion.

College Professors

At Elon College, I was fortunate to study physics under Alonzo Hook, the most revered college teacher I have ever known, and Wesley Alexander, a wonderful, patient man who loved his work and his students and taught me math. What I remember about Dr. Hook was his wisdom, loyalty, and dignity. A humble man of great presence, Dr. Hook was a true gentleman. He taught me that the kind of person I am is central to the type of teacher I hope to become and to the mentor whom I want my students to know and remember. Teaching is very much about living an honorable life.

Wesley Alexander taught me to listen more carefully to my students and really try to understand what they are saying. This builds rapport and trust, two traits that encourage learning. Dr. Alexander was never too busy to help me, and his door was always open. Professors Hook and Alexander were fine role models. Often I think teachers underestimate this part of their job. Without ever saying a word on the subject, both men reinforced my belief that students learn not just from what we say but from what they observe.

Two professors at the University of Minnesota likewise left indelible marks on my teaching. Donald Harper instilled in me the absolute importance of knowing what I am talking about, the essentiality of accuracy, and the importance of thorough classroom preparation and organization. Dr. Harper was exact and expected nothing less of his students. Preparation, he showed me, builds teacher self-confidence. I have made it a point never to go to class unprepared for the day's lesson. Highly successful teachers do not "wing it."

Without Fred Beier's encouragement, I would most likely never have become a college professor. As I neared graduation, Dr. Beier both encouraged me to pursue my Ph.D. and gave me an opportunity to see if I enjoyed college teaching. I am indebted to him for opening a window that has brought me such satisfaction in life. Additionally, he introduced me to the case teaching method, one of the most effective teaching tools I use in my classrooms. Case teaching opened my eyes to the Socratic method of teaching. It taught me that students need to be asked more often what they think. Discussion-oriented classes stimulate interest and enhance learning beyond anything that I have been able to achieve in straight lecture environments. Even in classes of three hundred students, I use the discussion format, practiced first in Dr. Beier's class in logistics.

Other Contributing Teachers

Before ending this review, I would like to praise four individuals who never taught me in the classroom but who still significantly shaped my teaching philosophy. The first three made big differences in the lives of our three children. The last laid the cornerstone for my career in teaching.

Joseph R. Berrigan, a two-time Meigs recipient and a contributor to this book, was our daughter Katie's all-time favorite teacher at The University of Georgia. What Katie loved about Dr. Berrigan was his positive attitude and his ability to generate student interest in his subject. She used to say that Dr. Berrigan came to every class happy to be with his students and excited about his field of history. To me this said that no attitude is more important to classroom success than the teacher's. Katie said she never wanted to miss his 7:50 A.M. class. What a compliment!

Neal Saye, an English professor at Georgia Southern University, absolutely changed our son Jeff's life. Dr. Saye, more than anyone else, helped Jeff believe in himself, recognize his abilities, work harder to accomplish his goals, and develop his potential. Jeff describes Dr. Saye as a teacher who really cares about the education his students achieve and who wants to make a positive impact on their lives. Jeff also praised Dr. Saye for taking time to explain things to him, for his encouragement, and for his passion for his work. As Jeff's father, I am very indebted to Neal Saye and motivated to help other people's children. Time, understanding, faith, and patience are four additional characteristics that should always be important parts of my teaching.

Dave, our third child, was fortunate to cross paths with Professor Frank Harrison, a UGA philosophy teacher who challenged him to live up to his potential. Essentially, Dr. Harrison told Dave to snap out of his temporary doldrums and get to work. Sometimes students need to hear the honest, even if painful, truth rather than be given a sympathetic ear or pat on the back. Outstanding teachers like Frank Harrison do not give up on students but rather dig into their bag of tricks to find whatever tool will work. Three children, three different exceptional teachers, and three approaches, but all worked to help develop our children's potential. Collectively, these three professors encouraged me to expand my teaching knowledge, particularly in the area of motivation.

The teacher, however, who had the most profound effect on my teaching philosophy was my mother, Ruth Horne Stephenson. Mom taught elementary school in Burlington, North Carolina, before she married my dad, moved to Rhode Island, and retired from teaching. On our annual trips to Burlington to visit my grandmother, old men (they seemed that way to a young boy, anyway) knocked at our door, saying that they had heard that Ms. Horne was back in town. They wanted to visit with her.

These men were Mom's former elementary students who respected her a great deal for having helped them as children. Mom was an expert at teaching individuals who had been rejected by other teachers and who, in several cases, had been told they would never amount to anything. She gave them hope, and they went on to successful lives and careers. What Mom taught me is that everyone has the capacity to learn even though all are not equally blessed with ability. Teachers have the job of doing their best for *every* student, not just the brightest. Some of the greatest teaching ever done occurs with some of these struggling students.

Conclusion

What then was accomplished by writing my statement of teaching philosophy? Actually, many things that were very beneficial to me. For the first time, I really put serious thought into my teaching purpose, and this forced me to recognize what I needed to do to accomplish my objectives. Writing the statement convinced me that regardless of any obstacles thrown in my path as a teacher, and there are many, I will continue to pursue my commitment to help my students. I am convinced now more than ever that teaching is an honorable profession and that I would have to search long and hard to find a career where I have as much opportunity to make a difference in society and in people's lives. I also became so much more aware of how dependent I was on the nurturing and love of so many individuals. What these teachers did for me is priceless, and I am energized to help as many other people as I possibly can. As I rediscovered what these individuals meant to me, I began contacting them to thank them. Many are getting along in years, but amazingly, Mrs. Jaswell and others still remembered me. They were so grateful for this effort, and as I talked with them, I, too, remembered how much the kind words of a former or current student mean to me.

I guess I would simply conclude that we make life more complex than we should. Most of us, regardless of career, position, or wealth, need appreciation, respect, and love, and it is these three things that are some of the most powerful and meaningful motivators in life. I will not forget what I learned from this exercise and try more often to say thanks, show respect, and give love to others, especially to all of my teachers both in and outside of the traditional classroom. What a wonderful gift teaching is to society. The reality is that everyone in one way or another is a teacher. May we all practice and appreciate it more thoughtfully and honor those individuals who made our lives better.

◆　◆　◆

Frederick J. Stephenson received his AB degree in mathematics from Elon College and his MS and Ph.D. degrees in transportation and logistics from the University of Minnesota. He is an associate professor in the Department of Marketing and Distribution in UGA's Terry College of Business. Additionally, he has taught at the University of Minnesota, Northeastern University, and Wake Forest University. Previously, he was a high school math teacher and a lieutenant in the U.S. Navy Supply Corps.

Since joining the faculty at The University of Georgia in 1978, Dr. Stephenson has received numerous teaching honors and awards, including twice being named a recipient of the Meigs Award for Excellence in Teaching, in 1988 and 1997, The University of Georgia's highest teaching honor, and twice being selected as the top teacher in the Terry College of Business. He has taught more than nine thousand undergraduate and graduate students and more than twenty different courses in the fields of transportation, logistics, and marketing at UGA. Currently, he twice annually teaches a mass section of three hundred students in marketing principles using a discussion-oriented approach. He also teaches an undergraduate section of marketing strategy and decision-making, the capstone course for undergraduate marketing majors, and a course in marketing strategy for MBA students. The latter two courses are case courses of thirty-five to fifty students.

Professor Stephenson's research primarily has addressed airline and trucking management strategies. He has published in leading journals in transportation and logistics and authored *Transportation USA*, a principles of transportation textbook. He, along with his colleague Kittsu Greenwood, founded UGA's Trucking Profitability Strategies Conference, considered North America's highest-rated educational seminar for CEOs and other top leaders in the trucking industry. Dr. Stephenson has served continuously as the TPS Conference Director since its beginning in 1986.

Dr. Stephenson loves life and nature, learning, hiking, backpacking, and landscape photography. He and his children have hiked to the bottom of the Grand Canyon, climbed Yosemite's Half Dome, and backpacked hundreds of miles on the Appalachian Trail. His other hobbies include whitewater rafting, traveling, reading, sports, and music. What means the most to him, though, is his family: Sharon, his best friend and wife of thirty-five years; their three children, Katie, Jeff, and Dave; son-in-law John; daughter-in-law Kendra; and granddaughters Haley and Sydney.

ENDNOTES

1. Lee Walczak et al., "The Politics of Prosperity," *Business Week*, August 7, 2000, p. 104.
2. Ben Wildavsky, "At Least They Have High Self-esteem," *U.S. News & World Report*, February 7, 2000, p. 50.
3. The Boyer Commission on Educating Undergraduates in the Research University, *Reinventing Undergraduate Education: A Blueprint for America's Research Universities*, 1998.
4. Carolyn J. Mooney, "Professors Feel Conflict Between Roles in Teaching and Research, Say Students Are Badly Prepared," *The Chronicle of Higher Education*, May 8, 1991, p. A17.
5. Mary Crystal Cage, "Regulating Faculty Workloads," *The Chronicle of Higher Education*, January 20, 1995, p. A30.
6. Ernest L. Boyer, "School Reform in Perspective," a speech before the Education Writers Association, Boston, April 16, 1993, as it appears on page 52 of *Ernest L. Boyer: Selected Speeches 1979–1995*. Princeton, N.J.: The Carnegie Foundation for the Advancement of Teaching, 1997.
7. George Orwell, "Why I Write," in *Such, Such Were the Joys,* Harcourt, Brace and Company, New York, 1953.
8. Ibid., "Reflections on Gandhi," in *Shooting an Elephant,* Harcourt, Brace and Company, New York, 1950.
9. Roger L. Geiger, *To Advance Knowledge: The Growth of American Research Universities, 1900–1940,* Oxford University Press, New York, 1986.
10. Robert C. Solomon and Jon Solomon, *Up the University: Re-creating Higher Education in America,* Addison-Wesley, Reading, Massachusetts, 1993.
11. The Boyer Commission on Educating Undergraduates in the Research University, *Reinventing Undergraduate Education: A Blueprint for America's Research Universities,* Carnegie Foundation for the Advancement of Teaching, 1998.
12. Sections of this paper were reprinted with permission from Josef M. Broder, "Empiricism and the Art of Teaching," *Journal of Agricultural and Applied Economics,* vol. 26, no. 1 (1994):1–18.
13. See Theodore J. Marchese, "The New Conversations About Learning," www.newhorizons.org/lrnbus_marchese.html (1998).
14. Quotation in the title is from John Milton's "L'Allegro."
   Sport that wrinkled Care derides
   And Laughter holding both his sides.
15. Caine, R., and G. Caine (1994). *Making Connections: Teaching and the Human Brain.* Menlo Park, N.J.: Addison-Wesley.

The Josiah Meigs Award for Excellence in Teaching

The University of Georgia's highest teaching award, the Josiah Meigs Awards for Excellence in Teaching, recognizes superior instruction at undergraduate and graduate levels. Josiah Meigs, whom the award honors, was the second president of The University of Georgia.

The Meigs Awards were first presented in 1982. They were the idea of Dr. Virginia Trotter, UGA's Vice President for Academic Affairs, and Dr. Ronald D. Simpson, UGA's Director of the Office of Instructional Development (now OISD). During the first six years, a faculty peer group selected two award winners, each of whom received a $1,000 one-time cash award. In 1989, William Prokasy, the new Vice President for Academic Affairs, with the support of UGA President Charles Knapp, expanded the program permitting the selection of a maximum of five Meigs recipients annually. Because recipients would now receive a $5,000 permanent pay raise ($6,000 in 1999), the 1982–88 honorees were made eligible for renomination subject to the new guidelines and selection by the Meigs committee, which consists of twelve faculty and student members. Nominations are made by the candidates' colleges.

From the earliest days of the Meigs Award, it has been the intent that honorees be tenured, experienced teachers at The University of Georgia. Thus, they are proven researchers as well as teachers. From

1982 through 1999, fifty-seven different UGA faculty members were honored as Meigs Teachers, including several earlier recipients who were chosen to receive the award for a second time.

Authors, Meigs Award Year(s), Fields and Colleges/Schools

Barsanti, Jeanne A.	1998	Small Animal Medicine	Veterinary Medicine
Barton, Michelle Henry	1999	Large Animal Medicine	Veterinary Medicine
Berrigan, Joseph R.	1986, 1991	History	Arts and Sciences
Broder, Josef M.	1989	Agricultural and Applied Economics	Agricultural and Environmental Sciences
Carlson, Ronald L.	1989	Law	Law
Carter, Lief H.	1984, 1989	Political Science	Arts and Sciences
Coenen, Dan T.	1998	Law	Law
Ennulat, Egbert	1992	Musicology and Organ	Arts and Sciences
Fink, Conrad C.	1992	Journalism	Journalism and Mass Communication
Ganschow, Thomas W.	1997	History	Arts and Sciences
Glynn, Shawn M.	1998	Educational Psychology	Education
Granrose, John	1983	Philosophy	Arts and Sciences
Hatfield, Larry L.	1990	Mathematics Education	Education
Hill, Richard K.	1987	Chemistry	Arts and Sciences
Hudson, Charles M.	1994	Anthropology	Arts and Sciences
Jaworski, Alan J.	1993	Botany	Arts and Sciences
Johnson, Loch K.	1988	Political Science	Arts and Sciences
Karnok, Keith J.	1996	Crop and Soil Sciences	Agricultural and Environmental Sciences
Logue, Calvin M.	1995	Speech Communication	Arts and Sciences
Manning, Brenda H.	1995	Elementary Education	Education
McAlexander, Hubert H.	1997	English	Arts and Sciences
McCarter, States M.	1993	Plant Pathology	Agricultural and Environmental Sciences
Morain, Genelle G.	1994	Language Education	Education
Price, Sharon J.	1990	Child and Family Development	Family and Consumer Sciences
Provost, William G.	1993	English	Arts and Sciences
Reed, O. Lee	1996	Legal Studies	Business
Reiff, Judith C.	1998	Early Childhood Education	Education
Rojek, Dean G.	1999	Sociology	Arts and Sciences
Shaffer, David R.	1990	Psychology	Arts and Sciences
Shedd, Peter J.	1993	Legal Studies	Business
Stephenson, Frederick J.	1988, 1997	Marketing and Distribution	Business
Sweaney, Anne L.	1999	Housing and Consumer Economics	Family and Consumer Sciences
Talarico, Susette M.	1986, 1990	Political Science	Arts and Sciences
Tesser, Carmen Chaves	1992	Romance Languages	Arts and Sciences
Walters, James	1984	Child and Family Development	Family and Consumer Sciences
Wilson, Katharina M.	1997	Comparative Literature	Arts and Sciences

AUTHOR INDEX